THE SOCIAL MEDIA DEBATE

This accessible, student-friendly book provides a concise overview of the primary debates surrounding the impact and effects of social media.

From Facebook, Twitter, and Instagram to Snapchat and TikTok, social media has become part of our everyday experience. However, its proliferation has brought a myriad of serious concerns about the long-term effects of social media on socializing and personal relationships and the impact on well-being and mental health (particularly in relation to children and adolescents), as well as issues linked to information and culture (such as privacy, misinformation, and manipulation). Featuring contributions by leading international scholars and established authorities such as Christian Fuchs, Henry Jenkins, Michael A. Stefanone, and Joan Donovan, editor Devan Rosen brings together key contemporary research from multiple disciplines in order to provide crucial insight into these debates.

This book will be an important resource for students and scholars of media and communication, as well as educators, parents, policy makers, and clinicians interested in the impacts of social media.

Devan Rosen is Professor of Emerging Media in the Roy H. Park School of Communications at Ithaca College. His research focuses on the social uses of new media, social network analysis, and distributed socio-technical systems. He has developed social and semantic network-analytic theories and methods for the analysis of dynamic social networks in online environments. His research on decentralized self-organizing systems, Flock Theory, has been featured as the basis for several episodes of the hit CBS show NUMB3RS.

Routledge Debates in Digital Media Studies

Series editors: Rachel Kowert and Thorsten Quandt

The *Routledge Debates in Digital Media Studies* series provides critical examinations of the active debates that surround the uses and effects of new media and technologies within society. Consisting of essays written by leading scholars and experts, each volume tackles a growing area of inquiry and debate in the field and provides readers with an in-depth and accessible overview of the topic in question.

The Video Game Debate 2
Revisiting the Physical, Social, and Psychological Effects of Video Games
Edited by Rachel Kowert and Thorsten Quandt

The Social Media Debate
Unpacking the Social, Psychological, and Cultural Effects of Social Media
Edited by Devan Rosen

For more information about this series, please visit: www.routledge.com/Routledge-Debates-in-Digital-Media-Studies/book-series/RDDMS

THE SOCIAL MEDIA DEBATE

Unpacking the Social, Psychological, and Cultural Effects of Social Media

Edited by Devan Rosen

Routledge
Taylor & Francis Group

NEW YORK AND LONDON

Cover image: © peepo / Getty Images

First published 2022
by Routledge
605 Third Avenue, New York, NY 10158

and by Routledge
2 Park Square, Milton Park, Abingdon, Oxon, OX14 4RN

Routledge is an imprint of the Taylor & Francis Group, an informa business

Library of Congress Cataloging-in-Publication Data
A catalog record for this title has been requested

ISBN: 978-0-367-77413-4 (hbk)
ISBN: 978-0-367-76751-8 (pbk)
ISBN: 978-1-003-17127-0 (ebk)

DOI: 10.4324/9781003171270

Typeset in Bembo
by Apex CoVantage, LLC

CONTENTS

List of Illustrations   *vii*
Acknowledgments   *ix*
List of Contributors   *x*

1   Introduction: The Rise of a New Media Paradigm   1
    Devan Rosen

2   Social Media as Social Infrastructures   5
    Sarah Myers West

3   Contemporary Social Capital: Relationships Versus Awareness   20
    Michael A. Stefanone and Jessica M. Covert

4   Don't be Antisocial: The Politics of the "Anti-Social" in
    "Social" Media   38
    Elinor Carmi

5   Social Media, Alienation, and the Public Sphere   53
    Christian Fuchs

6   Social Media Moderation: The Best-Kept Secret in Tech   77
    Ysabel Gerrard

7 Make It Trend! Setting Right-Wing Media Agendas
Using Twitter Hashtags   96
Gabrielle Lim, Alexei Abrahams, and Joan Donovan

8 Mis/Disinformation and Social Media   120
Melissa Zimdars

9 Locating Social Media in Black Digital Studies   137
Francesca Sobande

10 An Overview of Social Media and Mental Health   152
Sarah M. Coyne, Emily Schvaneveldt, and Jane Shawcroft

11 Adolescent Social Media Use and Mental Health: A
Personal Social Media Use Framework   170
Drew P. Cingel, Michael C. Carter, and Lauren B. Taylor

12 There Is No Easy Answer: How the Interaction of
Content, Situation, and Person Shapes the Effects of
Social Media Use on Well-Being   187
Philipp K. Masur, Jolanda Veldhuis, and Nadia Bij de Vaate

13 "What Does God Need With a Starship?": A Conversation
About Politics, Participation, and Social Media   203
Nico Carpentier and Henry Jenkins

14 Conclusion: Together We Ascend   220
Devan Rosen

Index   *228*

ILLUSTRATIONS

Figures

5.1	The media system as a part of the public sphere	55
5.2	Concept of the *Club 2.0*	70
7.1	Time series plots of #AOCLied (top) and #AlexandriaOcasioSmollett (bottom)	102
7.2	Twitter retweet networks for #AlexandriaOcasioSmollett (left) and #AOCLied (right)	103
7.3	Agenda seeding channels	106
7.4	Number of stories published mentioning #exposeCNN among right-leaning outlets	112
7.5	Daily mentions of right-wing Twitter influencers Jack Posobiec, Andy Ngo, and James O'Keefe during our study period	114

Tables

5.1	Antagonisms in three types of alienation	58
5.2	Main actors in the alienated and the humanist society	59
5.3	Three types of digital alienation and ten forms of colonialisation of the digital public sphere	61
5.4	Three antagonisms of digital alienation	61
5.5	Comparison of the economic power of the six largest internet corporations and the world's 30 poorest countries	62
5.6	Top ten most-viewed YouTube videos of all time	64
6.1	Overview and description of social media content moderation user outcomes	87

7.1   Summary statistics for #AOCLied and #AlexandriaOcasioSmollett   103
7.2   Breakdown of hashtags coined and amplified by the influencers   108
7.3   Number of media stories mentioning each hashtag and their
      overall share of total stories that week   109
12.1 Overview of influences on well-being at a given time   189

ACKNOWLEDGMENTS

The editor would like to express a heartfelt thank you to all the authors for contributing their time, talent, and voice to this volume. It is humbling to have the opportunity to work with such a remarkable group of individuals. To each one of you, thank you.

CONTRIBUTORS

Alexei Abrahams, PhD., is Data Scientist and Research Fellow with the Technology and Social Change Project at Harvard Kennedy School's Shorenstein Center. He researches cybersecurity, misinformation, and political conflict using big data and quantitative methods, often with a Middle East regional focus. He was previously an Open Technology Fund research fellow and worked at the Citizen Lab, University of Toronto. His work has been published in *Political Science Research and Methods, International Journal of Communication, the Washington Post, Just Security,* and *Lawfare,* among many other outlets. You can learn more about his work at *https://sites.google.com/site/alexeiabrahams.*

Nadia Bij de Vaate is PhD Candidate and Lecturer at the Department of Communication Science at the Vrije Universiteit Amsterdam. Her research is primarily focused on understanding how social media use impacts adolescents' mental health and body image. She is a member of the Media Psychology Program Amsterdam.

Elinor Carmi, PhD, is Lecturer in Media and Communication in the Sociology Department at City University, London, UK. Dr. Carmi is a feminist researcher, journalist, and ex-radio broadcaster who has a passion for data politics, digital rights, and feminism. She is currently working on two main projects: 1) Co-investigator on "Developing a Minimum Digital Living Standard for Households with Children," a Nuffield Foundation-funded project; 2) POST Parliamentary Academic Fellowship working with the UK's Digital, Culture, Media & Sport Committee on the project she proposed: "Digital literacies for a healthy democracy". Dr. Carmi also recently been part of two other projects: 1) Lead postdoc on "Me and My Big Data – Developing

Citizens' Data Literacies," a Nuffield Foundation-funded project; 2) Co-investigator on "Being Alone Together: Developing Fake News Immunity," a UKRI-funded project. In addition, in July 2020, Dr. Carmi was invited by the World Health Organisation (WHO) as a scientific expert to be part of the closed discussions to establish the foundations of Infodemiology. She also tweets @Elinor_Carmi.

Nico Carpentier, PhD, is Extraordinary Professor at Charles University (Prague, Czech Republic) and President of the International Association for Media and Communication Research (2020–2023). Moreover, he is a Research Fellow at Loughborough University. His latest monographs are *The Discursive-Material Knot: Cyprus in Conflict and Community Media Participation* (2017, Peter Lang, New York) and *Iconoclastic Controversies: A Photographic Inquiry into Antagonistic Nationalism* (2021, Intellect, Bristol).

Michael C. Carter is PhD Candidate in the Department of Communication at the University of California, Davis. His areas of research include adolescent well-being and social media use, media and suicide, and online health information seeking.

Drew P. Cingel, PhD, is Associate Professor in the Department of Communication at the University of California, Davis, where he directs the Human Development and Media Lab. Dr. Cingel studies the intersection between human development, media use, and media effects, focusing on children's moral development, as well as social media, adolescent development, and mental health. His work has been published in *Communication Research*, *Media Psychology*, and *New Media & Society*, among other journals.

Jessica M. Covert, PhD, is Visiting Instructor at the University at Buffalo. Dr. Covert's research primarily focuses on how social media use impacts individuals' perceptions of social exclusion and the resulting cognitive, emotional, and behavioral consequences. Further, her research explores how individuals differ in their ability to attend to information embedded in their social networks and how this attention influences access to social capital.

Sarah M. Coyne, PhD, is Professor of Human Development in the School of Family Life at Brigham Young University. Her research involves media, gender, body image, mental health, and child development.

Joan Donovan, PhD, is a leading Public Scholar and Disinformation Researcher, specializing in media manipulation, political movements, critical Internet studies, and online extremism. She is Research Director of the Harvard Kennedy School's Shorenstein Center on Media, Politics and Public Policy and Director of the Technology and Social Change project (TaSC). Through TaSC, Dr. Donovan explores how media manipulation is a means to control public conversation, derail democracy, and disrupt society. TaSC conducts research, develops methods, and facilitates workshops for journalists, policy makers, technologists, and civil society organizations on how to detect, document, and debunk media manipulation campaigns. Dr. Donovan is Cofounder of Harvard Kennedy School's *Misinformation Review*. Her research can be found in academic peer-reviewed journals such as *Social Media + Society*, *Journal of Contemporary Ethnography*, *Information, Communication & Society*, and *Social Studies of Science*. She is a columnist at *MIT Technology Review*, a regular contributor to *the New York Times*, *the Guardian*, National Public Radio (*NPR*), and *PBS* and is quoted often on radio and in print. Dr. Donovan has laid out the philosophical frameworks for how to research, report on, and understand this moment in Internet history and American politics. Her conceptualizations of strategic silence, meme wars, and media manipulation campaigns provide crucial frameworks for understanding how the United States got to this point. She coined many of the terms that the disinformation research field and mainstream media use to understand technology's impact on society.

Christian Fuchs is Professor of Media, Communication & Society at the University of Westminster, where he directs the Communication and Media Research Institute.

Ysabel Gerrard, PhD, is Lecturer in Digital Media and Society at the University of Sheffield. Her research on social media content moderation has been published in journals like *New Media and Society* and *Social Media + Society* and featured in venues like *the Guardian* and *WIRED*. Ysabel is Book Reviews Editor for *Convergence: The International Journal of Research into New Media Technologies*, Chair of ECREA's Digital Culture and Communication section, and a member of Facebook's Suicide and Self-Injury Advisory Board.

Henry Jenkins, PhD, is Provost's Professor of Communication, Journalism, Cinematic Art, and Education at the University of Southern California. He is the author or editor of 20 books on various aspects of media and popular culture, including *Textual Poachers: Television Fans and Participatory Culture*, *Convergence Culture: Where Old and New Media Collide*, *By Any Media Necessary: The New Youth Activists*, and *Popular Culture and the Civic Imagination: Case Studies of Creative Social Change*. You can follow his thoughts at his blog, henryjenkins.org, and his podcast, *How Do You Like It So Far?*

Gabrielle Lim is Researcher with the Technology and Social Change Project at Harvard Kennedy School's Shorenstein Center, as well as an associate at the Citizen Lab at the University of Toronto. She researches information technology and security, with a focus on media manipulation, censorship, surveillance, and civil society. Previously, she was a grantee of the Open Society Foundations, where her research focused on far-right extremism online, and a fellow at the Open Technology Fund, where she studied the securitization of "fake news" and censorship. Her research and writing have appeared in *Foreign Policy*, *Lawfare Blog*, *the New York Times*, and *the Atlantic*. You can learn more about her at gabriellelim.com.

Philipp K. Masur, PhD, is Assistant Professor of Persuasive Communication in the Department of Communication Science at Vrije Universiteit Amsterdam. He earned his PhD in the social sciences at the University of Hohenheim. His research focuses on different aspects of computer-mediated communication. More specifically, he investigates social influence and persuasion processes on social media, privacy, and self-disclosure in networked publics and communication effects on individual well-being.

Emily Schvaneveldt is MS Student at Brigham Young University in the MFHD program. Her research involves media, pornography, and sexual development.

Jane Shawcroft is MS Student at Brigham Young University in the MFHD program. Her research area involves media, parenting, and video games.

Francesca Sobande, PhD, is Lecturer in Digital Media Studies and Director of the BA Media, Journalism and Culture program at Cardiff University. Her work focuses on Black media experiences, digital remix culture, and the power and politics of popular culture. Francesca is the author of *The Digital Lives of Black Women in Britain* (Palgrave Macmillan, 2020), co-editor with Professor Akwugo Emejulu of *To Exist is to Resist: Black Feminism in Europe* (Pluto Press, 2019), and coauthor with layla-roxanne hill of *Black Oot Here: Black Lives in Scotland* (Bloomsbury, forthcoming 2022). She tweets at @chess_ess, and more about her work can be found at francescasobande.com.

Michael A. Stefanone, PhD, is Professor of Communication in the Department of Communication at the University at Buffalo. Dr. Stefanone's research addresses computer-mediated communication and social media, and he tries to situate technology use in evolving social contexts. Currently, his work explores the effects these technologies have on our relationships, access to resources like social capital, and the novel ways we present ourselves to others across media platforms. Also, his work explores differences in how we attend to our social worlds.

Lauren B. Taylor is PhD Candidate in the Department of Communication at the University of California, Davis, where she studies child and adolescent development and media use, focusing on the production and effects of user-generated content in relation to child psychosocial functioning, self-regulation, and developmental disorders.

Jolanda Veldhuis is Assistant Professor in the field of Health and Risk Communication as well as Media Psychology in the Department of Communication Science at Vrije Universiteit Amsterdam. Her research interests include media-by-peer interactions impacting body image and (mental) well-being, communication strategies to negotiate the effects of media exposure, group norms and individual processing of media, and social marketing communication applications (in the domain of health and environmental education). She is a member of the Media Psychology Program Amsterdam.

Sarah Myers West, PhD, is Postdoctoral Researcher at the AI Now Institute at New York University and has over a decade of experience working at the intersection of tech, labor, and platform accountability. Her current project examines histories of resistance and organizing in the tech industry, positioning today's wave of tech worker organizing in a long trajectory of labor and social movements. As one of the creators of the *Santa Clara Principles*, her work also critically examines the political economy of technology companies. She received her doctoral degree in 2018 from the Annenberg School for Communication and Journalism at the University of Southern California. Her writing is published in journals including *New Media & Society, Social Studies of Science, International Journal of Communication, Policy & Internet*, and *Business & Society*, and her research has been featured in *the Wall Street Journal, PBS, CBS, the Associated Press*, and *Motherboard*, among others.

Melissa Zimdars, PhD, is Associate Professor of Communication and Media at Merrimack College in North Andover, Massachusetts. She is the co-editor of the book *Fake News: Understanding Media and Misinformation in the Digital Age* (MIT Press, 2020). Zimdars has published in *Feminist Media Studies, Popular Communication, Television & New Media*, and *Flow*, and her work on misinformation has appeared in news outlets around the world, including *the Washington Post, the Boston Globe*, NPR, and BBC.

1

INTRODUCTION

The Rise of a New Media Paradigm

Devan Rosen

The Internet, from its outset, was a tool developed to digitally enable communication between individuals and to assist the electronic transfer of information between organizations. The evolution of digitally enabled social interactions eventually led to the information-dense platforms we now call "social media." The business of providing and supporting social media applications is a multibillion dollar industry driven by some of the most profitable and powerful companies in the world. About half of the total population of the world use social media, a proportion that is rapidly expanding. Facebook alone has garnered over 2.85 billion global users (Statista, 2021), a saturation achieved in a mere 17 years.

Social media have become part of our everyday experience. From Facebook, Twitter, and Instagram to Snapchat and TikTok, the landscape of options grows along with each generation of new users. However, its proliferation has brought a myriad of serious concerns about the negative effects social media have on our socialization patterns, social influence, spread of misinformation, and governing. There are also growing concerns about the long-term impacts of the use of social media on well-being, including social media addiction, privacy concerns, and a host of negative effects on our mental health. Moreover, social media present the most far-reaching and comprehensive navigable social network that has ever existed, allowing users to locate and interact with others and affiliation groups faster and more globally than any previous communication and information technology. It can give voice to those who were previously silenced, while simultaneously aiding the spread of distorted information with dire consequences.

However, as social media use has increasingly affected our politics, culture, and relationships, so have the debates over the causes and outcomes of these changes. The growing concerns over the effects of social media use have motivated vast amounts of

DOI: 10.4324/9781003171270-1

research across many scientific fields, and this volume brings together leading international scholars to discuss the primary concerns relating to social media.

The historical analysis of social media and the principal definitions have been discussed extensively across a wide array of publications over the past 15 years, and many of the authors in this volume introduce key concepts of social media as pertinent to their respective fields. As such, this introduction chapter will very briefly review the history and definitions of social media and then introduce the structure of this volume.

Rise of a New Media Paradigm

The social uses of networked information and communication technologies (ICT) for human interaction and information access began long before the current era of social media and even before the World Wide Web went online around 1991. Early bulletin board systems (BBS) emerged in the early 1980s and allowed users connected to a Unix-to-Unix copy dial-up network and navigate interest groups and discussions. The release of Usenet in the early 1990s further accelerated the utility of distributed networked communications. Usenet allowed users to read and post messages to *newsgroups* and introduced the concept of a *newsfeed* and indeed was a very *social* media. The emergence of the World Wide Web, html, graphical interfaces, and web browsers brought about increasingly user-friendly platforms of online interaction and, thus, increasingly widespread use.

Web-based platforms for social interaction continued to emerge through the 1990s, with the release of early social network websites like Classmates in 1995 and Six Degrees in 1997, an array of blogging and microblogging websites, and an ever-increasing cache of websites that allowed users to share their own content. These emerging platforms grew to be a dominant form of social interaction and information access during the ballooning popularity of social platforms in the "Web 2.0" era of the early 2000s, whose novelty and attraction were fueled heavily by the capital accumulation of the corporate Internet economy (Fuchs, 2021). It was in this period that these websites and applications started to be referred to as "social media" and the widespread adoption and diffusion began, all while the corporations that were deploying these services were undergoing financial elephantiasis and becoming central players in the global flow (and control) of information.

Although there are a variety of ways that social media have taken shape, it was the growth of social network sites (SNS) that largely accelerated the use of social media. Ellison and boyd (2013) offer a useful definition of SNS as:

> a *networked communication platform* in which participants 1) have *uniquely identifiable profiles* that consist of user-supplied content, content provided by other users, and/or system-level data; 2) can *publicly articulate connections*

that can be viewed and traversed by others; and 3) can consume, produce, and/or interact with *streams of user-generated content* provided by their connections on the site.

(p. 158)

From the earliest SNS like Six Degrees and Friendster to current industry leaders like Facebook, Instagram, and LinkedIn, SNS have normalized the dynamics that lowered barriers to communication, facilitated the sharing of information related to identity, and allowed individuals to easily distinguish their common interests and affiliations (Ellison, Steinfield, & Lampe, 2011). These key social dynamics helped users cultivate socially relevant interactions, established these new forms of socializing as normal, and paved the way for a torrent of social media platforms that have transformed the way we communicate, socialize, organize, and communicate.

Definitions of social media vary across fields and disciplines, but McCay-Peet and Quan-Haase (2017) offered a working definition of social media that is broad enough to be useful for an interdisciplinary volume like this one while also specific enough to elucidate the key concepts:

> Social media are web-based services that allow individuals, communities, and organizations to collaborate, connect, interact, and build community by enabling them to create, co-create, modify, share, and engage with user-generated content that is easily accessible.

(p. 17)

Unpacking and Peeking In

It is not within the scope of this volume to include an exhaustive suite of *all* the issues and debates related to social media, not even encyclopedias and handbooks are able to accomplish that. What we can include are some of the most pressing and timely debates, including impacts on how we socialize, effects on our well-being and mental health, impacts on politics and governing, and shifts in how information is spread, shared, and accessed.

The remainder of this volume will unpack key debates across 12 chapters. The following three chapters (Chapters 2–4) focus on the social: social media as social infrastructures, social capital, and the antisocial. These are followed by five chapters related to information and culture: content moderation, misinformation and digital ethics, social media in Black digital studies, influencers and news media agendas, and finally social media, alienation, and the public sphere. Next are three chapters on mental health and well-being: an overview chapter, a chapter on child and adolescent social media use and mental health, and a chapter on how the interaction of content, situation, and person shapes the effects of social media on well-being. The final chapter takes a conversation-style approach to discuss participatory ethics and social media. The volume concludes with some brief conclusions and next steps.

As social media continue to expand and emerge into new forms with ever-growing saturation and reach, so will the need to understand the ways we use these media forms and the effects that they have on our personal life experiences, our relationships, communities, governments, and cultures. This volume gathers a portion of what we know about social media and their effects to catalyze a greater understanding of how our lives are impacted.

References

Ellison, N. B., & boyd, d. (2013). Sociality through social network sites. In W. H. Dutton (Ed.), *The Oxford handbook of internet studies* (pp. 151–172). Oxford: Oxford University Press.

Ellison, N. B., Steinfield, C., & Lampe, C. (2011). Connection strategies: Social capital implications of Facebook-enabled communication practices. *New Media & Society*, *13*(6), 873–892. https://doi.org/10.1177/1461444810385389

Fuchs, C. (2021). *Social media: A critical introduction*. London: SAGE Publications Ltd. www.doi.org/10.4135/9781446270066

McCay-Peet, L., & Quan-Haase, A. (2017). What is social media and what questions can social media research help us answer? In L. Sloan & A. Quan-Haase (Eds.), *The SAGE handbook of social media research methods*. Thousand Oaks, CA: SAGE Reference. https://dx.doi.org/10.4135/9781473983847.n2

Statista. (August 27, 2021). Leading countries based on Facebook audience size as of July 2021. *www.statista.com*. Retrieved from www.statista.com/statistics/268136/top-15-countries-based-on-number-of-facebook-users/

2

SOCIAL MEDIA AS SOCIAL INFRASTRUCTURES

Sarah Myers West

At the heart of the social media debate are age-old questions: What knits us together as parts of a community? What do we need to become active, engaged members of our society and knowledgeable, curious citizens of the world? What does it mean to be part of a public, and how do we know if we are part of one? Social media companies have sought to position themselves as critical to the answers to these questions by creating what one founder called *social infrastructures* – the socio-technical means through which we interrelate and form communities. Whether or not we take this term at face value, the notion of social infrastructure leads to other corollary questions: What is the proper role for institutions to play in helping us to build the infrastructures of our social lives? Building social infrastructure imbues those who manage it with a considerable amount of power, which also leads to a final, critical question: How do we ensure that those who hold this power remain accountable to us?

There are no simple or easy answers to these questions, as social media companies, their users, and the politicians seeking to regulate them have found. These platforms may not have been designed to be social infrastructure at the outset – they weren't meant, necessarily, to be employed by millions of people, used to plan protests, leak secrets, livestream police brutality, or rally crowds to support extremist causes. According to Facebook's founder, it wasn't even created to be a company (though we can treat that statement with some skepticism).

But it is clear, in 2021, that social media companies have outsized power to influence how we access information, communicate with those around us, and develop our views of the world. As anyone who has lost a password or accidentally "liked" a post they didn't intend to, small tweaks to a platform interface can have significant downstream effects. Even more fundamentally, the infrastructures created by these companies and the policies developed to manage our behavior

DOI: 10.4324/9781003171270-2

on them navigate deep and existential questions about the information we can access, what we can share, and with whom we can share it, the answers to which have considerable influence on our lives.

It's important to keep in frame that where there is power there is resistance, and that regardless of what is on offer from the tech industry, people have always developed their own means of creating the information environments that they need. From local newspapers to samizdat, people work together to share what matters to them through the accounts of the experiences of their lives. And the advent of networked infrastructures offered an opportunity to do this in a new way – through email, bulletin board systems, and Internet relay chat in the early days, then through the creation of blogs, and, eventually, on social media platforms offered by large multinational tech companies. Social media took on distinctive meanings in the growing number of places in the world where the state does not encourage freedom of expression, because these platforms fostered the creation of alternative media sources that could provide accounts from the ground that did not always align to the state's views.

Though they often use rhetoric to distance themselves from this, social media platforms have *always* been political by their very nature. Sharing information and fostering associations between people can lead to mass protest, shift the outcome of an election, or cause a company to come under legal scrutiny. Because of this, nation-states tend to closely pay attention to the information environments within – and permeating across – their borders. For some, a healthy and robust information environment includes a press that educates its citizenry to hold the government accountable. For others, the role of information actors is to support the project of building the nation – or to consolidate the power of its figurehead. These differing views have created a complex and conflict-ridden geopolitical landscape for social media companies to navigate, but often, these companies do so with relatively little transparency or accountability to the communities they ostensibly serve.

This chapter examines the geopolitics of social media companies through a historical lens, focusing particularly on evolutions that occurred outside of the US and EU contexts that are taking up much of the companies' attention today. In it, I make three key points: First, that the evolution from a decentralized blogosphere to centralized social media platforms positioned these large multinational companies as power brokers. Second, this created a single point of failure that enabled nation-states to target social media platforms for surveillance, censorship, and eventually, the spread of disinformation. Third, this led social media companies to shift from policy making that was, at first, largely informal, idiosyncratic, and sometimes contradictory to develop a large, formalized bureaucratic infrastructure – but one largely decoupled from the significant base of users located outside of the US and the EU. Finally, in the conclusion, I consider possible levers for change that could make these social infrastructures more accountable to the societies that make them up. I suggest that to do so we can draw on historical examples of resistance to the tech industry built on international solidarity, working collectively to build upon what we've learned from critiques of social media to more expansively envision the social infrastructure we want and need.

Looking to history emphasizes something important about the infrastructural dimensions of social media platforms: that much of what now seems fixed and taken for granted about how these companies work is in fact the product of considerable experimentation. As scholars of science and technology studies (STS) have pointed out for so long, things could always be otherwise – and our responsibility as scholars and critics of technology is to understand the particularities, so we can be thoughtful about what we carry forward and advocate to the world we wish to live in. Though they are now large and formalized institutions, lacking the momentum of their early days, by taking stock of this history my hope is that we can revisit – and reconsider – the role of social media platforms in our lives at present. And maybe, if we can identify the right levers, we can shift the playing field around that experimentation so that we, the global public, however it may be constituted, play a bigger part in the process of figuring out what kinds of social media environments we want and need.

The Power Brokers

In the early days, many Silicon Valley-based technology firms saw themselves as giving power back to the people. Google's mission was "to organize the world's information and make it useful" and that of WhatsApp was "to let people communicate anywhere in the world without barriers". And, as Mark Zuckerberg wrote in a letter to investors accompanying the company's initial public offering, Facebook "aspires to build the services that give people the power to share and help them once again transform many of our core institutions and industries" (Zuckerberg, 2012). But, as is now clear, the evolution from a decentralized blogosphere to centralized social media platforms instead positioned a handful of large multinational companies as power brokers.

How did we get here? In the years immediately preceding and following the dot-com boom and bust, scholarship by communication researchers like Manuel Castells and Yochai Benkler observed the considerable changes affected by the emergence of networked communications infrastructures. This work described the emergence of what Castells called the "network society" and Benkler termed the "networked public sphere" (Castells, 1996; Benkler, 2006), terms that suggest a foundational shift in the makeup of social infrastructures wrought through technology.

Though both scholars refute claims that their ideas are rooted in technological determinism, arguing the relationship is not causal, the concept of networked power nevertheless aligned well with the self-conceptions of leaders within the tech industry, their flat business structures, and faith in meritocratic modes of self-governance. People like Kevin Kelly, the founding executive editor of the magazine *WIRED*, proclaimed that the migration online meant that "for the first time on our planet, hundreds of millions of minds were linked together in thousands of novel ways, each arrangement yielding potential benefit" (Kelly, 2018). Building upon communitarian ideals that emerged out of the hippie counterculture prevalent in the Bay Area, ideas about peer-to-peer sharing and participatory governance gained in popularity over the late 1990s and early aughts (Turner, 2006).

But despite the pervasiveness of these views, the underlying reality has been a remarkably persistent trend toward oligopoly within the Internet industry despite enormous change over the span of several decades. In the mid- to late-1990s, Internet firms proliferated under a period of rapid growth known as the dot-com bubble. Supported by an influx of venture capital, many of these dot-coms collapsed when their business models – which often depended on assumptions that offering services and products online alone would support growth – failed. The dot-coms that remained adopted cross-promotion and integration strategies that had been piloted by the telecommunications and entertainment conglomerates that preceded them. As scholars like Dan Schiller observed, what he described as "digital capitalism" did not emerge from the ether: global networked communications infrastructures were the product of neoliberal, market-driven policy that contributed to the empowerment of corporations (Schiller, 1999), driven particularly by policies enacted by US officials under the Clinton administration.

As early as 2003, it was clear that the self-image of openness and competitiveness promoted within Silicon Valley diverged from its reality: in a 20-year study of Internet firms, Eli Noam found that the industry was essentially oligopolistic and featured a notable concentration around a few large companies (Noam, 2003). The Web 2.0 titans then emerging, like Google, Facebook, and Amazon, largely focused on building out advertising and cross-platform experiences and bridging multiple emerging sectors of the Internet industry by acquiring start-ups. They also sought to ensure that their platforms were being used by a global community of users: in contrast to many Web 1.0 start-ups, which were often linked to physical retail infrastructures located in the US, social networks rapidly spread in use outside US borders. The early social network Friendster, for example, had over 65% of its users located in Asia by 2009, when it was acquired by an online payments provider based in Malaysia (Fiegerman, 2014).

As they sought to dominate global markets in mass communication, US technology firms treated connectivity as both a foundational value and a business imperative, the source of much of their power (Van Dijck, 2013; West, 2017a; Donovan, 2021). But connectivity is not a social good in and of itself – in fact, it has been demonstrated in many cases to cause harm. In 2016, Facebook executive Andrew Bosworth circulated a now infamous memo within the company in which he said "We connect people. Period. That's why all the work we do in growth is justified . . . Maybe it costs a life by exposing someone to bullies. Maybe someone dies in a terrorist attack coordinated on our tools" (Mac, Warzel, & Kantrowitz, 2018). While both Facebook CEO Mark Zuckerberg and Bosworth himself have since distanced themselves from the memo, it remains a remarkable expression of the runaway effects of connectivity and the willingness of company executives to take on the negative social consequences it can affect.

In the quest to optimize connectivity and user engagement, social media companies bought out their competitors or closely mimicked them, giving users fewer alternatives in the pursuit of network effects that issued a gravitational pull for a diminishing base of users who had not yet signed up for Facebook, Instagram, Twitter, or YouTube (Wu, 2018). When they reached a point of concentration in existing markets, they turned to outlandish initiatives designed to increase access to the Internet, like Facebook's Aquila project, an investment in drone technology that sought to "beam internet to remote parts of the world" (Zuckerberg, 2016), and Google's Project Loon, which used hot-air balloons to achieve similar ends. A more notorious endeavor by Facebook was its Free Basics program, in which the company brokered deals with telecommunications firms in 63 countries to offer zero-rated, or free, access to a limited number of services. Free Basics soon came under criticism by the governments of several countries and was ultimately banned in India when the country's telecommunications regulator ruled it violated net neutrality principles (Agrawal, 2016). While Facebook advertised Free Basics as an "onramp" to the global Internet, in fact it served primarily as a means through which the company – and its telco partners – could collect new swaths of profitable user data (West & Biddle, 2017).

Over time, this contributed to an Internet experience that, for many users, existed primarily and sometimes exclusively through proprietary platforms (Zittrain, 2009). In 2012, a survey of Internet users in Southeast Asia found that for many respondents, Facebook *was* the Internet. Among Indonesians, more people reported using Facebook than "the Internet", despite having to go online to access the social network. According to the researcher, follow-up focus groups conflated going onto Facebook with going online: "in their minds, the Internet did not exist; only Facebook" (LIRNEAsia, 2012). Similar results were reported in a survey on information and communication technology (ICT) use in Africa, with a discrepancy as high as 3–4% in Facebook use versus Internet use reported by mobile users (Calandro, Stork, & Gillwald, 2012).

As they emerged over the course of a decade, social media companies and the platforms they built and acquired were anything but flat or meritocratic: they exacerbated, rather than ameliorated, existing power disparities. Hindsight makes it easier to observe how, as Silicon Valley-based social media firms embarked on a "journey to connect the world," they positioned themselves as power brokers by creating a limited number of centralized commercial entities that mapped on top of existing communications networks.

A Single Point of Failure

Not all those affected by the spread of social media felt that communication and connectivity would be inherently beneficial. The quest to connect the world created a single point of failure that enabled nation-states to target these platforms as they sought to regulate the evolving communication ecosystem (Deibert, Palfrey, Rohozinski, & Zittrain, 2010). Waves of networked protests in Iran, Tunisia, Egypt, and Turkey highlighted the accelerant power of social media platforms to bring people together and out into the streets (Gerbaudo, 2012; Tufekci, 2017). While pundits advocated for what they claimed was the democratizing potential of social media platforms, encouraged by the companies themselves, detailed accounts from those on the ground tempered this exuberance by carefully documenting how social media was being used to serve the goals of reformers, revolutionaries, and authoritarian regimes alike (Tufekci & Wilson, 2012; Youmans & York, 2012).

Others began to observe more concerning trends: the emergence of new, networked forms of authoritarianism (Mackinnon, 2014; Morozov, 2012) as state actors began to redouble their efforts at censorship and surveillance by focusing on social media platforms (Pearce & Kendzior, 2012; Marechal, 2017). For example, in June 2017, Thai YouTube users reported that a subtitled copy of Charlie Chaplin's silent film "The Great Dictator" was no longer accessible. As Mong Palatino (2017) of Global Voices Advocacy reported, the Thai Academic Network of Civil Rights had urged that Thai citizens watch a scene from the film in which Chaplin urges that people take back power from the dictator in the lead-up to Thailand's commemoration of the anniversary of a revolution ending the country's absolute monarchy. Nearly two weeks later, users began reporting that they could no longer access the video, instead encountering a page displaying a message: "This content is not available on this country domain due to a legal complaint from the government".

The clip was blocked under Thailand's lese-majeste laws: under the Thai Criminal Code, it is illegal to defame or insult the royal family. In the years following a 2014 military coup, the country's government began assiduously enforcing lese-majeste; between 2014 and 2017, 105 people were arrested for violating the law versus six people prior to the coup. Social media platforms became a key site for enforcement; in May 2017, Palatino (2017) reported that Facebook removed 178 posts deemed in violation of lese-majeste, and the government threatened to take the company to court if it did not remove a further 131 posts it deemed in violation of the law.

But the strategy backfired: the removal of the Great Dictator clip ultimately drew more attention to the clip than the original message from the Thai Academic Network. Editors at the *Bangkok Post* wrote a piece deriding the decision, and Thai journalist Pravit Rohanaphruk, who had previously been jailed by the military for an "attitude adjustment", called the removal "hilariously insane and dictatorial" in a post on Twitter. The government reinstated the video, and views spiked into the thousands. As this suggests, censorship can sometimes produce a Streisand effect that leads to surges in usage through the deployment of circumvention technology (Jansen & Martin, 2015).

States began to experiment with other less blunt tools through which to establish digital information controls. In 2014, I interviewed a group of activists across ten different non-Western countries about how they navigated risks on social media, seeking to understand how they understood the mediating effect of these privatized platforms. As one activist I spoke to joked, "being censored in [my country] makes you famous, so it might be a good thing for me". Across disparate parts of the world, the activists reported that states were investing in tactics, such as astroturfing and disinformation, by monitoring the use of keywords, and funding the production of fake accounts to harass dissidents (West, 2017b; Forelle, Howard, Monroy-Hernandez, & Savage, 2015). The tactics weren't particularly sophisticated – one person remarked that they knew it was a government official when a message was posted in all caps – but often had the intended effect of intimidating the end user nonetheless, particularly in environments of ambiguity (Penney, 2021) when threats posted online were seen as a barometer for threats in physical spaces.

The ensuing suppression of speech on social media had a particularly strong effect in parts of the world where the press was, otherwise, not free. By 2015, the organization Freedom House issued its fifth consecutive Freedom on the Net report in which Internet freedom was on the decline. In it, they observed a concerning trend:

> [M]any governments have sought to shift the burden of censorship to private companies and individuals by pressing them to remove content, often resorting to direct blocking only when those measures fail . . . Governments have also grown more aggressive in presenting companies with ultimatums, threatening to revoke their operating licenses or block entire platforms if the specified content is not removed or hidden from view.
>
> *(Freedom House, 2015)*

The New Governors Have No Clothes

This growing pressure led tech companies to develop legal and policy infrastructures that would enable them to navigate a complex and shifting geopolitical environment. The companies weren't well versed in doing this from the start. In their early days, platforms expressed political orientations that tended to align with the values of free expression and association – orientations that Marvin Ammori observed aligned well with their business interests (2014). By 2017, in her careful documentation of content moderation mechanisms, legal scholar Kate Klonick observed that social media platforms had developed detailed systems, rooted in American legal frameworks that featured regularly revised rules, trained human decision-making, and relied on a system of external influence – all of which operated with little direct accountability to their users (Klonick, 2018).

YouTube's response to the posting of a video titled "The Innocence of Muslims" is an elucidating example. Styled as a movie trailer, the video contained material deemed offensive to the Muslim faith, and it led to violent protests in several regions around the world. The company made different decisions as to whether the video needed to come down depending on local laws, cultural norms, and market considerations. In India and Indonesia, it determined the video violated local laws and took it down. In Egypt and Libya, the video had led to violent protests, so the company did the same. But in other parts of the world, YouTube obstinately refused to remove the video, even in the face of encouragement by the Obama administration (which pushed for its removal globally in an attempt to quell the violence) (Miller, 2012). The Pakistani government blocked YouTube after the company refused to take it down, and the site was inaccessible in the country for three years.

The case is full of contradictions: the company decided that the video does not, on the whole, violate its site guidelines on hate speech. It voluntarily opted to remove the video in accordance with a policy to take cultural norms into account – but not in all countries, for reasons that remain largely unclear. And it withstood a hit to its revenue by waiting out a ban for several years in Pakistan. While the case was widely viewed as an important precedent in platforms' mediation of free expression, it is hard to know what, if anything, to take away from the company's decision-making – other than its idiosyncratic nature. Long-time researcher and advocate Jillian York observed that, over a decade of interfacing with policy representatives of Silicon Valley-based tech firms, policy decision-making was often a reflection of the personal politics of individual members of these teams rather than a clearly articulated viewpoint (York, 2021). This may explain why they so frequently made policy decisions that appeared to be sometimes outright contradictory.

Undergirding these seemingly contradictory decisions is a technical infrastructure that has proven important to many social media companies seeking to navigate different international norms and legal regimes: geoblocking or geographic-based restrictions on content. Twitter's adoption of its 'Country Withheld Content' policy is a case in point. In 2014, Turkish Prime Minister Recep Tayyip Erdogan banned Twitter after a set of leaks about corruption within the government was posted on the platform. Turkish Twitter users began using Domain Name System addresses that belonged to Google in order to attempt to circumvent the ban, even painting the addresses as graffiti on buildings, until the government blocked access to them as well (Hurriyet Daily News, 2014). The company initiated a mode of circumvention using SMS, so that users could text their tweets to a set of numbers while they worked to get their services back online (Twitter, 2014).

Before long, #TwitterIsBlockedInTurkey began trending on the site globally. But after six days, Twitter opted to use geoblocking while it contested the legal orders enacting the ban, removing the tweets for users only within a specific jurisdiction (Gadde, 2014). And weeks after Turkey's highest court demanded that Twitter be brought back online, representatives from the company met with Turkish officials to broker a deal that included using geoblocking to prevent certain posts from being seen within the country and appointing a local representative devoted to handling requests from the Turkish government (Yeginsu & Arango, 2014). Twitter's implementation of a technical infrastructure to facilitate geographically limited blocking, accompanied by its implementation of local staff devoted to handling government requests, is symptomatic of what became an increasingly formalized bureaucratic infrastructure for content moderation.

Often, these companies learned their lessons in countries outside of US and EU contexts, making the Global South the testing grounds for their policy decisions (Arun, 2018). Such dynamics are evocative of neocolonial practices in the health care and clinical research worlds in which pharmaceutical companies reap the benefits of conducting medical testing in locales where they can pay less for human labor (Kim, Oleribe, Njie, & Taylor-Robinson, 2017; Farrell, 2006). Similarly, social media companies have demonstrated over time an investment in resources in countries deemed to be more lucrative to them and an unwillingness to invest similar resources in parts of the world deemed to be less valuable – even in the face of considerable evidence that the platform is being used to cause harm (BSR, 2018).

This was revealed most clearly by Sophie Zhang, a whistleblower who worked for Facebook handling instances of disinformation in countries around the world. In a memo published internally within the company before she was fired, Zhang revealed a resistance within Facebook to take action, even when abuses of the platform were escalated through international channels. In Zhang's view, the company's willingness (or reluctance) to address issues of fraudulent behavior and the spread of disinformation was closely tied to the company's assessment of a particular country's market value.

> With no oversight whatsoever, I was left in a situation where I was trusted with immense influence in my spare time. A manager on Strategic Response mused to myself that most of the world outside the West was effectively the Wild West with myself as the part-time dictator – he meant the statement as a compliment, but it illustrated the immense pressures upon me.
>
> *(Silverman, Mac, & Dixit, 2020)*

This had significant downstream effects in parts of the world deemed to be of marginal value to Facebook. For example, veteran journalist Arzu Geybullayeva wrote that Azerbaijan's government has long abused loopholes in Facebook's content moderation to create fake engagement to boost the property of pro-government content and target critics for harassment (Geybullayeva, 2021). Individuals acting on behalf of the ruling party, which is classified by Freedom House as a "consolidated authoritarian regime", created thousands of inauthentic accounts to harass the opposition. It took a year following initial reporting of the issue in Azerbaijan for Facebook to take any action, and according to reports by Azerbaijan Internet Watch, it remains an ongoing problem.

Similar dynamics can be observed at the interface level – for example, when Google rolled out its new social media platform Google+, it required that users employ their real names. Turning on the service led to a wave of bans from the platform for users whose names were in non-Roman alphabets, including those with Arabic and Chinese characters (Carmody, 2011). In the interviews I conducted, a lack of sufficient language support had both benefits and detractions for users from non-Anglophone nations: for example, one person I interviewed from the MENA region ran into challenges navigating her legal rights on the platform when the terms of service for Twitter were, at the time, available only in English. She offered to translate the English terms into Arabic for other users, but the company ignored her request. On the other hand, *not* having language support was useful to another user based in South Asia whose Facebook account was shut down due to a real name violation. The lack of language support let him submit a fake ID to bring his account back online and continue using a pseudonym in safety.

This haphazard treatment of countries in the Global South is in stark contrast to the more formal bureaucratic apparatuses that social media companies have amassed for international policy decision-making in the United States and European Union, including by making significant investments in lobbying: in the first half of 2020, Facebook, Amazon, Apple, and Google spent a combined $20 million on lobbying US politicians and, together with Microsoft, $23 million in lobbying in the European Union (Schwartz, 2020; Satariano & Stevis-Gridneff, 2020). Their neglect of the rest of the world leaves the users of these platforms vulnerable to well-documented and wide-ranging harms.

Conclusion

I began this chapter with a set of questions that frames much of the social debate at present. I'd like to conclude by focusing on the final two: What is the proper role for institutions – not just governments, but also companies – to play in helping us to build out the infrastructures of our social lives? And how do we hold such institutions accountable to those they claim to serve?

Governance of our activities across the Internet is, in many respects, now enacted through commercialized platforms via their policy decisions and technical interfaces. While we still have a fairly decentralized (though decidedly commercial) networked communications infrastructure, the bulk of our experiences online are largely consolidated on a handful of social media platforms. This concentration has enabled nation-states to use what levers are available to them to shape our online behavior through the use of platform bans, as in the case of Pakistan's ban of YouTube in the "Innocence of Muslims" case, legal requests, as in Thailand's enforcement of its lese-majeste laws to remove the Great Dictator video, and lobbying, as in Turkey's advocacy for Twitter to establish a local representative in the country. Also, governments use extralegal resources, such as disinformation, astroturfing, and harassment and threats issued to end users with the hope of exerting greater control over the information shared by their citizens over social media networks. As legal scholars have observed, social media companies have demonstrated greater responsiveness to acceding to demands in parts of the world where these levers hold greater influence over the companies' bottom line (Ammori, 2014). This has important downstream consequences for the role social media can play as social infrastructures. But, as is clear across these examples, these dynamics have proven to be far from perfect mechanisms for creating a just society: rather, they have contributed to the spread of false information, hate speech, and inciting content across the web. Placing the onus for accountability solely on government and corporate actors has proven to be an insufficient foundation for enacting meaningful change.

One of the primary levers for accountability from outside – one that I draw on for much of the evidence that makes up the case studies for this chapter – is the generation of incisive, critical research and analysis of companies' and governments' activities published in highly visible venues that shape global conversations about platform accountability. Publicity has proven a critical means through which companies' behavior can change. This is itself difficult work that relies on investigative journalism, rigorous research, and intrepid whistleblowing that bring to light what would otherwise be largely opaque aspects of what social media companies do in the world and the effects they render on our geopolitical environment.

However, there are limitations to this approach, most of all its tendency to reinforce the needs of those who already have visibility and a platform. Here is where I think nurturing a stronger base for international solidarity and collective action can prove critically important. There are many examples of international solidarity campaigns to draw on for developing strategies and tactics, leveraging what we know about geopolitics to advocate for social infrastructures that are more responsive to the needs of users wherever they reside, but particularly in parts of the world where governments are less encouraging of the development of independent media.

For example, we might look to the divestment and boycotting campaigns staged at Polaroid and IBM around South Africa's apartheid regime for inspiration on how to handle social media companies' treatment of the violence enacted against Palestinians. We could learn from groups like Computer People for Peace and Computer Professionals for Social Responsibility, which forged international coalitions to leverage technical expertise in support of ending tech-facilitated militarization. And we could draw on more contemporary campaigns like #NoTechForICE that employ refusal of labor for social media companies that facilitate abuses of power. There is much to be learned from these examples of collective action that can work in tandem with the critical study of social media to forge a new path for global connection.

References

Agrawal, R. (2016). Why India rejected Facebook's 'free' version of the Internet. *Mashable*. Retrieve from http://mashable.com/2016/02/09/why-facebook-free-basics-failed-india/#yxIopvOQZuq5

Ammori, M. (2014). The "New" New York Times: Free speech lawyering in the age of google and twitter. *Harvard Law Review, 127*(8), 2259–2295. https://harvardlawreview.org/2014/06/the-new-new-york-times-free-speech-lawyering-in-the-age-of-google-and-twitter/

Arun, C. (2018, Mar 28). Rebalancing regulation of speech: Hyper-local content on global web-based platforms. *Berkman-Klein center for internet and society*. Retrieved from: https://medium.com/berkman-klein-center/rebalancing-regulation-of-speech-hyper-local-content-on-global-web-based-platforms-1-386d65d86e32

Benkler, Y. (2006). *The wealth of networks: How social production transforms markets and freedom*. New Haven, CT: Yale University Press.

BSR. (2018, October). *Human rights impact assessment: Facebook in Myanmar*. Retrieved from https://about.fb.com/wp-content/uploads/2018/11/bsr-facebook-myanmar-hria_final.pdf

Calandro, E., Stork, C. and Gillwald, A. (2012). Internet going mobile: Internet access and usage in 11 African countries. *ResearchICT Africa*. Retrieved from https://researchictafrica.net/publication/internet-going-mobile-internet-access-and-usage-in-11-african-countries/

Carmody, T. (2011). Google+ Identity Crisis: What's at stake with real names and privacy. *Wired*. Retrieved from www.wired.com/2011/07/google-plus-user-names/

Castells, M. (1996). *The rise of the network society*. Malden, MA: Blackwell Publishers.

Deibert, R., Palfrey, J., Rohozinski, R., & Zittrain, J. (2010). *Access controlled: The shaping of power, rights and rule in cyberspace*. Cambridge, MA: Massachusetts Institute of Technology Press.

Donovan, J. (2021). Statement for hearing on "Algorithms and amplification: How media platforms' design choices shape our discourse and our minds." Senate Committee of the Judiciary Subcommittee on Privacy, Technology, and the Law. Retrieved from www.judiciary.senate.gov/imo/media/doc/Donovan%20Testimony%20(updated).pdf

Farrell, H. (2006). Regulating information flows: States, private actors and e-commerce. *Comparative Research in Law & Political Economy, 2*(1). Retrieved from https://digital-commons.osgoode.yorku.ca/cgi/viewcontent.cgi?referer=https://scholar.google.com/&httpsredir=1&article=1163&context=clpe

Fiegerman, S. (2014, February 3). Friendster founder tells his side of the story, 10 years after Facebook. *Mashable*. Retrieved from https://mashable.com/2014/02/03/jonathan-abrams-friendster-facebook/

Forelle, M. C., Howard, P., Monroy-Hernandez, A., & Savage, S. (2015). *Political bots and the manipulation of public opinion in Venezuela*. arXiv. Retrieved from https://arxiv.org/pdf/1507.07109.pdf

Freedom House. (2015, October). *Freedom on the net 2015*. Retrieved from https:// freedomhouse.org/sites/default/files/2020-02/FH_FOTN_2015Report_Overview-EssayFinal.pdf

Gadde, V. (2014, March 26). Challenging the access ban in Turkey. *Twitter*. Retrieved from https://blog.twitter.com/official/en_us/a/2014/challenging-the-access-ban-in-turkey.html

Gerbaudo, P. (2012). *Tweets and the streets: Social media and contemporary activism*. London: Pluto Press.

Geybullayeva, A. (2021, April 19). How Azerbaijan's government abused Face-book's loopholes – for years. *Global Voices*. Retrieved from https://globalvoices. org/2021/04/19/how-azerbaijans-government-abused-facebooks-loopholes-for-years/?utm_source=twitter.com&utm_medium=social&utm_campaign=targetings-Testglobalvoicestest&utm_content=Arzu-Geybullayeva&utm_term=733846#0_8_9 097_7947_2307_228180578

Hurriyet Daily News. (2014, March 22). *Turkey widens Internet censorship*. Retrieved from www.hurriyetdailynews.com/turkey-widens-internet-censorship-63954

Jansen, S., & Martin, B. (2015). The Streisand effect and censorship backfire. *International Journal of Communication*, *9*, 656–671. Retrieved from https://ro.uow.edu.au/ cgi/viewcontent.cgi?referer=https://scholar.google.com/&httpsredir=1&article=289 0&context=lhapapers

Kelly, K. (2018, September 18). How the Internet gave all of us superpowers. *WIRED Magazine*. Retrieved from www.wired.com/story/wired25-kevin-kelly-internet-superpowers-great-upwelling/

Kim, J. U., Oleribe, O., Njie, R., & Taylor-Robinson, S. D. (2017). A time for new north-south relationships in global health. *International Journal of General Medicine*, *10*, 401–408.

Klonick, K. (2018). The new governors: The people, rules, and processes governing online speech. *Harvard Law Review*, *131*(6), 1598–1670.

LIRNEAsia. (2012). Facebook = Internet?. *LIRNEAsia*. Retrieved from https://lirneasia. net/2012/05/facebook-internet/

Mac, R., Warzel, C., & Kantrowitz, A. (2018, March 28). Growth at any cost: Top Face-book executive defended data collection in 2016 memo – And warned that Facebook could get people killed. *Buzzfeed*. Retrieved from www.buzzfeednews.com/article/ ryanmac/growth-at-any-cost-top-facebook-executive-defended-data

Mackinnon, R. (2014). *Consent of the networked: The worldwide struggle for internet freedom*. New York: Basic Books.

Marechal, N. (2017). Networked authoritarianism and the geopolitics of information: Understanding Russian Internet policy. *Media and Communication*, 5(1): 29–41.

Miller, C. C. (2012, September 14). Google has no plans to rethink video status. *The New York Times*. Retrieved from www.nytimes.com/2012/09/15/world/middleeast/ google-wont-rethink-anti-islam-videos-status.html

Morozov, E. (2012). *The net delusion: The dark side of internet freedom*. New York: PublicAffairs Books.

Noam, E. (2003). The internet: Still wide open and competitive? *TPRC 2003*. Retrieved from https://papers.ssrn.com/sol3/papers.cfm?abstract_id=2056037

Palatino, M. (2017, June 27). At Thailand's request, YouTube blocks video clip of Charlie Chaplin's 'The Great Dictator'. *Global Voices Advocacy*. Retrieved from https://advox. globalvoices.org/2017/06/27/at-thailands-request-youtube-blocks-video-clip-of-charlie-chaplins-the-great-dictator/

Pearce, K.E., & Kendzior, S. (2012). Networked authoritarianism and social media in Azerbaijan. *Journal of Communication*, 62(2): 283–298.

Penney, J. (2021). Understanding chilling effects. *Minnesota Law Review, 106*. Retrieved from https://papers.ssrn.com/sol3/papers.cfm?abstract_id=3855619

Satariano, A., & Stevis-Gridneff, M. (2020, December 14). Big tech turns its lobbyists loose on Europe, alarming regulators. *The New York Times*. Retrieved from www.nytimes.com/2020/12/14/technology/big-tech-lobbying-europe.html.

Schiller, D. (1999). *Digital capitalism: Networking the global market system*. Cambridge, MA: Massachusetts Institute of Technology Press.

Schwartz, B. (2020, July 31). Big Tech spends over $20 million on lobbying in first half of 2020, including on coronavirus legislation. *CNBC*. Retrieved from www.cnbc.com/2020/07/31/big-tech-spends-20-million-on-lobbying-including-on-corona-virus-bills.html

Silverman, C., Mac, R., & Dixit, P. (2020, September 13). "I have blood on my hands": A whistleblower says Facebook ignored global political manipulation. *Buzzfeed*. Retrieved from www.buzzfeednews.com/article/craigsilverman/facebook-ignore-political-manipulation-whistleblower-memo

Tufekci, Z. (2017). *Twitter and tear gas: The power and fragility of networked protest*. New Haven, CT: Yale University Press.

Tufekci, Z., & Wilson, C. (2012). Social media and the decision to participate in political protest: Observations from Tahrir Square. *Journal of Communication*, *62*(2), 363–379. https://doi.org/10.1111/j.1460-2466.2012.01629.x

Turner, F. (2006). *From counterculture to cyberculture: Stewart Brand, the whole earth network, and the rise of digital utopianism*. Chicago: University of Chicago Press.

Twitter. (2014, March 20). Retrieved from https://twitter.com/policy/status/446775722120458241

Van Dijck, J. (2013). *The culture of connectivity: A critical history of social media*. Oxford: Oxford University Press.

West, S. M. (2017a). Data capitalism: Redefining the logics of surveillance and privacy. *Business & Society*, *58*(1), 20–41.

West, S. M. (2017b). Ambivalence in the (Private) Public Sphere: How global digital activists navigate risk. In *7th USENIX Workshop on Free and Open Communications on the Internet*. Retrieved from www.usenix.org/conference/foci17/workshop-program/presentation/west

West, S.M., & Biddle, E. (2017, July 27). Facebook's free basics doesn't connect you to the global internet – but it does collect your data. *Global Voices Advocacy*. Retrieved from https://advox.globalvoices.org/2017/07/27/facebooks-free-basics-doesnt-connect-you-to-the-global-internet-but-it-does-collect-your-data/

Wu, T. (2018). *The curse of bigness: Antitrust in the New Gilded Age*. New York: Columbia Global Reports.

Yeginsu, C., & Arango, T. (2013, April 16). Turkey greets Twitter delegation with list of demands. *The New York Times*. Retrieved from www.nytimes.com/2014/04/17/world/europe/a-list-of-demands-greets-twitter-delegation-in-turkey.html

York, J. (2021). *Silicon values: The future of free speech under surveillance capitalism*. London: Verso Books.

Youmans, W., & York, J. C. (2012). Social media and the activist toolkit: User agreements, corporate interests, and the information infrastructure of modern social movements. *Journal of Communication, 62*(2), 315–329.

Zittrain, J. (2009). *The future of the Internet and how to stop it.* New Haven, CT: Yale University Press.

Zuckerberg, M. (2012). Facebook's S-1 Letter from Zuckerberg urges understanding before investment. *TechCrunch.* Retrieved from https://techcrunch.com/2012/02/01/facebook-ipo-letter/

Zuckerberg, M. (2016). The technology behind Aquila. *Facebook.* Retrieved from www.facebook.com/notes/670584150260175/

3

CONTEMPORARY SOCIAL CAPITAL

Relationships Versus Awareness

Michael A. Stefanone and Jessica M. Covert

Introduction

Humans always find themselves involved in social groups. Today, communication and social exchange within and across these groups is typically mediated by technology. Contemporary social media platforms are the conduit for a slew of social exchange today including conversations with our family and friends, romantic partners, as well as interest groups, political parties/candidates, and corporations. Social media is characterized best as the set of tools that facilitates production and distribution of content produced by everyday individuals and formal organizations of all kinds.

Self-interest guides much of human behavior both offline and online. For example, we present ourselves strategically by sharing selfies to maximize the probability of achieving interpersonal goals (Stefanone, Yue, & Toh, 2019). Moreover, we routinely use specific platforms to promote ourselves professionally, among a wide range of other goals. Of course, these goals and behaviors are consistent with a rational choice perspective on the human condition.

The nature and structure of these relationships are often framed in terms of social capital. Consequently, there is currently pervasive interest in the relationship between these platforms and related content, (online) social networks, the nature of interpersonal relationships mediated by social network sites (SNS), and the changing role people now play in the production and consumption of mass-mediated messages. Considering that social media platforms facilitate the accumulation of expansive networks of acquaintances, there are pressing questions about the relationships between behavior guided by self-interest and access to resources like social capital.

Social capital is a rather vast conceptual framework employing social network analysis as an analytical framework and a variety of evolving operationalizations

DOI: 10.4324/9781003171270-3

regarding the size, structure, and intensity of personal relationships across contexts (e.g., within formal organizations, etc.). Conversations about social capital often center on perceptions of resource availability. For example, if your friends are lawyers, doctors, and politicians, you likely have access to more social capital, compared to someone like an immigrant or a refugee who is new to a country or city and has few friends. This research operationalizes categories of relationships in terms of bridging (i.e., weak tie, casual relationships) and bonding (strong, emotionally close ties) capital (Adler & Kwon, 2002) and continues to explore the impact our relationships have on our beliefs and behavior (Ellison, Wohn, & Greenhow, 2014).

One of the critical distinctions emerging in the literature on social capital has been between perceptions of resource availability and *actual* enacted support. Stefanone, Kwon, and Lackaff (2012) argued that although there is significant research on social capital, there is little research focusing on *online* social capital and the kinds of actual support available via mediated networks. They conducted one of the first field studies to evaluate actual supportive behavior (or, enacted support) in response to requests for help via social media, and results suggest a disconnect between perceptions and behavior.

The research on perceptions and actual behavior led the authors of this chapter to start thinking about the consequences of persistent, readably accessible data about our social worlds which extends far beyond our immediate physical environment. Never before have we had access to comprehensive databases of social behavior like we do today. The sheer volume of social data available raises questions about whether systematic differences exist in our ability to attend to and process this information.

To begin addressing these questions, we have been working over the past nearly ten years to conceptualize and explicate a novel construct related to the "social capital" family of ideas – we call this new construct *network monitoring*. In short, we propose that network monitoring offers a framework for thinking about and measuring the extent to which individuals focus on what's occurring around them socially – in real time – and their aptitude in terms of processing that information. This work grew out of and is an extension of scholarship on cognitive social structures (CSS) (Casciaro, 1998). Thus, the purpose of this chapter is to outline the development of the network monitoring construct by providing a historical context and summary of recent findings.

In the following, we first present a broad overview of one important theory of self-interest: instrumental action. This review sets the stage for more in-depth analysis of related scholarship framed in the context of social capital. Armed with knowledge about the intersection between rational choice theories explaining human behavior and the nature of the structures of relationships that surround us, we present *network monitoring* as an alternative way to think about social resources in networked society.

Self-Interest and Instrumental Action

Social scientists concerned with self-interest as a motivation for social action (Coleman, 1986) suggest individuals make what they believe to be rational choices while pursuing interpersonal and social objectives (Monge & Contractor, 2003). Of course, humans are not always objective, systematic beings (e.g., Frijda, 1986). However, rational choice theorists (e.g., Homans, 1950) outline the processes through which individuals systematically weigh outcomes based on sets of alternative actions and make decisions based on straightforward cost–benefit analyses. This approach suggests that people actively attend to and process the information available to them with the purpose of maximizing their individual outcomes. When it comes to understanding the characteristics and flow of social information, social network analysis is a critically important tool.

Social Network Analysis

It is helpful at this point to briefly review social network analysis to establish a baseline understanding of key vocabulary. The premise that behavior and action are interpretable only in relation to the positions of actors in social structures underlies much social scientific inquiry. Social structures can be defined as "persisting patterns of social relationships among social positions" (Laumann, 1966). The traditional network approach focuses on relationships between actors rather than on the attributes of actors in different social network positions.

Abstractions of social network structures centered on an individual are known as "ego centered" networks, and include social relationships of all kinds (Mitchell, 1969). In pursuing an egocentric approach to network analysis, the breadth and intensity of social relationships are measured for a group of individuals, resulting in a collection of ego networks, one for each individual studied. Thus, ego refers to focal actors in networks (Wellman, 1993). An egocentric network can be conceptualized also as a representation of an individual's potential sphere of influence. The range of an ego network represents the breadth or variety of one's social network. Within ego networks, social relationships differ in contact intensity. Strong-tie contacts are characterized by frequent, reciprocal communication and include resources for social and emotional support. Often, strong ties constitute relationships with family and close friends. Weak ties, on the other hand, are characterized by infrequent communication, low reciprocity, and a lack of emotional closeness. Granovetter's (1973, 1982) seminal work on the "strength of weak ties" suggests that acquaintances (weak ties) could offer an advantage over friends and colleagues (strong ties) in obtaining useful information such as job opportunities. Whether strong or weak ties are the source of supportive resources, those resources are typically employed for instrumental goals.

Instrumental Action

The literature on self-interest and behavior largely stems from research on status attainment (e.g., Blau & Duncan, 1967). The theory of instrumental action offers an alternative perspective by explicating the nature of relationships and embedded resources (e.g., social capital). While status attainment was operationalized as a function of "given" social network properties, status attainment should also be viewed as a product of strategic relationship choices.

Lin's (1982) theory of instrumental action describes behaviors that seek to achieve goals that benefit the individual taking action. These behaviors are thus defined as instrumental in nature and are restricted to actions involving interpersonal relationships. From this perspective, resources embedded in social networks are used to maintain or promote an individual's self-interest (i.e., survival, wealth). Thus, the theory focuses on instrumental action initiated for the purpose of gaining valued resources that reside in social systems.

Moreover, Lin's theory predicts that actors occupying certain network positions have greater access to social resources and, therefore, have greater success using resources for instrumental purposes. For example, individuals positioned high in formal hierarchies, determined by status, prestige, power, etc., are assumed to have greater accessibility and command of resources by virtue of their network characteristics. Network characteristics associated with position in a hierarchy include greater range and visibility of the network. For example, weak ties tend to lead to better social resources than strong ties (Granovetter, 1982). Thus, those network positions that facilitate access to numerous weak ties should facilitate the development of novel and diverse information sources. We refer to these types of resources that are derived from social relationships as social capital (Burt, 1992; Lin, 2001).

Obviously, the tools we use to develop and maintain relationships have changed in meaningful ways over the past 20 years, particularly in light of the popularity of social media. Subsequently, there has been increasing scholarly activity directed at these processes and behaviors. We provide an overview and background on more recent research on social capital with emphasis on specific dimensions which have become prominent in the literature including bridging and bonding capital.

Social Capital

Lin (2001) proposes a clearly operationalizable definition of social capital as "investment in social relations by individuals through which they gain access to embedded resources to enhance expected returns of instrumental or expressive actions" (p. 39). Lin's definition is particularly useful because it elucidates the social nature of capital. According to Adler and Kwon (2002), social capital is understood as "the good will that is engendered by the fabric of social relations . . . mobilized to facilitate action (p. 17)." Other scholars emphasize that social capital is embedded in interpersonal relationships that develop during the pursuit of instrumental goals (e.g., Coleman, 1988; Kadushin, 2004). In sum, social capital can be defined as networked resources that are created, maintained, and leveraged through relationships occurring via mediated communication (Wellman & Frank, 2001).

Social support is one type of resource that is accessed through social networks and refers to availability of emotional and material support from others. Barrera (1986) suggests that social support research should clearly differentiate among three major concepts: social embeddedness, perceived social support, and enacted support. Social embeddedness refers to the structures of relationships connecting people. This is typically measured with social network analytic techniques which facilitate the quantification of structural properties of communication networks (Walker, Wasserman, & Wellman, 1994; Wellman, Carrington, & Hall, 1988; Wellman & Gulia, 1999; Wellman & Wortley, 1990).

Perceived social support is one of the broadest and most prevalent operationalizations in the social support literature (Barrera, 1986) and reflects idiosyncratic perceptions of support, rather than social structure. Perceived social support has been found to correlate with a range of psychosocial and physiological responses and behaviors including coping (Tao, Dong, Pratt, Hunsberger, & Pancer, 2000), academic achievement (Eggens, van der Werf, & Bosker, 2008), and even blood pressure (O'Donovan & Hughes, 2007). More recently, research on social network sites has adopted measures differentiating between bridging and bonding support (Williams, 2006).

Finally, enacted support refers to the actual provision or reception of support. Barrera (1986) notes that enacted support is often measured using self-report data. As such, much extant research has in fact measured perceived-received support. Valid measures of enacted support should therefore utilize behavioral observation or dyadic analysis.

As mentioned earlier, different perspectives on the nature of social relationships and resources have led to the identification and operationalization of two related forms of social capital: *bonding and bridging*. Bonding capital is understood as embedded in internal or closely connected social ties (Adler & Kwon, 2002), and research shows that perceptions of bonding capital increase credibility assessments, garner consensus from others, and enhance emotional support (Williams, 2006). Bonding capital can be particularly advantageous for collective endeavors (Klandermans, 1984; McAdam & Paulsen, 1993; Opp & Gern, 1989). For example, Coleman (1988) focused on a student revolution in Korea to discuss the collective returns of bonding social capital within small clandestine groups. Gould (1991) also illustrated the importance of neighborhood relations in exerting contagious motivation toward protest participation. Thus, bonding capital is related to group solidarity, which in turn should be related to enacted, mutual social support.

Bridging capital is associated with diverse social ties (Adler & Kwon, 2002) and is understood as linkage capital because it facilitates connections to otherwise disparate social groups. The advantage of bridging capital lies in its ability to connect people to novel, nonredundant social resources. For example, information flow between groups providing instrumental resources may be limited in homogeneous networks exhibiting insulating properties opposed to heterogeneous networks where subgroups are connected by liaisons (Granovetter, 1973). Accordingly, bridging social capital is understood as benefits stemming from network diversity.

Hampton, Lee, and Her (2011) explored the relationship between offline and online behavior and network diversity and framed their investigation in the context of advantages associated broadly with "accessible social capital" (p. 14). They found that Internet use, and in particular the use of SNS, had positive relationships with network diversity (or, bridging capital). Also, their results suggest a negative relationship between SNS use and the number of offline neighborhood ties people maintained, which suggests a replacement process whereby resources obtained by local, offline relationships are now accessible by mediated interpersonal relationships. Their results are consistent with Wellman's (2001) argument that in a networked society, physical proximity is becoming less important in terms of access to social capital. However, questions persist regarding the extent to which actual, enacted support resources accrue to users today.

Bonding and bridging social capital develop through regular activity that (in)directly facilitates interaction with other people. Thus, the social nature of contemporary Internet use lends itself to the accumulation of bonding and bridging capital (Wellman, Haase, Witte, & Hampton, 2001). The widespread use of social media increases perceived social capital (Ellison, Steinfield, & Lampe, 2007) which can create opportunities to expand the size of recruitment pools for instrumental action. The level of interpersonal and collective capital built online may contribute to instrumental action online and offline.

Much of the scholarship reviewed earlier relies on self-report survey data. However, there has been efforts to address actual behavior related to social capital. Operationalized as enacted support, we review a stream of research aimed at evaluating actual behavior related to the mobilization of social capital via social media text. This review is presented in part to explain the proposed need to begin to start thinking about social capital not in terms of position in networks, or raw network connections facilitated by social media, but rather in terms of cognitive processes related to attention to our social worlds.

Enacted Support

Grounded in the theory of instrumental action (Lin, 1982) and limited to instrumental support, Stefanone et al. (2012) established a baseline for assessing actual networked resources by exploring the accessibility of social capital embedded in online networks. The motivation for this study was due to a lack of research examining the relationship between perceived social capital and the *actual* capacity of generating enacted support. The authors approached the problem of actual enacted support by conducting a field study based on two sets of hypotheses. The first set explored the provision of instrumental support via relationships mediated by SNS. Research suggests that perceptions of online social capital are positively associated with an individual's psychological well-being.

The second set of hypotheses was posited by considering specific relationship characteristics between SNS friends independent of perceptions of bonding social capital online. Many network scholars have discussed the multidimensionality of relationship characteristics including Marsden and Campbell (1984), who found that tie strength – operationalized as emotional closeness and communication frequency – are distinct constructs. Wellman and Wortley (1990) also treated tie strength and contact frequency as distinct variables. Of particular interest to this study was the distinction between relational explanations which include "the strength of the relationship or . . . access that two persons have to each other" (p. 560). Here, strength is characterized by voluntary, intimate relationships. On the other hand, access is related directly to communication frequency and interaction (Galaskiewicz, 1985). In light of this evidence, it is likely that tie strength and contact frequency operate as two separate variables that explain the provision of support.

Results showed that of the 600 requests for help issued via Facebook, about 80% went unanswered. Further, perceptions of bridging and bonding capital did not explain whether social network friends responded to requests for help. These results are important because they point to a disconnect between the perceptions we maintain about social resources and the actual mobilization of these resources. To our knowledge, this was the first study to evaluate social capital based on a behavior metric while controlling for participant's perceptions of bridging and bonding capital. Ultimately, this study provided the motivation to begin reconceptualizing the social capital framework in terms of individual differences in cognitive resources dedicated to the social world.

Social media and online networking sites have functionally enhanced our ability to maintain a broader spectrum of relationships ranging from the most intimate to extremely superficial. This exploratory study focused on social capital operationalized as enacted online support and began to explore the utility of vast networks articulated via SNS like Facebook.

We propose that social media afford us persistent access to social network and relationship-related information beyond our immediate social worlds. Social media users have unprecedented access to network-related data, and it may be the case that these individuals are building a more comprehensive understanding of the online and offline social networks they routinely navigate and thus capitalizing on the opportunities posed by generally public and persistent information about their associations. However, comparatively fewer academic resources have been dedicated to understanding the precise motivational and cognitive processes that modulate this kind of understanding and knowledge.

Proficiency in understanding the complexities and nuances of the social structures that surround us is a useful skill, and it is likely that some people are naturally better at understanding their social worlds regardless of online social network data.

As the body of research concerning (online) social networks and social media continues to grow, scholars have sustained interest in communicative dynamics within and across mediated networks and outcomes like opportunity and control (Friedkin, 1983). Much research has been dedicated to investigating how individuals use social networking sites in order to access social capital, although the results are mixed (e.g., Stefanone et al., 2012). Importantly, results demonstrate a weak relationship between perceptions of social capital and actual behavior. This raises important questions including: 1) Are there systematic differences in our ability and motivation to attend to social information? and, 2) If so, are there consequences for "managing and negotiating" our social worlds in pursuit of "capital"? We address these fundamental questions next.

Network Monitoring

Relatively little research has been conducted regarding the ways in which individuals actually understand the structure and composition of the complex and dynamic social networks surrounding them. Relatedly, little is known about which individual differences likely demonstrate systematic relationships with attending to, processing, understanding, and ultimately leveraging knowledge about the structure and dynamics of relationships comprising one's social sphere. Investigating these processes starts with both an understanding of the intrinsic motivation to pursue this knowledge and the ability to gain, consolidate, and subsequently mobilize it in the pursuit of strategic personal, social goals. The ability to measure declarative knowledge of social structure – the purpose of our network monitoring research – will eventually facilitate research on procedural knowledge whereby individuals actively pursue social goals.

In order to gain the greatest access to potentially rewarding relationships, individuals must be able to accurately perceive, interact with, and predict the behavior of others in their networks. Recall that network monitoring is composed of more than an individual's knowledge of how he or she stands in relation to the other members of their social network. Network monitoring is defined as the extent to which individuals understand the structure of their social world and the relationships within it. The construct of network monitoring suggests that individuals who best gauge the relationships between other members of their social networks are better able to negotiate their self-presentation and interactions with others not only in relation to individuals but also in relation to the network as a whole. For example, network monitoring enhances the ability of high self-monitors to acquire the kind of bridging social capital that can result in better job offers or other benefits and opportunities. This suggests that network monitoring, as well as understanding other-based reciprocity and the tendency to self-monitor, all contribute to an individual's comprehensive understanding of dynamic social networks.

Our work on network monitoring is based on large part on extant literature in the domain of CSS.

Cognitive Social Structures

As aforementioned, traditional approaches to social network analysis examine the existing patterns between actors in a network. However, there is a competing perspective known as CSS (Krackhardt, 1987), which suggests that there is merit in examining how individuals attend to and understand the information about their social network. It is important to note that social cognition is not a new phenomenon. Early ideas such as Lewin's (1951) field theory argue that individuals' behaviors are often influenced by their subjective experiences with their social environment. Heider's (1958) balance theory suggests that individuals experience discomfort when they perceive individuals in their social network to not like one another. However, there has been a recent resurgence of research examining how individuals attend to and understand information about their social network.

This contemporary approach to social network analysis argues that cognitive monitoring of social networks has additional benefits at both the individual and global levels. For example, individuals who have the motivation and/or ability to acquire knowledge about others can use that information to mobilize resources embedded in their networks (Brands, 2013). Flynn, Reagans, Amanatullah, and Ames (2006) argue that understanding one's social network is important to the development and maintenance of relationships. Dunbar (2008) argues that on a large-scale level understanding the cognitive components of social network analysis helps advance the human race. In the following, we will outline the foundational ideas explaining this contemporary perspective.

CSS are defined as individuals' cognitive representations of social networks. CSS emphasize *perception*, such that each individual has their own idea of the relational dynamics between other actors in a given social network. Often, there are discrepancies between the actor's perceptions of and the actual structure of the network. For example, some individuals have an accurate understanding of who knows who and to what degree. Alternatively, one can have a skewed perception of the network and believe that some network connections are closer than they actually are. Building upon this idea, Casciaro (1998) proposed that individuals differ in *network perception accuracy* defined as one's ability to correctly perceive the informal dynamics between individuals in a group. Network perception accuracy can further be broken down into two levels: local and global. Local network perception accuracy refers to one's perception of their direct relationships with others in a social network, and global accuracy refers to one's perception of the complete set of relationships linking all members of a social network (Casciaro, Carley, & Krackhardt, 1999).

Research suggests that network perception accuracy is a complex cognitive task as it requires individuals to collect substantial information about those in their social network. Individuals must process through this information by filtering out the irrelevant noise and making sense of that tied to their social network (Casciaro et al., 1999). Casciaro et al. (1999) argue that network perception accuracy requires individuals to have not only the cognitive capacity to obtain information about those in their network but also high levels of mental organization and flexibility to make sense of this information. Brands (2013) further elaborates that individuals can rely on schemas or knowledge structures acquired via experiences to make judgments as to what social information is considered (ir)relevant. Schemas serve as also filters, retaining information consistent with our knowledge structures while discarding information that is incongruent (Bem, 1981). Brand (2013) identifies three main relational schema that influence how individuals process information embedded in their social environment: perception of hierarchy, equivalence, and groups.

Scholars have sought to identify additional elements that influence individuals' network perception accuracy, such as situational factors and individual differences. For example, Casciaro (1998) proposed that one's formal position within an organization impacts access to social information. Specifically, individuals holding higher-level positions end up feeling increasingly disconnected from the informal networks within organizations. Additionally, scholars have begun identifying and examining individual differences such as need for affiliation (Casciaro, 1998), positive affectivity (Casciaro et al., 1999), in addition to network monitoring (Covert, Stefanone, Foucault-Welles, Yue, & Toh, 2018) that help systematically explain differences in network perception accuracy.

Recall that network monitoring stems from theories of self-interest which suggest that individuals engage in rational thought when interacting with others (Monge & Contractor, 2003). This line of research proposes that individuals seek to maximize their benefits and minimize their costs by monitoring their social environment. Network monitoring measures the extent to which individuals dedicate their cognitive resources toward understanding their environment to strategically obtain network resources (Covert et al., 2018). Network monitoring builds on previous constructs including self-monitoring and network attention, which we review next.

Self-Monitoring

Individuals high in self-monitoring can engage in optimal self-presentation as a function of attending to and observing others' behavior. Specifically, individuals with the ability to self-monitor can control and manage their behavioral expressions and nonverbal displays of emotion (Snyder, 1979). High self-monitors can understand the social rules acceptable within their environment and strategically behave in accordance with these norms (Snyder, 1974). Low self-monitors consistently behave in ways that are "true to themselves" across all social contexts, while high self-monitors' behaviors vary as a function of the situation. High self-monitors are more likely to achieve their goals because they can gauge the expectations and responses of others, and therefore behave in accordance with these social norms. Network monitoring builds upon the social monitoring literature by further suggesting that individuals not only have self-awareness, but they also attend to others' interactions.

Network Attention

Badawy, Stefanone, and Brouer (2014) proposed a novel construct called social network attention – originally referred to as awareness – which suggests that individuals differ in their ability to understand the dynamics of their interpersonal relationships. Individuals high on network attention have the tendency to dedicate their cognitive resources toward their social environment and therefore, have the ability to understand the structure and equity statuses of members of their social network. Stefanone, Iacobucci, and Svetieva (2016) further examined the effect network attention had on one's ability to attend to, process, and understand relational dynamics in novel social situations.

Stefanone et al. (2016) found that individuals high on network attention had higher levels of network perception accuracy when given a test assessing one's perception of the dynamics among a group of unknown individuals. The stimulus material were scenes of varying complexity pulled from two movies, *Who's Afraid of Virginia Woolf* (1966) and *Key Largo* (1948). These older movies were used to minimize the likelihood that participants were familiar with the plots. The test administered to participants evaluated their understanding of the past, current, and future relationship dynamics of the characters in the video clips.

Covert and Stefanone (2020) furthered this research by examining how network attention influences one's ability to attend and respond to social exclusion signals. Specifically, participants were given written hypothetical scenarios where they were excluded from or included in conversations between their close friends on social media. Results found that those high on network attention experienced negative emotions in the excluded condition and positive emotions in the included condition. Although there are ecological validity concerns with this methodology, we can see that those high on network attention care about managing their social networks carefully to ensure social capital accruement. All these findings suggest that it is likely that there are systematic differences in individuals' attention to their social network.

Network monitoring is a trait building upon self-monitoring and network attention research. Specifically, network monitoring comprises four conceptually distinct dimensions which measure the cognitive and behavioral components of social network attention: network structural awareness, social awareness, advantage, and actualization (Covert et al., 2018). Network structural awareness assesses the degree to which one understands the structure of relationships between members of their network. Individuals high on network structural awareness can identify which members of their network actually know each other. Network social awareness assesses the extent to which one acquires social information about those in their social circle. For example, those high on network social awareness are knowledgeable of the news and gossip spreading throughout their network. Network advantage assesses individuals' networking and matchmaking abilities. Specifically, those high on network advantage can broker connections between those who do not know each other. Finally, network actualization assesses the degree to which one can turn their social resources into benefits. Individuals high on network actualization understand which of their network members can provide them resources when needed.

Covert et al. (2018) investigated network monitoring in the context of social exclusion to examine how this trait influences individuals' attention and response to exclusion signals. Note that fulfilling the need to belong is fundamental to human behavior – much of our actions are motivated by the desire to achieve acceptance and affiliation from others (Baumeister & Leary, 1995). Baumeister and Leary (1995) suggest that when individuals encounter social exclusion signals or instances where one's belongingness is threatened, they experience cognitive, emotional, and/or behavioral consequences. Thus, individuals dedicate much of their cognitive resources toward understanding and managing their social networks to quickly respond to and remedy any instances of social exclusion. However, it is likely that those high on network monitoring are particularly sensitive to social exclusion signals as they dedicate much of their cognitive resources toward understanding and managing their social network.

Covert et al. (2018) replicated Covert and Stefanone's (2020) methodology by employing hypothetical written scenarios of social exclusion and inclusion on social media. Covert et al. (2018) argued that those high on network monitoring should be more sensitive to social exclusion signals as these individuals dedicate much of their cognitive resources toward understanding and navigating their social network. Results from this study found that specific dimensions of network monitoring – network social awareness and advantage – were significant predictors of negative affect in the excluded condition. Specifically, those who surveil their social environment and seek to bridge members of their social network are particularly sensitive to experiencing social exclusion on social media. Results from this study showcase that those high on network monitoring care about encountering social exclusion signals as it affects one's social capital accruement.

Network Monitoring as a Distinct Construct

Thorndike (1920) argued that in order to further research on theories of self-interest and advance knowledge about how individuals develop and acquire social capital, scholars should focus on distinguishing various social effectiveness traits from one another. Thus, Covert and Stefanone (2021) replicated Stefanone and colleagues' (2016) original work utilizing the network monitoring construct in addition to assessing participants on political skill – a well-known and tested organizational construct that assesses individual differences in one's ability to understand social situations with the ability to modify one's behaviors to situational demands (Ferris, Kolodinsky, Hochwarter, & Frink, 2001). Ferris and colleagues (2005) proposed political skill as a multidimensional construct including four dimensions: networking ability, interpersonal influence, social astuteness, and apparent sincerity.

Networking ability measures the extent to which individuals can develop and utilize their social network at work. Individuals with high networking ability spend time building their diverse network for advantageous purposes. Interpersonal influence captures one's ability to situationally adapt their behavior to different influence targets and contexts. Individuals high on interpersonal influence are good at getting others to like them. Social astuteness examines one's ability to understand the interpersonal dynamics of social situations. Individuals high on social astuteness can manage and attend to the nonverbal cues and facial expressions in social situations. Finally, apparent sincerity measures the extent to which individuals can convey communication sincerity, authenticity, and honesty to others. Research suggests that individuals high on political skill can recognize and capitalize opportunities not only for self-promotion, (Andrews, Kacmar, & Harris, 2009) but also for the organization (Blass & Ferris, 2007). Additionally, evidence suggests that political skill is associated with favorable ratings of others within organizations (e.g., Jawahar, Meurs, Ferris, & Hochwarter, 2008).

Although political skill is important for organizational growth, Covert and Stefanone (2021) argue that it is important to understand how individuals generally attend to and understand the dynamics of their social world – not just within an organizational context. Specifically, research suggests that individuals who are able to understand and maximize the social capital opportunities within their social world have more success with their interpersonal relationships (e.g., Rushton & Irwing, 2011). Covert and Stefanone (2021) employed the experimental design from Stefanone et al. (2016), where participants were exposed to short video vignettes of novel social situations with varying levels of complexity (low and high) and evaluated their accuracy and confidence on a test assessing the interpersonal dynamics of the characters' relationships. Results suggest that although network monitoring and political skill are related, they are conceptually distinct constructs. Further, results indicated that both network monitoring and political skill predicted accuracy in the low complexity condition only. Interestingly, network monitoring was the only significant predictor of confidence.

Together, these findings suggest that network monitoring may be a better global indicator of how much attention one dedicates to their social environment. It is possible that individuals high on network monitoring have more confidence in their responses as they have experience of previous success in their lives in regard to acquiring and understanding information about those in their social network. Note that network monitoring is a measure developed to understand general attention to one's social world while political skill was developed originally as a measure of strategic influence and control of others within organizations.

These findings are important in the context of social media as these platforms provide individuals access to a plethora of information about those in their social network. If individuals have the cognitive capacity and motivation to capitalize on this wealth of information, they have ample opportunity for social capital accruement to obtain both organizational and interpersonal goals. Thus, it is important for research to further examine these individual differences in attention to and processing of social information.

Conclusion

Humans are social beings who are motivated to maximize the opportunities embedded within their social networks to promote goal attainment. Social capital is a fruitful avenue of research as it helps explain how individuals obtain, process, and act upon the information readily available in both their offline and online networks. Throughout this chapter, we highlighted key concepts surrounding social capital and how social media influences the way we think about and acquire resources within our networks. We discussed the key terms and ideas surrounding the traditional approach to social capital known as social network analysis. Further, we highlighted a more contemporary approach to social capital which features scholarship on CSS to illustrate how individuals think about their social networks and capitalize on the opportunities embedded in those relationships. Finally, we reviewed the literature surrounding a novel construct known as network monitoring, which seeks to assess individual differences in attention to and understanding of one's social world.

After conducting this review on social media and social capital, we believe that the field of communication would benefit from researching this phenomenon in a multitude of ways. As previously mentioned, research on enacted support typically utilizes self-report measures. This is problematic as it measures individuals' *perceptions* of the resources embedded in their network and one's actual reception of support. Scholars can gain a more global understanding of how individuals obtain support from their networks by continuing to develop and validate new measures of enacted support such as behavioral observation or dyadic analysis.

Moreover, research on social media and social capital should continue teasing out the various individual differences regarding how individuals attend to the social information that is readily available in both offline and online realms.

As evidenced earlier, network monitoring influences an individual's attention to social exclusion and their ability to assess the informal dynamics between a group of unknown individuals. Future research should continue to examine network monitoring and other social effectiveness constructs in other capacities to gain a more global understanding of how individuals attend to and process social information. By understanding these constructs, we can further develop theories of self-interest and understand more about how individuals navigate their social networks and accrue social capital.

Finally, the authors of this chapter believe that if we can gain a more in-depth understanding on the various ways individuals attend to and process this online information, then we can use this information to train individuals on various ways to advantageously mobilize on the social capital embedded in both their offline and online networks. This is specifically important for those individuals belonging to underrepresented or unfairly treated social groups that could benefit from understanding and accessing the social capital embedded in their network.

References

Adler, P. S., & Kwon, S. W. (2002). Social capital: Prospects for a new concept. *Academy of Management Review, 27*(1), 17–40.

Andrews, M. C., Kacmar, K. M., & Harris, K. J. (2009). Got political skill? The impact of justice on the importance of political skill for job performance. *Journal of Applied Psychology, 94*(6), 1427–1437.

Badawy, R. L., Stefanone, M. A., & Brouer, R. (2014, January 6–9). I'm not just wasting time online! Development of Situational Awareness measure. In *Proceedings of the 47th Annual Hawaii International Conference on Systems Science* (HICSS). Hawaii: Big Island.

Barrera, M. Jr. (1986). Distinctions between social support concepts, measures, and models. *American Journal of Community Psychology, 14*(4), 413–445.

Baumeister, R. F., & Leary, M. R. (1995). The need to belong: Desire for interpersonal attachments as a fundamental human motivation. *Psychological Bulletin, 117*(3), 497–529.

Bem, S. L. (1981). Gender schema theory: A cognitive account of sex typing. *Psychological Review, 88*(4), 354.

Blass, F. R., & Ferris, G. R. (2007). Leader reputation: The role of mentoring, political skill, contextual learning, and adaptation. *Human Resource Management, 46*(1), 5–19.

Blau, P. M., & Duncan, O. D. (1967). *The American occupational structure.* New York: Wiley.

Brands, R. A. (2013). Cognitive social structures in social network research: A review. *Journal of Organizational Behavior, 34*(1), 82–103.

Burt, R. S. (1992). *Structural holes: The social structure of competition.* Cambridge, MA: Harvard University Press.

Casciaro, T. (1998). Seeing things clearly: Social structure, personality, and accuracy in social network perception. *Social Networks, 20*(4), 331–351.

Casciaro, T., Carley, K. M., & Krackhardt, D. (1999). Positive affectivity and accuracy in social network perception. *Motivation and Emotion, 23*(4), 285–306.

Coleman, J. C. (1988). Social capital in the creation of human capital. *American Journal of Sociology, 94*, 95–120.

Coleman, J. S. (1986). Social theory, social research: A theory of action. *American Journal of Sociology, 91*, 1309–1335.

Covert, J. M., & Stefanone, M. A. (2020). Does rejection still hurt? Examining the effects of network monitoring and exposure to online social exchange signals. *Social Science Computer Review, 38*(2), 170–186.

Covert, J. M., & Stefanone, M. A. (2021). *Covert surveillance: Understanding individual differences in attention to the social world* (Unpublished manuscript).

Covert, J. M., Stefanone, M. A., Foucault-Welles, B., Yue, Z., & Toh, Z. (2018, July). #thanksfortheinvite: Examining attention to social exclusion signals online. In *Proceedings of the 9th International Conference on Social Media and Society* (pp. 51–63). Copenhagen: ACM.

Dunbar, R. I. (2008). Cognitive constraints on the structure and dynamics of social networks. *Group Dynamics: Theory, Research, and Practice, 12*(1), 7.

Eggens, L., van der Werf, M., & Bosker, R. (2008). The influence of personal networks and social support on study attainment of students in university education. *Higher Education, 55*, 553–573.

Ellison, N. B., Steinfield, C., & Lampe, C. (2007). The benefits of Facebook "friends": Social capital and college students' use of online social network sites. *Journal of Computer-Mediated Communication, 12*(4), 1143–1168.

Ellison, N. B., Wohn, D. Y., & Greenhow, C. M. (2014). Adolescents' visions of their future careers, educational plans, and life pathways: The role of bridging and bonding social capital experiences. *Journal of Social and Personal Relationships, 31*(4), 516–534.

Ferris, G. R., Kolodinsky, R. W., Hochwarter, W. A., & Frink, D. D. (2001, August). *Conceptualization, measurement, and validation of the political skill construct* [Conference presentation]. Academy of Management's 61st Annual National Meeting. Washington, DC, United States.

Ferris, G. R., Treadway, D. C., Kolodinsky, R. W., Hochwarter, W. A., Kacmar, C. J., Douglas, C., & Frink, D. D. (2005). Development and validation of the political skill Inventory. *Journal of Management, 31*(1), 126–152.

Flynn, F. J., Reagans, R. E., Amanatullah, E. T., & Ames, D. R. (2006). Helping one's way to the top: Self-monitors achieve status by helping others and knowing who helps whom. *Journal of Personality and Social Psychology, 91*(6), 1123.

Friedkin, N. E. (1983). Horizons of observability and limits of informal control in organizations. *Social Forces, 62*(1), 54–77.

Frijda, N. H. (1986). *The emotions.* Cambridge: Cambridge University Press.

Galaskiewicz, J. (1985). *Social organization of an Urban Grants economy: A study of business philanthropy and nonprofit organizations.* Orlando, FL: Academic Press.

Gould, R. V. (1991). Multiple networks and mobilization in the Paris Commune, 1871. *American Sociological Review, 56*, 716–729.

Granovetter, M. (1973). The strength of weak ties. *American Journal of Sociology, 78*, 1360–1379.

Granovetter, M. (1982). The strength of weak ties: A network theory revisited. In P. V. Marsden & N. Lin (Eds.), *Social structure network* (pp. 105–130). Beverly Hills, CA: SAGE.

Hampton, K. N., Lee, C. J., & Her, E. J. (2011). How new media affords network diversity: Direct and mediated access to social capital through participation in local social settings. *New Media & Society, 13*(7), 1031–1049.

Heider, F. (1958). *The psychology of interpersonal relations.* New York: Wiley.

Homans, G. C. (1950). *The human group.* New York: Harcourt, Brace & World.

Jawahar, I. M., Meurs, J. A., Ferris, G. R., & Hochwarter, W. A. (2008). Self-efficacy and political skill as comparative predictors of task and contextual performance: A two-study constructive replication. *Human Performance, 21*(2), 138–157.

Kadushin, C. (2004). Too much investment in social capital? *Social Networks, 26,* 75–90.

Klandermans, B. (1984). Mobilization and participation: Social-psychological expansions of resource mobilization. *American Sociological Review, 49,* 583–660.

Krackhardt, D. (1987). Cognitive social structures. *Social Networks, 9,* 109–134.

Laumann, E. O. (1966). *Prestige and association in an urban community.* Indianapolis, IN. Bobbs-Merrill.

Lewin, K. (1951). *Field theory in social science.* New York: Harper.

Lin, N. (1982). Social resources and instrumental action. In P. V. Marsden, & Y. N. Lin (Eds.), *Social structure and network analysis* (pp. 131–145). Beverly Hills, CA: Sage.

Lin, N. (2001). Building a network theory of social capital. In N. Lin, K. Cook, & R. Burt (Eds.), *Social capital: Theory and research* (pp. 3–30). New York: Aldine de Gruyter.

Marsden, P. V., & Campbell, K. E. (1984). Measuring tie strength. *Social forces, 63*(2), 482–501.

McAdam, D., & Paulsen, R. (1993). Specifying the relationship between social ties and activism. *American Journal of Sociology, 99,* 640–667.

Mitchell, J. C. (1969). *The concept and use of social networks.* Manchester: Manchester University Press.

Monge, P. R., & Contractor, N. S. (2003). *Theories of communication networks.* Oxford: Oxford University Press.

O'Donovan, A., & Hughes, B. (2007). Social support and loneliness in college students: Effects on pulse pressure reactivity to acute stress. *International Journal of Adolescent Medicine and Health, 19,* 523–528.

Opp, K. D., & Gern, C. (1989). Dissident groups, personal networks, and spontaneous cooperation: The East German revolution of 1989. *American Sociological Review, 58,* 659–680.

Rushton, P., & Irwing, P. (2011). The general factor of personality: Normal and abnormal. In T. Chamorro-Premuzic, S. von Stumm, & A. Furnham (Eds.), *The Wiley-Blackwell handbook of individual differences* (pp. 132–161). London: Wiley Blackwell.

Snyder, M. (1974). Self-monitoring of expressive behavior. *Journal of Personality and Social Psychology, 30*(4), 526–537.

Snyder, M. (1979). Self-monitoring processes. *Advances in Experimental Social Psychology, 12,* 85–128.

Stefanone, M. A., Iacobucci, A., & Svetieva, E. (2016, January). Developing the network awareness construct: Evidence supporting the ability to understand social situations. In *2016 49th Hawaii International Conference on System Sciences (HICSS)* (pp. 2028–2037). IEEE.

Stefanone, M. A., Kwon, K. H., & Lackaff, D. (2012). The relationship between perceptions of online capital and enacted support. *Journal of Computer-Mediated Communication, 17,* 451–466.

Stefanone, M. A., Yue, Z., & Toh, Z. (2019). A social cognitive approach to traditional media content and social media use: Selfie-related behavior as competitive strategy. *New Media and Society, 21*(2), 317–335.

Tao, S., Dong, Q., Pratt, M. W., Hunsberger, B., & Pancer, M. S. (2000). Social support: Relations to coping and adjustment during the transition to university in the People's Republic of China. *Journal of Adolescent Research, 15,* 123–144.

Thorndike, E. L. (1920). Intelligence and its uses. *Harper's Magazine, 140,* 227–235.

Walker, J., Wasserman, S., & Wellman, B. (1994). Statistical models for social support networks. In S. Wasserman & J. Galaskiewicz (Eds.), *Advances in social network analysis* (pp. 53–78). Newbury Park, CA: SAGE.

Wellman, B. (1993). An egocentric network take. *Social Networks, 15,* 423–436.

Wellman, B. (2001). Physical place and cyber-place: Changing portals and the rise of networked individualism. *International Journal for Urban and Regional Research, 25*(2), 227–252.

Wellman, B., Carrington, P., & Hall, A. (1988). Networks as personal communities. In B. Wellman & S. D. Berkowitz (Eds.), *Social structures: A network approach* (pp. 130–184). Cambridge: Cambridge University Press.

Wellman, B., & Frank, K. (2001). Network capital in a multi-level world: Getting support from personal communities. In N. Lin, K. Cook, & R. Burt (Eds.), *Social capital: Theory and research* (pp. 233–273). Hawthorne, NY: Aldine de Gruyter.

Wellman, B., & Gulia, M. (1999). The network basis of social support: A network is more than the sum of its ties. In B. Wellman (Ed.), *Networks in the global village* (pp. 83–118). Boulder, CO: Westview Press.

Wellman, B., Haase, A. Q., Witte, J., & Hampton, K. (2001). Does the Internet increase, decrease, or supplement social capital? Social networks, participation, and community commitment. *American Behavioral Scientist, 45*(3), 436–455.

Wellman, B., & Wortley, S. (1990). Different strokes from different folks: Community ties and social support. *American Journal of Sociology, 96,* 558–588.

Williams, D. (2006). On and off the net: Scales for social capital in an online era. *Journal of Computer Mediated Communication, 11*(2), article 11.

4

DON'T BE ANTISOCIAL

The Politics of the "Anti-Social" in "Social" Media

Elinor Carmi

Introduction

Social media have become an inseparable part of our lives, whether we like it or not. But one of the things that many of us take for granted revolves around what exactly *is* "social" in social media? What does being social mean within these platforms? Who gets to decide, influence, and shape what is social on these platforms? And how do they make specific behaviors or feature design social? This chapter aims to address these questions.

A good way to interrogate the social is by exploring how the antisocial is created. This approach was used by scholars such as philosopher Michel Foucault and anthropologist Mary Douglas, who examined different cultures and spheres of life by focusing on the "deviant." By focusing on the abnormal they aimed to show how the norm and normal were constructed, who were the main people or organizations involved in these processes, what were the purposes and motives behind them, and what strategies did they use. For example, Foucault (1973, 1975) focused his research on the way the mad, the sick, the prisoner, and sexuality have been constructed through various discursive practices (measurements, architecture, training, institutions) to shine a light on our understanding of the normative forms of these life spheres. Similarly, Douglas's (1966) famous research from the 1960s on dirt shows how different cultures used "unclean" and "dirty" to construct different norms and values. Douglas shows that dirt is "matter out of place", and that dirt represents disorder in specific cultures, times, and places. This means that "dirt" goes against an order (conceived as "clean" or "pure") that was promoted as the ideal norm and value, and it was constructed by powerful institutions and people.

What Foucault and Douglas show is that nothing is abnormal, bad, or negative, but rather, that social constructions turn specific behaviors objects and spaces

DOI: 10.4324/9781003171270-4

as such because it serves a specific purpose. Importantly, those who create these deviant manifestations hold powerful positions in society in establishing specific ways of thinking, acting, and organizing. In other words, the social and antisocial are intertwined, they complement each other so that specific orders, norms, and values will be developed, maintained, managed, and controlled.

The premise of this chapter is that nothing is inherently social or antisocial, but the strategies that make them one or the other create a specific kind of mediated territory that aims to shape us in particular ways. The questions in this chapter aim to challenge things that we take for granted about the platforms we use every day. They are meant to push us to peel off the layers of design and interactions and try to figure out how things that look natural and objective to us became this way. This chapter will explore two ways in which social media platforms construct and enact what is the antisocial: practices and interface design. In each dimension, we will focus on what are considered to be antisocial behaviors, features, design, and metrics, and importantly, what they say about how the "social" is conceived. As Nick Couldry and José van Dijck argue in regard to examining social media:

> It must mean at least researching how social media platforms (and the plural production cultures that generated them) have come to *propose* a certain version of "the social", and how users go on to *enact* it. It must also mean researching how this social/media dialectic is generating *ethical or normative* concerns, how a more effective ethics of social life *through* media can be developed, and registering the fractured spaces from where alternative proposals of "the social" might be built.
>
> *(Couldry & Van Dijck, 2015, p. 2)*

This chapter focuses precisely on the type of sociality that platforms *propose* but argues that it is more than just proposing; often, it is more about forcing, controlling, and covertly influencing how we perform and understand the social. One of the main challenges of writing and doing research on media and technology is that everything changes so fast. Like other writings on social media, some of the examples in this chapter may not exist by the time you read it. But the examples here are meant to point to broader questions about how media and technology companies shape, manage, control, and influence the options of living on the platforms they develop. In short, this chapter is about power and agency.

Practices – Behaving Antisocially

Social media platforms gradually entered our lives from 2004, and people developed different kinds of relationships with them and in them. Throughout time every social media platform, from Facebook, Instagram, Twitter, and TikTok, has created rules about the things you cannot do. These things change all the time, but in this section, we will explore what types of behaviors are forbidden or hidden on social media and what does it say about the values of these platforms. These practices can be broadly divided into two main groups: the first is practices whereby people or bots operated by people act in what are considered to be malicious behaviors toward others such as trolling, spamming, and spreading misinformation. The second group is practices whereby people go against the connectivity ideal of social media and do various disconnectivity actions such as unfriending, unliking, or disconnecting from social media temporarily (digital detox) or permanently.

Stop Harassing Me

Antisocial behaviors conducted with or in media have been an ongoing phenomenon which received many names throughout the years: hackers, trolls, harassers, spammers, pirates, and scammers. An example of this can be seen in one of the earliest guidelines for email etiquette, written in 1985 by Norman Shapiro and Robert Anderson. They wanted the new technology of email to be used in an efficient, productive, and appropriate way, so they suggested people to "avoid responding while emotional", and "if a message generates emotions, look again" (Shapiro & Anderson, 1985). This was later called 'flaming' as Esther Milne (2012) shows and was considered to be 'antisocial behaviour'. But as Milne shows in her work on early email communication practices, 'flaming' has many meanings that revolve around the normative way of behaving on the Internet.

Specific people and organizations have taken or given the authority to categorize what is an appropriate online activity to construct what they perceive to be the normative behavior on the Internet. A good example for this is hackers, who trick, manipulate, and challenge the way media works but often get framed as bad actors, malicious violators, and sometimes even terrorists. Digital anthropologist Gabriella Coleman (2014) argues that what computer hackers do is reorder a network infrastructure, meaning that they challenge, object, and negotiate the intended use and structure of media networks. Hackers' behavior can be interpreted only in relation to what is expected from us to do with media – to obey and follow specific rules to make things 'work properly'. Therefore, calling specific behavior as antisocial is a powerful instrument to draw boundaries between legitimate and illegitimate behaviors of actors who are participating in this mediated space.

Similarly, trolls are often considered to be deceptive, disruptive, and manipulative – they ruin the order of the 'normal' Internet. However, as Whitney Phillips argues (2017), trolls are not that radically different from sensationalist corporate media, for the former trolling is part of a leisure activity and for the latter a business model. Trolls, as she observes:

> are quite skilled at navigating and in fact harnessing the energies created when politics, history, and digital media collide. In short, rather than

functioning as a counterpoint to 'correct' online behavior, trolls are in many ways the grimacing poster children for the socially networked world.

(Phillips, 2015, p. 8)

What Phillips emphasizes is that trolling is not one type of behavior but a spectrum that spans multiple types of behavior that can be more or less aggressive and be continuous or momentary. Some trolls work individually, some work in groups, but self-defining trolls would act as such as a way of self-expression of their identity. Trolls, as Phillips argues, are motivated by lulz, which means enjoying or laughing at someone you dislike or experiences of bad luck.

Similarly, as I argue about spamming, it involves many types of behavior, and it is difficult to distinguish between spamming and 'normative' behavior by advertisers or even the platforms themselves. For example, as I show in my book *Media Distortions* (Carmi, 2020a), Facebook offers the option to buy Likes and at the same time calls click-farms, which are factories that employ either humans or bots to click on things for a cost – spam. But one of the best examples is about the way the World Wide Web functions and how one type of spam gets legitimized whilst the other is criminalized. The web is funded by advertising, which is based on surveillance of people's behavior across time and platforms (Zuboff, 2015). This data is then collected and packaged and repackaged as profiles and segments to be sold through real-time bidding between multiple data brokers. The tool that enables this surveillance exploitative market is web-cookies. Web-cookies were made possible by the digital advertising industry after severe lobbying to legislators in the European Union and Internet standard bodies such as the Internet Engineering Task Force (I.E.T.F.). Their aim was to make a distinction between legitimate unsolicited bulk communication (web-cookies) and an illegitimate one (spam). As I argue:

> Framing spam as dangerous was a good diversion that allowed the cookie campaign to pass without objection. This was achieved by portraying spam as a form of communication that was not requested, sent for economic purposes in covert ways, which had the ability to track people and invade their private space while exploiting their data. The exact same definition, however, can also be applied to cookies. It is just a matter of which economic purpose is considered to be the legitimate one. In other words, spam and cookies are the same communication practice.
>
> *(Carmi, 2020a, p. 143)*

Once more as these scholars show, the main purpose of defining and constructing specific behaviors and content as antisocial comes from platforms' aim to make more profit. Whether these are hackers, trolls, or spammers – maintaining the business model is the strongest drive for making a distinction between social and antisocial. In the next section, we will explore how people themselves make actions that go against these aspirations.

I Don't Like This Anymore

When social media took over our lives, they started to shape new kinds of expectations from people. The experiences of always being 'connected', always being available, and having to 'share' every detail of our lives were portrayed as an emancipation for the 'user'. Finally, people were able to share their thoughts without the old media gatekeepers. But along these portrayals of democratizing media and expression of the people, at the same time, many people did not feel 'empowered' by having to constantly be online and sharing a lot of information about their lives. Therefore, some people started to develop different practices of resistance to social media by leaving, disconnecting, or pausing their participation in various degrees.

So what are disconnections? Ben Light and Elija Cassidy (2014) argue that they can come in many shapes and forms such as unfriending, logging off, removing timeline content, untagging content, and disconnecting from apps. Light and Cassidy also argue that disconnections can happen with humans and nonhumans:

> Disconnectors are those human and non-human actors that engage with us and engage us in disconnective practice. Disconnection Modes refer to the varying natures of automated and manual disconnective activity we undertake with SNS. Importantly, these modes can be enacted with and by those actors we might see as non-human.
>
> *(Light & Cassidy, 2014, p. 1173)*

Disconnections are a way to disrupt the always connected 'nature' that social media inscribed in their design, it goes against the way we are shaped into sociality.

Leaving Facebook, as Eric Baumer et al. (2013) describe, can take several practices such as leaving, limiting use, deactivating and deleting their accounts, and resisting joining to begin with, or non-use as Baumer et al. call it. The main motivations for these disconnection practices are concerns around privacy, data use and misuse, decrease in work productivity, and social and professional pressures. Because being online on social media has quickly become a norm, when people decide to disconnect, their behavior can be perceived as antisocial. As Baumer et al. highlight 'social pressures can similarly stigmatize non-use as a deviant behavior; one would leave Facebook only "if something was wrong". Just as various pressures can lead to non-volitional non-use, such pressures can also lead to non-volitional use' (Baumer et al., 2013, p. 3265). Social media norms of what it means to be social can create pressures on people who defy, challenge, or refuse to accept them.

Many people, as Pepita Hesselberth (2018) argues, feel uncomfortable with the ubiquitous presence of networked devices that demand that people will always be connected and available. Disconnectivity, as she shows, has also been discussed as a form of media resistance under the conditions of neoliberal reform. These discourses, then, go against the cultures of connectivity which are presented to us as if there is 'no outside' of them. As José van Dijck argues ironically in her book on Cultures of Connectivity, '[o]pting out of connective media is hardly an option. *The norm is stronger than the law*; if not, it would be too hard for any regime to control its citizens' (Van Dijck, 2013, p. 174). Norms of social media's ideal of sociality engineer society.

Social media platforms have become a nuisance, interfering in multiple spheres of our lives, as Tero Karppi (2018) argues in his book about disconnections. As he observes,

> [D]isconnections, per se, are important and even elemental. Disconnec-
> tions, in our network culture, take different forms: a break, a manifesto, an
> act, a form of resistance, a failure. They express the vulnerabilities of social
> media and bring us to the volatility of social media business models based
> on establishing, enabling, and sustaining connectivity.
>
> *(Karppi, 2018, p. 2)*

Karppi highlights that disconnection becomes a problem for social media platforms, which want to keep people who use them more engaged since this is their core business model. Therefore, as Karppi argues, social media platforms aim to control people's experience and at the same time to keep value and attention in the system.

Some people choose to disconnect only temporarily. As Ana Jorge (2019) says in her examination of Instagram interruptions, such temporary disconnection are attempts of people to self-manage themselves and maintain their well-being. As she observes, people feel overwhelmed by the acceleration of time on social media, therefore, temporary interruptions allow them to gain control and have a better experience when they come back. However, Jorge emphasizes that digital disconnections have become a performance of people which ultimately conforms with social media's connectivity values. People who use Instagram and perform a 'balanced' way of life also judge others who do not act this way. This kind of behavior reinforces the idea that people are individually responsible for their social media use, and if they feel unwell from it, it is their fault. Also, such performances, as Jorge argues, do not advocate for alternative platforms or force social media platforms to be accountable for the way they impact people.

Finally, many researchers, journalists, policy makers, and activists rely on social media platforms for research informing their projects. Therefore, there are huge consequences on the kind of data that these platforms make available to them which then, in turn, shapes what they can know, ask, and examine. As Nicholas John and Asaf Nissenbaum (2019) show in their paper, it was impossible for them to get data from multiple social media companies about people's disconnectivity patterns. This is dangerous, as they argue, because it means that the theories and insights that scholars produce are shaped by what is available to them and hence lean more on notions of positivity and connectivity. As they observe,

> [A]ny theory of social life that ignored phenomena such as breaking up, quitting a workplace, changes in taste, or dropping out would at best be partial, and any methodology that a priori rendered such phenomena invisible would surely be discounted. However, unfriending, unfollowing, unliking, leaving a group, muting a conversation, and more, are all meaningful social actions to which SNSs' APIs are blind.
>
> *(John & Nissenbaum, 2019, p. 9)*

By hiding disconnectivity from people and researchers, as John and Nissenbaum argue, social media platforms misrepresent all facets of our social and antisocial engagements. It is precisely how we should examine, understand, and perform what is meaningful to us – the social – that social media companies want to shape, control, and manage.

Dark Patterns

In the previous sections we have talked about what kinds of behavior are considered to be antisocial and what does that mean about social media's political economy, norms, and values. But behaviors are not the only thing that can be deviant, different kinds of design can also have different norms and values engineered into them. That could be from interface design, to features offered, colors of buttons or text, language used, and metrics. These deviant designs can broadly be called dark patterns. Dark patterns is a concept that was coined by Harry Brignull in 2010 to represent deceptive interface designs. What dark patterns mean in our context is that the design of social media can nudge and sometimes force us to do specific things. Dark patterns influence what we can and cannot do and consequently also shape how we understand these environments.

In this section we will focus on three main interface designs that constitute dark patterns and the kind of norms and values social media intend for us to perform and understand by designing them: metrics, newsfeed, and terms of use.

I'm Counting on This

Media companies have been using metrics for years. Companies usually used metrics along with advertisers for different purposes – understanding how many people watch or read their content, whether it is cinema, radio, newspapers, or television. This has been called audience measurement. It has been important for media companies to understand that for various reasons, but the main reason is to match audiences to advertisements according to these metrics. As Joseph Turow argues '[w]hen the internet came along, media buyers saw its interactive environment as terrific terrain for expanding their numerical understanding of audiences – and for using the measures and labels directly to sell products' (Turow, 2012, p. 20). But social media took metrics a step further and started to design different metrics that enable people to indicate if they like, share, or comment on something. These new metrics quickly became a social value to assess popularity, reputation, status, and worth. Nancy Baym (2013), for example, examines how social media metrics affect the music industry and specifically the relationships between the fans and artists. As she argues, these metrics are not real representations, they skew the way algorithms work to amplify (sometimes through bought likes) or demote specific behaviors:

> [T]he more a post or user receives comments, likes or follows, the more likely algorithms are to make them visible to other users. To some extent, counts reflect opaque algorithmic decision making as much as they reflect expressions of interest. Another skew in social media counts is that they are designed to reflect only positive affect, another element of the politics of platforms.
>
> *(Baym, 2013, n.p.)*

Importantly, as Baym shows, Facebook enables only 'positive' interactions, these can be expressed through the 'Like' button. Such platform affordances flatten our experience in and understanding of sociality in these mediated spaces. Similarly, Benjamin Grosser (2014) has shown in his net art project, the Facebook Demetricator, the politics of metrics on Facebook. The Facebook Demetricator is a browser add-on which removes the metrics the platform shows on its interface such as friends, pending notifications, events, friend requests, messages/chats waiting, photos, places, and others. It also removes the timestamp, meaning when the post or comment was created. Grosser created this feature to examine how interface designs influence our behavior and persuade or pressure us to act in specific ways. He emphasizes that:

> Not all metrics collected by Facebook are visible in the interface, however. This raises the question of what specific metrics Facebook reveals to its users and which ones it keeps to itself. How do these hidden and revealed metrics differ, and what drives the company's decisions to show or conceal data?
>
> *(Grosser, 2014, n.p.)*

Grosser tested the Facebook Demetricator on several people who installed his plug-in and experienced Facebook without metrics. The results were that people engaged less and felt less pressure to do so. This means that the interface design of metrics is meant to push people for more engagement. In addition, the timestamp, as Grosser shows, presents and engineers an ideological prioritization of the new, creating a sense of urgency to not miss anything that has happened on the platform. He points four strategies Facebook metrics employ: competition, emotional manipulation, reaction, and homogenization. Through these strategies Facebook prescribes, structures, and manages social interactions while suppressing, hiding, or not enabling others. But beyond that, Grosser argues that the broader picture is that the metrification of our interactions and relationships makes us understand our digital lives in a market narrative.

In addition to shaping and controlling how we behave, metrics, as Benjamin Jacobsen and David Beer (2021) show also influence our memories. They show how quantifying memories affects memory making and memory practices in what they call quantified nostalgia, the way:

> [M]etrics are variously performative in memory making, and how regimes of ordinary measures can figure in the engagement and reconstruction of the digital past in multiple ways, shaping both how people engage with it in the present, how they remember it, and how they feel about those automated memories.
>
> (Jacobsen & Beer, 2021, p. 2)

What they argue is that quantified nostalgia is a way for social media platforms to produce an ideal type of memory that is meant to raise these feelings with the person using them. In this way, social media platforms try to shape our feelings and emotions and in turn our behaviors toward a specific sociality, in their case – one that evokes more engagement and hence more profit.

Another design feature that has managed to conceal the way it influences us because it looks objective is the 'newsfeed'. In the next section, I will examine how it continuously changes according to social media platforms' economic incentives, despite their 'antisocial' impacts on people.

Nothing is Organic in This Feed

Many people open their mornings and finish their days by scrolling on their newsfeeds. That is the space social media companies turned into your daily updates of everything that is important to you. From news articles to posts from your friends and family, status changes, groups on stuff you care about like protests and LGBTQI rights, and onto advertisements from brands you liked, you get a feed of what is relevant to your profile. Or at least, that is what social media platforms claim they are doing. Many people still think that algorithms are objective and hence think that what they see and engage with on their 'feed' depends on what interests them, what 'the algorithm' thinks is best for their personalized experience. But as this section will show, constructing the notion of 'organic feed' is a calculated strategy meant to hide the politics and economic incentives that stand behind the ordering of your feed.

Various scholars have exposed the way algorithms are biased, from Eli Pariser's famous book on filter bubbles (2011) showing how algorithms and their ideal way of ordering through personalization puts people in 'filter bubbles' where they engage with people and content that they agree with rather than being exposed to diverse opinions. Other scholars like Virginia Eubanks (2018) and Safiya Noble (2018) show how algorithms and automated decision-making discriminate the poor (in Eubanks's work) and women of color (in Noble's work). In addition, Anna Jobin and Malte Ziewitz (2018) talk about how metaphors like 'organic' hide the way Google search is influenced by economic incentives and fueled by a two-sided market whereby 'users search for useful information, advertisers search for users'. As these works show, algorithms are far from being neutral or objective, and as a society we need to have a better understanding of the entities, organizations, political, and economic incentives behind them.

Newsfeeds are built from algorithms, and while they can amplify and prioritize specific things, they can also demote, decrease, filter, and disable specific behaviors that the platforms that develop them consider to be 'antisocial'. As I argue elsewhere 'platforms don't just moderate or filter "content"; they alter what registers to us and our social groups as "social" or as "experience". Their design influences behavioral patterns across different conversations, groups, and geographical areas, with different frequencies and paces' (Carmi, 2020b). This means that behaviors, content, and interactions that can harm the business model of social media platform are categorized as antisocial, and the design of these platforms will use any interface option available to them to remove those things.

A great example for that can be seen in the way Facebook has been conducting endless experiments on its newsfeed algorithms, as *the New York Times* journalist Kevin Roose (2020) argues. A particular interesting experiment was to understand how to promote what they define as 'civility' where they reduced content on people's newsfeed that they defined as 'negative'. The outcome, however, was that with the algorithmic tweak people were less likely to come back to the platform and hence Facebook decided to reintroduce 'negative' content. What these moves suggest is that although decreasing/removing negativity from people's newsfeed has a better impact on people's well-being because they engage less with platforms, social media platforms cannot afford to integrate this change. Sociality in this case has to include negative impacts on people's lives because they help the platforms make profit, which is, as this experiment shows, the strongest value. Negative or antisocial content in this case, is therefore an essential part of social media companies' business model.

As this experiment shows, there is a delicate balance that platforms have to maintain between their desire to make more profit by people who engage more on their platforms and spread negative and potentially harmful content, which can also include disinformation and misinformation. As journalists Jasper Jackson and Alexandra Heal (2021) from the Bureau for Investigative Journalism showed, the platform enables creators to make a profit from spreading misinformation about the COVID-19 pandemic. These tools are, for example, via 'fundraising' or the 'shopping' sections where these pages can sell different related products. As Jackson and Heal observe, Facebook profits from popular individuals and brands spreading misinformation because it takes about 5–30% on its 'Star currency', which is a tool that enables fans 'tip' creators who stream live videos. But ultimately Facebook benefits from people who keep on engaging with misinformation because they stay logged into the service and this experience exposes them to more advertisements. Of course, Pages that spread misinformation is against the company's policy, but when it comes to enforcement it seems that platforms are more lenient, especially when it means they make more profit. So although social media platforms have rules about harmful content, they still prioritize it on their newsfeed because content that is emotional drives more engagement and hence profit.

Some of these filtering and removing content that goes against the platform's rules are not conducted by algorithms but rather by commercial content moderators (CCM), as Sarah Roberts coined them (2019). These are workers who are usually hired by third-party companies to filter and remove content or profiles/P that go against the platforms' rules. These rules can vary between profanity, inciting hate, and pornography. But as scholars who investigate the roles of CCM argue (Gillespie, 2018), since they work behind our screens, most of the times we have no idea what content or things they take away and how does that affect how we behave and understand platforms. Some of the disputes revolve around the fact that the values of the company are to make profit, and hence any content that might upset advertisers, such as women's nipples and nudity (Myers–West, 2017), will be removed from the platform to maintain the economic circulation. As Roberts argues:

> The internal, extremely detailed policies by which the commercial content moderation workers adjudicated content were not available to the public but, rather, were treated as trade secrets to be used internally, and ultimately functioned in the service of brand management for MegaTech . . . It could also trigger difficult questions about the values undergirding those policies, a fact of which the moderation admins were certainly aware.
>
> *(Roberts, 2019, p. 93)*

The purpose behind making their work hidden is to make it seem as though the algorithms are doing this work, and that this points to objectivity and neutrality of how our newsfeed order our experiences. However, the main goal is to make platforms unaccountable to the things that they remove and design interfaces that make our experience 'frictionless' and at the same time constructing a certain type of sociality. The rules that social media platforms make are often found in their terms of use, which are another form of dark pattern, as the next section will reveal.

Tl:dr

A crucial dark pattern that underpins and authorizes a lot of what we have discussed in this chapter comes from the new type of contract that social media introduced, what we all know as 'terms of use'. As Mark Lemley said about terms of use on the Internet, they 'control (or purport to control) the circumstances under which buyers of software or visitors to a public Web site can make use of that software or site' (Lemley, 2006, p. 460). As Lemley argues, the online environment introduced an easier way to create contracts in the shape of clickwrap licenses agreements. These types of contracts are a development of shrink-wrap contracts that Lemley says were prevalent in the 1980s and 1990s and included licenses for physical copies of software. Once people loaded the software and ran the program that meant that they 'agree' to the terms of the contract. In these agreements people who visit websites sign electronically by clicking 'I agree' to a set of terms, which present a 'take-it-or-leave-it' kind of situation. But as Wauters, Lievens, and Valcke (2014) argue, this "situation may tilt the interests in favour of the provider and result in a lower degree of protection for the user" (ibid., p. 293). Terms of use, as these scholars observe, help to protect social media platforms from possible threats and what they perceive as antisocial behavior from the people who use their platforms.

We can think of social media design as a contract, as Woodrow Hartzog argues (2010). As he says 'website features and design should, in some contexts, be considered enforceable promises. Code-based negotiations for confidentiality can form implied-in-fact contracts or give rise to a claim for promissory estoppel' (Hartzog, 2010, p. 1638). Some of the main issues with these contracts that make them part of dark patterns are that they are long, jargon laden, and they change constantly. Since people use dozens of apps, services, and websites, this means that reading all the terms of use can take weeks if not months.

One of the exploitative natures of terms of use is that people do not understand what is being done with their data, even if they try. As Hartzog adds

> [B]road, sweeping agreements that control the use of personal information lack the specificity to be truly effective in providing meaningful control over the flow of personal information because users often disclose both sensitive and innocuous personal information on the same website.
>
> *(Hartzog, 2010, p. 1652)*

Importantly, as Jared Livingstone shows (2011), people have no bargaining power around these contracts, so it is a 'take-it-or-leave-it' situation where social media platforms cement their powerful position. What terms of use do is legitimize social media platforms' behavior through a contract that binds people in many rules they are not aware of because they have not read or understood what is written in it. In other words, terms of use authorize social media platforms' antisocial behavior.

Conclusion – Antisocial Complex

The social cannot exist without the antisocial, this is what this chapter was all about. While our lives become inseparable from social media platforms, it is important to continuously challenge and question what they tell us is the 'social'. This can be through specific behaviors or platform design that influences, nudges, and manages our understanding, feelings, and agency toward a specific kind of sociality. The type of things we are told are negative, bad, problematic, unacceptable, or inappropriate can tell us a lot about what are the norms and values of these platforms. But just like society constructs specific rules and norms, so do social media platforms. These are not neutral, objective, or permanent but rather constantly negotiated, challenged, and changed according to multiple motives, mainly economic and political.

Not taking the 'social' for granted is especially important as most of our interactions happen in these platforms. Whether we are communicating with our family, friends, or customers or read about politics and engage with our local neighborhood or politicians – it is important to understand that our social networks are mediated by biased infrastructures that want us to engage and understand our networks, ourselves, and these spaces in specific ways.

References

Baumer, E. P., Adams, P., Khovanskaya, V. D., Liao, T. C., Smith, M. E., Schwanda Sosik, V., & Williams, K. (2013, April). Limiting, leaving, and (re) lapsing: An exploration of Facebook non-use practices and experiences. In *Proceedings of the SIGCHI Conference on Human Factors in Computing Systems* (pp. 3257–3266).

Baym, N. K. (2013). Data not seen: The uses and shortcomings of social media metrics. *First Monday, 18*(10). https://doi.org/10.5210/fm.v18i10.4873

Carmi, E. (2020a). *Media distortions: Understanding the power behind spam, noise, and other deviant media.* New York: Peter Lang.

Carmi, E. (2020b). The organic myth. *Real Life Magazine.* Retrieved from https://reallifemag.com/the-organic-myth/

Coleman, G. (2014). *Hacker, hoaxer, whistleblower, spy: The many faces of Anonymous.* London: Verso Books.

Couldry, N., & Van Dijck, J. (2015). Researching social media as if the social mattered. *Social Media+ Society, 1*(2). https://doi.org/10.1177/2056305115604174

Douglas, M. (1966). *Purity and danger.* New York: Routledge and Kegan Paul.

Eubanks, V. (2018). *Automating inequality: How high-tech tools profile, police, and punish the poor.* New York: St. Martin's Press.

Foucault, M. (1973). *The birth of the clinic: An archaeology of medical perception.* New York: Vintage Books.

Foucault, M. (1975). *Discipline and punish* (A. Sheridan, Trans.). Paris, FR: Gallimard.

Gillespie, T. (2018). *Custodians of the Internet: Platforms, content moderation, and the hidden decisions that shape social media.* New Haven, CT: Yale University Press.

Grosser, B. (2014). What do metrics want? How quantification prescribes social interaction on Facebook. *Computational Culture, 4.*

Hartzog, W. (2010). Website design as contract. *American University Law Review, 60*(6), 1635–1672.

Hesselberth, P. (2018). Discourses on disconnectivity and the right to disconnect. *New Media & Society, 20*(5), 1994–2010. https://doi.org/10.1177/1461444817711449

Jackson, J., & Heal, A. (2021). Misinformation market: The money making tools Facebook hands to Covid cranks. *The Bureau for Investigative Journalism.* Retrieved from www.thebureauinvestigates.com/stories/2021-01-31/misinformation-market-the-money-making-tools-facebook-hands-to-covid-cranks

Jacobsen, B. N., & Beer, D. (2021). Quantified nostalgia: Social media, metrics, and memory. *Social Media+ Society, 7*(2). https://doi.org/10.1177/20563051211008822

Jobin, A., & Ziewitz, M. (2018). Organic search: How metaphors help cultivate the web. *HIIG.* Retrieved from https://serval.unil.ch/resource/serval:BIB_723BFBD04A10.P001/REF.pdf

John, N. A., & Nissenbaum, A. (2019). An agnotological analysis of APIs: Or, disconnectivity and the ideological limits of our knowledge of social media. *The Information Society, 35*(1), 1–12. https://doi.org/10.1080/01972243.2018.1542647

Jorge, A. (2019). Social media, interrupted: Users recounting temporary disconnection on Instagram. *Social Media+ Society, 5*(4). https://doi.org/10.1177/2056305119881691

Karppi, T. (2018). *Disconnect: Facebook's affective bonds.* Minneapolis, MN: University of Minnesota Press.

Lemley, M. A. (2006). Terms of use. *Minnesota Law Review, 91*(2), 459–483.

Light, B., & Cassidy, E. (2014). Strategies for the suspension and prevention of connection: Rendering disconnection as socioeconomic lubricant with Facebook. *New Media & Society, 16*(7), 1169–1184. https://doi.org/10.1177/1461444814544002

Livingston, J. S. (2011). Invasion contracts: The privacy implications of terms of use agreements in the online social media setting. *Albany Law Science & Technology Journal, 21*(3), 591–636.

Milne, E. (2012). *Letters, postcards, email: Technologies of presence.* New York: Routledge.

Noble, S. U. (2018). *Algorithms of oppression: How search engines reinforce racism.* New York: New York University Press.

Pariser, E. (2011). *The filter bubble: What the Internet is hiding from you.* London: Penguin UK.

Phillips, W. (2015). *This is why we can't have nice things: Mapping the relationship between online trolling and mainstream culture.* Cambridge, MA: MIT Press.

Roberts, S. T. (2019). *Behind the screen.* New Haven, CT: Yale University Press.

Roose, K. (2020). Facebook struggles to balance civility and growth. *The New York Times.* Retrieved from www.nytimes.com/2020/11/24/technology/facebook-election-misinformation.html

Shapiro, N. Z., & Anderson, R. H. (1985). *Towards an ethics and etiquette for electronic mail.* California: Rand Publication Series.

Turow, J. (2012). *The daily you.* New Haven, CT: Yale University Press.

Van Dijck, J. (2013). *The culture of connectivity: A critical history of social media*. Oxford: Oxford University Press.

Wauters, E., Lievens, E., & Valcke, P. (2014). Towards a better protection of social media users: A legal perspective on the terms of use of social networking sites. *International Journal of Law and Information Technology*, *22*(3), 254–294. https://doi.org/10.1093/ijlit/eau002

West, S. M. (2017). Raging against the machine: Network gatekeeping and collective action on social media platforms. *Media and Communication*, *5*(3), 28–36. https://doi.org/10.17645/mac.v5i3.989

Zuboff, S. (2015). Big other: Surveillance capitalism and the prospects of an information civilization. *Journal of Information Technology*, *30*(1), 75–89. https://doi.org/10.1057/jit.2015.5

5

SOCIAL MEDIA, ALIENATION, AND THE PUBLIC SPHERE

Christian Fuchs

Introduction

Over the past 15 years, the term "social media" has become widely established. It generally functions as a collective term for social networking sites such as Facebook and LinkedIn, video platforms such as YouTube, photo-sharing platforms such as Instagram, blogs and microblogs such as Twitter and Weibo, messaging apps such as WhatsApp, livestreaming platforms, video apps, and wikis such as Wikipedia. It often remains in question what exactly qualifies as "social" in these media and, by implication, why more traditional information and communication media such as email, telephone, television, and books should not also be considered as social. The problem here seems to be that in sociology there are conflicting ideas and understandings about what is social, not just one (Fuchs, 2017, Chapter 2; Fuchs, 2021, Chapter 2).

Internet platforms such as Facebook and Google, which dominate the social media sector, are among the largest corporations in the world at present. Meanwhile, social media has become an indispensable part of politics and public communication. Right-wing politicians use various internet platforms and spread propaganda and false news through these media. The Arab Spring and the various Occupy movements have proven that social media such as Facebook, Twitter, and YouTube are important in social movements. No politician, party, NGO, or social movement today does without profiles on social media. Therefore, the question arises as to the connection between social media and the public sphere. The chapter sheds light on this question.

The next section introduces a concept of the public sphere as a concept of critique. The third section uses the concept of the public sphere to critique capitalist internet platforms. The last section of the chapter deals with potentials of a public internet.

DOI: 10.4324/9781003171270-5

The Public Sphere as a Concept of Critique

The public sphere is a vital component of any political and social system. Habermas understands "public" to mean spaces and resources that are "open to all" (Habermas, 1989, p. 1). Hence, we speak, for example, of public service media, public opinion, public education, public parks, etc. The concept of the public has to do with the common good, with the idea that there are facilities that are not only used and owned by a privileged few but from which everyone enjoys benefits.

Public institutions and goods are often, but not necessarily, regulated and organised by the state. There may be certain requirements for access. For example, public service media in many countries are financed by a legally regulated broadcasting fee. Such access conditions should be affordable for everyone and there should not be any discrimination by class, income, origin, gender, etc. to access these public resources. Accordingly, a park to which only white people had access at the time of segregation in the United States or South Africa was not a public good.

The public sphere has to also do with public debate about society, interests, and decisions that are collectively and bindingly taken by all. It therefore has an inherently political character. The public sphere mediates between other spheres of society and functions as a kind of interface between economy, culture, politics, and private life. An ideal, typical public sphere is one in which "critical publicity" (Habermas, 1989, p. 178) and "critical discussion" (p. 95) take place. If criticism is being silenced or suppressed, there is no public sphere.

The public sphere is a sphere of public political communication which mediates between other subsystems of society, that is, the economy, politics, culture, and private life. The public sphere is a medium of political communication. The public sphere enables people to inform themselves about, discuss, and participate in politics.

The media system is part of the public sphere in modern society. Figure 5.1 illustrates a model of the role of the media in the modern public sphere (cf. Fuchs, 2016). Media organisations produce publicly available content in the media system. Such content is generally used to inform about news, educate, and entertain. Through public news, members of the political system inform themselves about important events in society and politics. News is a trigger of political communication. People talk about what is happening in politics and ideally participate in the decision-making processes themselves. In a capitalist society, different interest organisations such as employers' associations, workers' associations such as trade unions, lobby organisations, political parties, NGOs, private individuals, social movements, etc. try to have an influence on the media companies' reporting. Such lobbying happens, for example, through interviews, press releases, lobbying, advertising, public relations, the interlocking of organisations, etc. The media system interacts with the economy, politics, and culture.

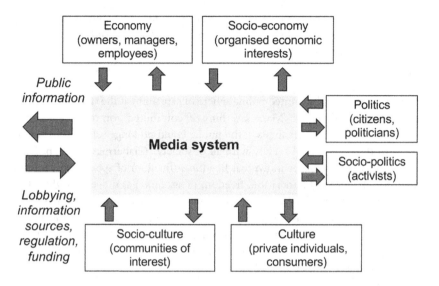

FIGURE 5.1 The media system as a part of the public sphere. Note: The figure is a further development of Figures 5.1 and 5.2 in Habermas, 2008.

The base of economic resources for the media to operate with is enabled by citizens (through purchase, broadcasting fee, subscriptions, etc.), the state (e.g., media funding), as well as business organisations (advertising). Politics regulates the framework conditions under which the media operate. Culture is a context of world views and ideologies that shape the climate of society and thus also have an influence on the media.

For Habermas, the public sphere is autonomous from capital and state power, that is, from economic and political power. "Laws of the market were suspended as were laws of the state" (Habermas, 1989, p. 36) in the public sphere. State censorship that interferes with the making of political opinion and private ownership of the means of production of public opinion is against the democratic character of the public sphere. For Marx, socialism is an alternative to the capitalist economy and the bourgeois state. Marx describes the Paris Commune, which existed from March to May 1871, as a socialist form of public sphere. It was an attempt to organise politics and the economy democratically:

> The Commune was formed of the municipal councillors, chosen by universal suffrage in the various wards of the town, responsible and revocable at short terms. The majority of its members were naturally working men, or acknowledged representatives of the working class. The Commune was to be a working, not a parliamentary body, executive and legislative at the same time. . . . Public functions ceased to be the private property of the

> tools of the Central Government. Not only municipal administration, but the whole initiative hitherto exercised by the state was laid into the hands of the Commune.
>
> *(Marx, 2010a, p. 331)*

Marx was critical of the limited public sphere of capitalism at the same time: "The public sphere with which Marx saw himself confronted contradicted its own principle of universal accessibility – the public could no longer claim to be identical with the nation, civil society with all of society" (Habermas, 1989, p. 124). Liberal ideology postulates individual freedoms (freedom of speech, freedom of expression, freedom of association, freedom of assembly) as universal rights. The particularist and stratified character of capitalist class society undermines these universal rights. It breeds inequality and thereby unequal access to the public sphere. In bourgeois society, there is an antagonism between the freedom of private property and individual freedoms. There are two inherent limitations to the public sphere, as discussed by Habermas:

- The restriction of freedom of expression and public opinion: if people do not have the same level of formal education and material resources at their disposal, then this may constrain their access to the public sphere (cf. Habermas, 1989, p. 227).
- The restriction of freedom of assembly and association: powerful political and economic organisations "enjoy an oligopoly of the publicistically effective and politically relevant formation of assemblies and associations" (cf. Habermas, 1989, p. 228).

Habermas argues that the bourgeois public sphere is colonialised and feudalised as a result of these limitations. It is not a proper public sphere but rather a political space structured by class. The public sphere entails a concept of immanent critique that lends itself to the critique of the deficits and problems of modern society. Habermas does not claim that the public sphere exists everywhere but that it should exist. Immanent critique compares purported ideals with reality. If it finds that reality contradicts its own ideals, it reveals that there is a fundamental contradiction, and that reality must be changed to overcome this incongruity. The bourgeois public sphere creates its own limits and thus its own immanent critique.

Public spaces and publics exist not only in the West. It is a misguided claim that the public sphere is a Western-centric or Eurocentric concept. Such criticism also risks justifying undemocratic regimes that are anti-Western and promote authoritarianism under the guise of opposition to Western-centrism and Eurocentrism. The public teahouse is an ancient cultural practice and space that can be found in many parts of the world. Di Wang (2008) compares the Chinese teahouse of the early 20th century to British public houses. It is a public space that people from all classes and backgrounds would frequent for a variety of reasons. The Chinese word for teahouse is 茶馆 (*cháguǎn*). Chengdu is the capital of the Sichuan province in southwest China. "Teahouses in Chengdu . . . were renowned for their multiclass orientation. One of the 'virtues' of Chengdu teahouses was their 'relatively (sic!) equality'" (He Manzi, *Wuzakan*, p. 192 as quoted in Wang, 2008, p. 420). Although women were excluded at first, they gained full access from about 1930 onwards. These teahouses served not only as cultural spaces but also as political meeting places where political debates took place and political plays were performed, attracting the interest of not only citizens but also government informers. Wang discusses the importance of teahouses in the 1911 railway protests in Chengdu. Public meeting places are spheres of citizen engagement that can become spheres of political communication and protest.

The various Occupy movements – which emerged after the global economic crisis that began in 2008 – were movements in which protests and the occupation of spaces converged. They generated self-managed publics for political communication. The creation of these publics did not take place only in the West but in many parts of the world in times of global capitalist and social crisis. A common aspect of these protests was that in many of them the tactic of transforming spaces into public and political spaces was used and that these protests took place in a general social crisis. Resistance is as old as class society. Publics have been created as resistant publics throughout the history of class societies, so the public sphere exists wherever people gather to organise collectively and express their anger and displeasure at exploitation and domination.

One of the connections between Habermas's *Structural Transformation of the Public Sphere*[1] and his *Theory of Communicative Action*[2] is the way it points to the functioning of stratification processes in modern society. When Habermas (1989) speaks of the "refeudalization" of the public sphere in his earlier work (pp. 142, 158, 195, 231), he would refer to it as the concept of *colonialization of the public sphere* in his later work, which includes "monetarization and bureaucratization" (Habermas, 1987, pp. 321–325, 343, 364, 386, 403). According to Habermas (1987, p. 323), these two processes "instrumentalise" the lifeworld and thus the public sphere. In my own approach, I assume that there are not two but three ways how the exercise of power may colonialise and re-feudalise the public sphere (cf. Fuchs, 2008, 2011, 2015, 2020a):

- Through *commodification* and *class structuration*, the logics of money, capital, and the commodity form permeate people's everyday lives and lifeworlds.
- Through the *process of domination*, society is organised in such a way that particular interests prevail and a few people or groups or individuals obtain advantages at the expense of other people.
- Through *ideologisation*, partial interests, exploitation, and domination are rendered as natural and necessary by presenting reality in a distorted or manipulated way.

The commodity form, domination, and ideology are the three main forms of stratification in a capitalist society. The critical theory of the public sphere is a critique of the commodity form, a critique of domination, and a critique of ideology. A critical theory of the public sphere is therefore a critique of alienation. What was referred to by Horkheimer (2013) as "instrumental reason", "technological rationality"[3] by Marcuse (1982, p. 141), and "reification" by Lukács (1971, pp. 83–222), may assume three forms in capitalism:

- Class structuration and the commodity form instrumentalise people's labour power and people's needs in capitalist consumption.
- Political domination instrumentalises people's political agency in such a way that they do not make decisions themselves but leave them to dominant groups.
- Ideology tries to bend and instrumentalise people's consciousness and their subjective interests.

Karl Marx emphasised that the logic of accumulation shapes capitalism (cf. 2010b). This logic has its origin in the capitalist economy. But it also shapes modern politics and modern culture, which are about the accumulation of political and cultural power. The accumulation of power assumes the form of the accumulation of capital, decision-making power, and defining power. As a result of accumulation, there are asymmetries of power, namely class structures, structures of domination and ideology (see Table 5.1).

Alienation means that people are confronted with structures and conditions that they are unable to control and influence themselves. People do not have control over the economic, political, and cultural products that influence their lives and everyday life. Alienation means "*loss* of the object, his product" (Marx, 2010c, p. 273). Alienation means "vitality as a sacrifice of life, production of the object as loss of the object to an alien power, to an *alien* person" (Marx, 2010c, p. 281). Use values, collectively binding decisions, and collective meanings are social products of human practices. In the capitalist society, however, they are controlled only by a few, resulting in the existence of objectively alienated conditions.

TABLE 5.1 Antagonisms in three types of alienation

Types of Alienation	Dominant Subjects	Dominated Subjects
Economic alienation: exploitation	Ruling class, exploiters	Exploited class
Political alienation: domination	Dictator, dictatorial groups	Excluded individuals and groups
Cultural alienation: ideology that leads to disrespect	Ideologues	Disrespected individuals and groups

TABLE 5.2 Main actors in the alienated and the humanist society

	Alienated Society	*Humanist Society*
Economy	The exploiter	The socialist
Politics	The dictator	The democrat
Culture	The ideologue/demagogue	The solidary friend

Source: Based on Fuchs, 2020a, p. 140, Table 4.4.

Table 5.2 illustrates the antagonism between alienated and humanist society along the three social dimensions of economy, politics, and culture. In the alienated society, the main actors are the exploiter in economy, the dictator in politics, and the ideologue/demagogue in culture. Humanism is the alternative design to the alienated society. In a humanist society, the main actors are the socialist in economy, the democrat in politics, and the solidary friend in culture.

Capitalist Colonialisation of the Digital Public Sphere

In discussions about the internet and social media, it is fairly often stated that an *electronic democracy*, a *digital/virtual public sphere*, and a participatory culture are emerging through the possibilities of prosumption (i.e., the phenomenon that users on the internet consume and produce at the same time so that media consumers become producers of content) and user-generated content (UGC). These arguments are widespread in the academic debate as well.[4] A far-reaching democratisation of society, including the capitalist economy, is inferred from a technical change in society, although class antagonism, political antagonisms, and ideological lines of conflict continue to exist and have even deepened. Is today's internet and social media a new public sphere that expands democracy or a new form of colonialisation of the public sphere?

Users of today's internet and social media face ten problems[5]:

1. **Digital Capitalism/Digital Class Relations:** Digital capital exploits digital labor. It results in capitalist digital monopolies and contributes to the precarisation of life.
2. **Digital Individualism**: The logic of the capitalist internet encourages users to accumulate attention with and approval of individual profiles and postings on social media. Its logic is to treat people as mere competitors, undermining interpersonal solidarity.
3. **Digital Surveillance**: State institutions and capitalist corporations employ digital surveillance of people as part of the complex digital and surveillance industry.

4. **Antisocial Social Media**: Social media are unsocial and antisocial media. Edward Snowden's revelations and the Cambridge Analytica scandal have shown that capitalist social media are a danger to democracy. Right-wing ideologues and demagogues propagate digital authoritarianism on social media.

5. **Algorithmic Politics**: Social media are shaped by automated, algorithmic policies. Automated computer programs ("bots") replace human activity, post information, and generate "likes". This has made it more difficult to distinguish which information and which endorsement comes from a human or a machine.

6. **Filter Bubbles**: Fragmented online publics are organised as filter bubbles in which opinions are homogeneous and disagreements either do not exist or are avoided.

7. **Digital Tabloidisation**: The digital *culture industry* has organised social media as digital tabloids that are controlled by digital corporations. Online advertising and tabloid entertainment dominate the internet, displacing engagement with political and educational content.

8. **Influencer Capitalism**: On social media, the so-called influencers shape public opinion, creating power asymmetries in terms of online attention and visibility and living in a commodified online culture that paints the world as an endless shopping mile and a mall (see Fuchs, 2021, Chapter 7).

9. **Digital Acceleration**: Due to digital acceleration, our attention capacity is challenged by superficial information that comes at us at very high speed. There is too little time and too little space for conversation and debate on social media.

10. **False/Fake News**: Post-truth politics and fake news are spreading globally through social media. In the age of new nationalisms and authoritarianism, a culture has emerged in which false/fake news is spread online, many people distrust facts and experts, and there is an emotionalization of politics through which people do not rationally examine what is real and what is fiction but assume something is true if it suits their state of mind and ideology (cf. Fuchs, 2020a, 2018).

These ten tendencies have led to a digital public sphere that is both colonialised and feudalised by capital, state power, and ideology and characterised by economic, political, and cultural asymmetries of power. The internet certainly has potentials for socialising human activities in the form of communication, cooperative work, community building, and the creation of digital commons. However, class relations and structures of domination colonialise the humanistic potentials of the internet and society. In contemporary capitalism, people are confronted with an antagonism between precarity and austerity. The internet and social media are now defined by class structures and inequalities.

Social media today are not sufficiently social. They are dominated by capitalist corporations, demagogues, and ideologues, even though they carry potentials for a world and for forms of communication beyond capitalism. Digital alternatives such as Wikipedia, digital workers' cooperatives, alternative online media such as *Democracy Now!*, digital commons such as *Creative Commons*, or free software are the manifestation of a truly social and socialised internet. Within capitalism, however, such projects often remain precarious and can only challenge the power of the dominant corporations and actors (Google, Facebook, Apple, Microsoft, Amazon, etc.) in a very limited way. The history of alternative projects within capitalism is a history of resource scarcity and precarious, often unpaid and self-exploitative labour.

In Table 5.3, the ten problems of social media and the internet in digital capitalism which had already been elaborated are assigned to the three types of alienation. There are thus economic, political, and cultural types of digital alienation.

In Table 5.4, digital alienation is presented as three types of antagonisms: class antagonism, in which digital capital exploits digital labor; political antagonism between digital dictators and digital citizens; and the cultural antagonism between digital ideologues and digital people. Alienation is the instrumentalisation of

TABLE 5.3 Three types of digital alienation and ten forms of colonialisation of the digital public sphere

Economic Digital Alienation: digital exploitation	(1) Digital class relations, digital monopolies, (2) Digital individualism, digital accumulation, digital competition
Political Digital Alienation: digital domination	(3) Digital surveillance, (4) Antisocial social media, digital authoritarianism, (5) Algorithmic politics, (6) Online filter bubbles
Cultural Digital Alienation: digital ideology	(7) Digital boulevard, digital culture industry, (8) Influencer capitalism, (9) Digital acceleration, (10) Online false/fake news

TABLE 5.4 Three antagonisms of digital alienation

Type of Alienation	Dominant Subject	Dominated Subject
Economic alienation: exploitation	Digital capital	Digital labour
Political alienation: domination	Digital dictators	Digital citizens
Cultural alienation: ideology that leads to disrespect	Digital ideologues	Digital humans

human beings. In digital alienation, people are instrumentalised with the aid of digital technologies such as the internet, mobile phones, social media, apps, big data, Industry 4.0, artificial intelligence, cloud computing, etc.

For a detailed analysis of the digital antagonisms through which the public sphere is colonialised and feudalised in digital capitalism, turn to the literature provided later.[6] However, a few examples are mentioned here.

The world's largest internet corporations in 2020 were Apple, Microsoft, Alphabet/Google, Amazon, Alibaba, and Facebook. In the Forbes list of the 2,000 largest corporations in the world, they ranked ninth (Apple Inc.), thirteenth (Alphabet/Google), fifteenth (Microsoft Corp), twenty-second (Amazon.com Inc), thirty-first (Alibaba Group), and thirty-ninth (Facebook) in the same year. Digital goods sold by these corporations include hardware (Apple), software (Microsoft), online advertising (Google, Facebook), and digital services such as online shopping (Amazon, Alibaba). The overall sales of these six corporations amounted to *US$1,012.8 billion* in 2020, which is altogether even more than the gross domestic product of the 30 least developed countries in the world, whose combined GDP in 2019 was *US$984.5 billion* (HDR, 2020; United Nations, 2020). Table 5.5 shows the world's poorest countries and their GDP as well as the world's richest internet corporations and their revenues.

TABLE 5.5 Comparison of the economic power of the six largest internet corporations and the world's 30 poorest countries

HDI Rank 2020	Country	GDP (in Billion US$, 2019)	Forbes 2000 Rank 2020	Internet Corporation	Revenues (2019, in Billion US$)
189	Niger	12,911.69	9	Apple	267.7
188	Central African Republic	2,220.31	13	Alphabet/ Google	166.3
187	Chad	11,314.95	15	Microsoft	138.6
185	Burundi	3,012.33	22	Amazon	296.3
185	South Sudan	11,997.80	31	Alibaba	70.6
184	Mali	17,279.57	39	Facebook	73.4
182	Burkina Faso	15,990.80			
182	Sierra Leone	4,121.73			
181	Mozambique	15,291.45			
180	Eritrea	2,065.00			
179	Yemen	22,581.08			
178	Guinea	12,296.67			
175	Democratic Republic of the Congo	50,400.75			

HDI Rank 2020	Country	GDP (in Billion US$, 2019)	Forbes 2000 Rank 2020	Internet Corporation	Revenues (2019, in Billion US$)
175	Guinea-Bissau	1,339.45			
175	Liberia	3,070.52			
174	Malawi	7,666.70			
173	Ethiopia	95,912.59			
172	Gambia	1,826.07			
170	Haiti	14,332.16			
170	Sudan	30,513.46			
169	Afghanistan	19,291.10			
168	Senegal	23,578.08			
167	Togo	5,490.27			
166	Djibouti	3,324.63			
165	Lesotho	2,376.33			
164	Madagascar	14,114.63			
163	Tanzania	63,177.07			
162	Cote d'Ivoire	58,539.42			
161	Nigeria	448,120.43			
160	Rwanda	10,354.42			
	Total (Billion US$):	984.51146		**Total (Billion US$):**	1,012.9

Data sources: Human Development Index Rank – HDR (2020); GDP in current US$ for various countries – World Bank (2020); in current US$ Forbes (2020)

Five digital corporations combined are more economically powerful than 22 states. And these corporations have monopolies in operating systems (Microsoft), search engines (Google), online shopping (Amazon and Alibaba), and social networking (Facebook). The internet economy is dominated by a few global corporations. Hence, we cannot assume that digital capitalism has led to an end of monopoly or to a plural economy. The concentration of capital is a tendency inherent to capitalism.

Table 5.6 provides data on the ten most-viewed YouTube videos in 2020. YouTube is the world's most-used internet platform after Google's search engine (cf. Alexa, 2021). In discussions about the digital public sphere, it is often claimed that UGC means that everyone has a voice on social media and that the public sphere has become pluralistic and participatory. On the internet, everyone is indeed able to produce and publish digital content easily – but there are asymmetries of visibility and attention. Entertainment dominates over education and politics. In terms of content, social media are primarily digital tabloid media. Online visibility and attention are dominated by multimedia corporations and celebrities. Nine of

TABLE 5.6 Top ten most-viewed YouTube videos of all time

Position	Title	Video Type	Owner	Views
1.	Luis Fonsi – Despacito	Music	Universal Music (Vivendi)	6.5 billion
2.	Ed Sheeran – Shape of You	Music	Warner Music	4.5 billion
3.	Wiz Khalifa – See You Again	Music	Warner Music	4.3 billion
4.	Masha and the Bear – Recipe for Disaster	Children's entertainment	Animaccord Animation Studio	4.1 billion
5.	Pinkfong Kids' Songs & Stories – Baby Shark Dance	Children's music	SmartStudy (Samsung Publishing)	4.1 billion
6.	Mark Ronson – Uptown Funk	Music	Sony Music	3.7 billion
7.	Psy – Gangnam Style	Music	YG Entertainment (distributed by Universal)	3.4 billion
8.	Justin Bieber – Sorry	Music	Universal Music (Vivendi)	3.2 billion
9.	Maroon 5 – Sugar	Music	Universal Music (Vivendi)	3.1 billion
10.	Katy Perry – Roar	Music	Universal Music (Vivendi)	2.9 billion

Source: Refer to Wikipedia, 2020.

the ten most-viewed YouTube videos are music videos. The copyright of five of these videos is controlled by Universal Music. Warner Music, Sony, and Samsung also have a major share in YouTube. This example shows that internet platforms have not created a participatory culture, but rather that attention and publicity on the internet is controlled by media corporations and celebrities.

The Cambridge Analytica scandal dominated the world news in the first half of 2018. Cambridge Analytica was a consulting firm founded in 2013 that was, among other things, active in the field of using big data. Steve Bannon, a former advisor of ex-president Donald Trump and known for extreme right-wing positions, used to be the vice president of this company. Cambridge Analytica bought access to personal data of around 90 million people collected on Facebook via a personality test. This data was collected from participants' Facebook profiles. Cambridge Analytica then used this data in Donald Trump's election campaign to spread personalised fake news. The Cambridge Analytica scandal is remarkable in several respects:

• It shows that right-wing extremists will resort to any means at their disposal to spread their ideology. This includes false/fake news and surveillance.

- It shows that Facebook accepts dangers to democracy to cash in on data. Facebook operates on the logic that ever-growing amounts of data processed and collected on the internet will turn out to be profitable for the corporation, which uses them to personalise advertising, that is, tailor it to individual user behavior and then sell it.
- It shows that the neoliberal deregulation of the economy has led to internet corporations being able to act as they wish.
- It shows the connection between digital fascism, digital capitalism, and digital neoliberalism, which poses a threat to democracy.

The three examples highlight individual dimensions of the ten forms of colonisation of the digital public sphere mentioned in Table 5.3. The first example shows the power of internet corporations and illustrates aspects of digital monopolies (aspect 1 of the ten problems of today's internet). The second example dealt with the digital attention economy on YouTube. This is an expression of the digital boulevard and the digital culture industry (Problem 7), where celebrities dominate attention and visibility (Problem 8). The Cambridge Analytica illustrates a combination of several of the ten problems, namely digital capitalism (Problem 1), digital surveillance (Problem 3), digital authoritarianism (Problem 5), and online false/fake news (Problem 10).

The three examples demonstrate that the assumption that the internet and social media are a democratic, digital public sphere is a myth and an ideology that trivialises the real power of internet corporations and phenomena such as online false/fake news and online fascism. But the question remains whether a democratic internet is possible. The next section deals with this question in the context of public service media.

Toward a Public Service Internet

The digital public sphere assumes the form of the colonialised and feudalised public sphere through the logic of accumulation, advertising, monopolisation, commercialisation, commodification, acceleration, individualism, fragmentation, automation of human activity, surveillance, and ideologisation. The internet and social media are dominated by commercial culture. Platforms are mostly owned by large profit-oriented corporations. Public service media operate on the basis of a different logic. However, the idea of a public service internet has not yet caught on and sounds strange to most people as there are hardly any alternatives to the commercial internet today.

Media have (a) a political–economic and (b) a cultural dimension: on the one hand, they need resources such as money, legal frameworks, staff, and organisational structures in order to exist. In this respect, they are economic organisations. However, they are special economic organisations that are also cultural organisations since they produce meanings of society that serve public information, communication, and opinion-forming. Since opinion formation and communication also include political opinion formation and political communication, media organisations have implications for democracy and the political system. As cultural organisations, all media organisations are also public as they *publish* information. As business organisations, on the other hand, only certain media organisations are public while others assume a private-sector status, that is, they are organisations that have private owners and operate for profit. Public service media and civil society media are however not profit-oriented and are collectively owned by the state or a community. Table 5.1 illustrates these distinctions. Public media are public in the sense of the cultural public and the political–economic public. They publish information and are owned by the public.

Communication scholar Slavko Splichal provides a precise definition of public service media:

> In normative terms, public service media must be a service *of* the public, *by* the public, and *for* the public. It is a service *of* the public because it is financed by it and should be owned by it. It ought to be a service *by* the public – not only financed and controlled, but also produced by it. It must be a service *for* the public – but also for the government and other powers acting in the public sphere. In sum, public service media ought to become "a cornerstone of democracy".
>
> *(Splichal, 2007, p. 255, emphases in the original)*

The means of production of public service media are in public ownership. The production and circulation of content is based on a non-profit logic. Access is universal, as all citizens are given easy access to the content and technologies of public service media. In political terms, public service media offer diverse and inclusive content that promotes political understanding and discourse. In cultural terms, they offer educational content that contributes to the cultural development of individuals and society.

Due to the special qualities of public service media, they may also offer a particularly valuable democratic and educational contribution to a democratic online public sphere and digital democracy – if they are given the necessary material and legal opportunities.

Signed by more than 1,000 individuals, the Public Service Media and Public Service Internet Manifesto calls for the defence of the existence, funding and independence of public service media and the creation of a public service Internet (Fuchs & Unterberger, 2021). Among those who have signed the Manifesto, which was initiated by Christian Fuchs and Klaus Unterberger, are Jürgen Habermas, Noam Chomsky, the International Federation of Journalists, the European Federation of Journalists, the International Association for Media and Communication Research (IAMCR), and the European Communication and Research Education Association (ECREA).

Two ideas to expand digital democracy and the creation of public service Internet platforms are the *public service YouTube* and *Club 2.0*.

The Public Service YouTube

Digital media change the traditional relationship between media production and media consumption. While in classical broadcasting these two aspects are separate, on the internet, consumers can become producers of information (so-called *prosumers*, i.e., producing consumers). UGC offers the possibility for the audience to become a producing audience. As a result, the educational and democratic mandate of public service broadcasting can be expanded in the form of a participatory mandate. Participation here means offering an online platform through which citizens can make user-generated audiovisual content publicly available.

YouTube *de facto* holds a monopoly in user-generated video distribution platforms. Public service media have the necessary experience and resources to develop, offer, and operate online video and online audio platforms. This could create real competition to YouTube's dominance. YouTube is often criticised for distributing false/fake news, hateful, terrorist and far-right content, and relatively little is done about it because video content is not screened by humans when uploaded. YouTube works based on the logic of "the more user-generated content, the better; the more advertising opportunities, the more profit". YouTube's advertising and profit orientation leads to blindness to the quality of the content. A public YouTube, on the other hand, could fulfil the public democratic mandate by not allowing videos on all topics ("anything goes") to be uploaded but by opening up certain politically and democratically relevant topics (e.g., as accompaniment to certain TV or radio programmes) for uploading at certain times and for a limited period of time.

For this purpose, it should be provided that all submitted contributions are published and archived and thus made accessible to the public without time limit, so that a user-generated democratic online public is created. However, the videos submitted should be checked by trained moderators before release to see if they contain racist, fascist, sexist, or otherwise discriminatory content. Such content should not be released.

The individualism of today's social media could be tackled by deliberately addressing and encouraging social, cultural, and civic contexts such as school classes, university seminars, adult education centers, workplace communities, civil society organisations, etc. to submit collectively produced videos.

Public service media have large archives with masses of self-produced content. These could be digitised and made available on a public service video and audio platform. The Creative Commons (CC) licence allows content to be reused. The CC-BY-NC licence allows content to be reproduced, redistributed, remixed, modified, processed, and used for *non-commercial* purposes, provided the original source is acknowledged.[7] The CC-BY-NC licence is very well suited for digitised content from the archives of public service media that are made publicly available. In this way, the creativity of the users of public service audio and video platforms may be encouraged, as they are granted permission to generate and distribute new content with the help of archive material. This could allow the public service educational mandate to become a digital creativity mandate. There is also the possibility that at certain points in time, topics are specified, and users are given the opportunity to process certain archive material and upload their new creations with the help of this material. A selection of the content submitted in this way could be broadcast on television or radio on a regular basis or on specific occasions. All submitted contributions could be provided on the platform.

Public service video and audio platforms can be offered in individual countries (as BBCTube, PBSTube, ARDTube, ZDFTube, ORFTube, SRGTube, etc.). However, it might also make sense for public media broadcasters to cooperate and jointly offer such platforms or to technically standardise their individual platforms and connect them together. The fact that in the field of television there are collaborations, for example, between the channels France Télévisions, ARD, and ZDF for ARTE or between the ORF, ZDF, and STRG for 3sat, show that it is useful to collaborate similarly in the field of online platforms. A European public alternative to YouTube could rival the commercial YouTube in terms of popularity and interest and could be a real competitor to the Californian internet giant Google/Alphabet which owns YouTube. Concrete projects are often postponed or not initiated at all because of being too small and because they would have to start at a European level. If the legal conditions were being provided, it might be easier to start at the national level to then set an international example and, in a further step, embark on a European project.

A *public service* YouTube that aims at the user-generated production of democratic content promotes the political participation and cooperation of citizens as well as the concrete, active, and creative engagement with democratic content through digital production and cooperative production. Participatory democracy entails infrastructure, space, and time for democratic processes. A public service YouTube would offer the material possibility and infrastructure for practising digital democracy.

The Club 2.0

The journalists Kuno Knöbl and Franz Kreuzer designed the concept for the Club 2 on behalf of the Austrian Broadcasting Corporation (ORF). Club 2 was a discussion programme that was usually broadcast on Tuesday and Thursday. Its basic concept was to broadcast a controversial live discussion on television with potentially unlimited airtime. It was first broadcast on 5 October 1976, and the last on 28 February 1995. About 1,400 programmes were broadcast on ORF.

The concept of Club 2 may sound rather odd to many people today, as we are so used to formats with short duration and high speed and a lack of time to engage with media and feeling rushed in our everyday lives. Open, uncensored, controversial live discussions that engage their viewers differ from accelerated media in terms of space and time: Club 2 was a public space where guests met and discussed with each other in an atmosphere that offered unlimited time. Its airtime was a public experience during which a socially important topic was discussed. Club 2 allowed for democratic publicity in public service broadcasting.

Space and time are very important for the political economy of the public sphere. However, a social space that offers enough discussion time is no guarantee for an engaged, critical, and dialectical discussion that transcends one-dimensionality, delves into the depth of an issue, and points out the common ground and differences between different positions. The public sphere must be wisely organised and managed in terms of space and time so that suitable people will attend, the atmosphere will be suitable, adequate questions are being asked, and it needs to be provided that all guests have their say, listen to each other, and that the discussion can proceed undisturbed, and so on. An unrestricted space, a dialectically controversial and intellectually demanding space, and a clever organisation are three important aspects to create such a public sphere. They are preconditions of slow media, non-commercial media, decolonised media, and media of public interest.

Is a new version of the Club 2 possible today? How could it look and be designed? If we speak of a second version ("2.0"), it means that on the one hand the Club 2 should be revitalised in a new form in order to strengthen the public sphere in times of authoritarian capitalism. On the other hand, "Club 2.0" means that we must take into account that society does not stand still. Society has developed dynamically and thus new public communication realities such as the internet have emerged. A *Club 2.0* therefore relies on a somewhat updated concept that leaves the basic rules unchanged but at the same time expands the concept. Whether a *Club 2.0* will not just remain a possibility but will become a reality is thus not merely a technical question but also one of political economy. It is a political question because its implementation necessitates a break with the logic of commercial, entertainment-oriented television dominated by reality TV. *Club 2.0* is hence also a political choice in favour of public service media formats. Its implementation is moreover an economic matter as it requires a break with the logics of colonised media, such as its high speed, superficiality, scarcity, algorithmisation and automation of human communication, post-facticity, spectacle, etc. Plus, the implementation of a *Club 2.0* is a question of resources and changing power relations in the media system.

Figure 5.2 illustrates a possible concept for the *Club 2.0*. It relies on a simple idea and is open to change and development. Here are some of its crucial aspects:

- **Basic Rules of *Club 2.0***: *Club 2.0* uses and extends the traditional principles of Club 2. The television broadcast is based on the proven Club 2 rules, which are crucial to the quality of the format. *Club 2.0* broadcasts are open-ended, live, and uncensored.

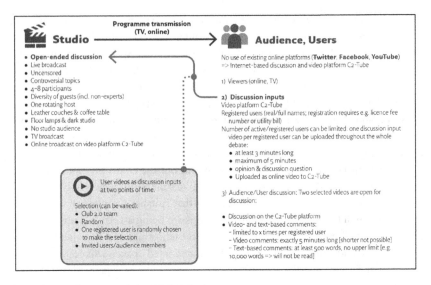

FIGURE 5.2   Concept of the *Club 2.0*

- **Cross-Medium**: *Club 2.0* is a cross-medium that combines live television and the internet and thereby transcends the boundary between these two means of communication.
- **Online Video**: Club 2.0 is broadcast live online via a video platform.
- **Autonomous Social Media, Not Traditional Social Media**: Existing commercial social media (YouTube, Twitter, Facebook, etc.) are not suitable because they are not based on the principles of slow media and public interest media. The use of YouTube would result in commercial breaks that would interrupt and ruin the discussion.
- **Autonomous Video Platform C2 Tube**: *Club 2.0* needs its own online video platform (C2-Tube). C2-Tube allows viewers to receive the debate online and via a range of technical devices.
- **Interactivity**: C2-Tube has also interactive possibilities that can be used to a certain degree.
- **User-Generated Discussion Inputs**: Users have the possibility of generating discussion inputs and actively contributing to the programme. This characteristic is linked to a non-anonymous registration of users on the platform. Anonymity encourages Godwin's Law, which states: "As an online discussion grows longer, the probability of a comparison involving Nazis or Hitler becomes more likely".[8] The number of registered and active users can be limited. The selection of active users could be random for example. Alternatively, all registered users could be invited to participate in the discussion. User-generated discussion inputs should preferably have a video format. The

number of user-generated discussion inputs uploaded onto the platform should be limited (ideally to one upload per active user). Since information overload hinders a proper discussion, it would make sense to set certain limits to make for a decelerated, relaxed culture of debate. Active users should be able to contribute to discussions on the platform.

- **Interface Between the Studio Discussion and the Video Platform**: At certain times during the live broadcast, a user-generated video is selected and shown as input for the studio discussion. Users could utter their opinion on the topic in such videos and they could contribute a discussion question. In a two- to three-hour discussion, about two of these user-generated inputs could be included. It is unavoidable that a selection mechanism is employed to decide which user-generated videos are suitable for the live broadcast. There are various ways to do this such as a random selection, selection by the production team, selection by a randomly determined registered user, selection by a special guest, etc.
- **Discussion Among Users**: *Club 2.0* allows users to discuss the topic of the programme. It could take place during and or after the live broadcast. The videos that were selected as discussion inputs could then be opened for discussion on C2 Tube. Comments should be allowed in video and written form. There should be a minimum length for written comments and possibly a maximum length for video comments. To implement the slow-media principles and avoid the Twitter effect of accelerated standstill, the number of comments per user per discussion should be limited.
- **The Forgetting of Data**: Video data are very storage-intensive. This begs the question of what should happen to all those videos that are uploaded to the platform but not broadcast and not opened for discussion. Since they are of less practical importance for public discussion, they could be deleted after a certain time. Users would need to be reminded that uploading a video in many cases entails forgetting the data eventually. Contemporary social media store all data and metadata forever. *Forgetting data* is therefore also a crucial counter-principle. Online discussions consisting of written and video comments can be either archived and kept or deleted after a certain period of time.
- **Privacy Protection**: Most social media monitor users for economic and political purposes, to achieve monetary profits through the sale of personalised advertising, and to establish a surveillance society that promises more security but undermines privacy and installs a regime of categorical suspicion of all citizens. *Club 2.0* should therefore be very privacy-friendly and store only a minimum of data and metadata necessary to run the platform. This is to ensure that user data is not sold and that exemplary data protection routines are used. Data protection should therefore be one of the design principles of *Club 2.0*. However, this does not mean that privacy protection should take the form of anonymous discussion, as anonymity can encourage

online bullying or hooliganism, especially on politically controversial issues. Data protection is therefore much more about the storage and use of data.

- **Social production**: Today's dominant social media are highly individualistic. In contrast, the production of user-generated videos for *Club 2.0* could take the form of cooperative social production which transcends individualism and creates truly social media, so that *Club 2.0* is integrated into educational institutions where people learn and create knowledge together by elaborating discussion inputs and collective positions and producing them in video form. This requires that the topics of certain *Club 2.0* programmes are known some time in advance. This could be achieved by publishing a thematic programme. Groups of users can prepare videos together, which they can upload to the platform on the evening of the relevant *Club 2.0* programme as soon as the upload option is activated.

All in all, *Club 2.0* is a concept to provide a democratic digital public sphere. It manifests a combination of elements of deliberative and participatory democracy. *Club 2.0* offers space and time for controversial political communication and enables citizens to participate collectively and individually in the discussion through videos and comments. The communicative aspect of deliberative democracy and the participatory idea of grassroots democracy are connected in the *Club 2.0* model.

Conclusions

Jürgen Habermas's concept of the public sphere in his *Structural Transformation of the Public Sphere* is often portrayed by critics as too idealistic, idealising, Eurocentric, as well as anti-pluralistic. These critics fail to realise that Habermas's concept of the public sphere is, above all, an immanent concept of critique which allows to confront the prevalent state of society with its democratic possibilities.

In this chapter and many others, I have argued for an interpretation of Habermas based on Marx and Marx's theory of alienation. This distinguishes three forms of alienation that colonise and feudalise the public sphere: 1) economic alienation (commodification and class structuring), 2) political alienation (glorification), and 3) cultural alienation (ideologisation).

The critical theory of the public sphere is suitable as one of the foundations of a critical theory of the internet and social media, that is, of communicative action in the age of digital capitalism. A critical theory of the digital public sphere points out that the internet and social media do not constitute a democratic public sphere in digital capitalism. Humans are confronted with problems such as digital class relations, digital individualism, digital surveillance, digital authoritarianism, algorithmic politics, online filter bubbles, the digital culture industry, digital tabloids, influencer capitalism, digital acceleration, and online false/fake news in digital capitalism.

A critical theory of the digital public sphere should avoid digital defeatism and digital luddism. Digital technologies interact with society. Society's antagonisms are expressed in them. A digital public sphere is not just a democratisation of the internet but must go hand in hand with a reinforcement of democracy in the fields of economy, politics, and culture. There are already non-capitalist forms of economy today. In the field of media, public service media play an important role alongside progressive alternative media. This chapter has pointed out that the development of a public service internet is a democratic alternative to the capitalist internet and digital capitalism.

Right-wing and far-right forces have frequently attacked public broadcasting throughout the past years. In Switzerland, a referendum on the abolition of broadcasting fees was held in 2018 as a result of an initiative by the neoliberal party Jungfreisinnigen. In Austria, the Freedom Party of Austria (FPÖ), when it was the governing party, wanted to replace broadcasting fees with tax funding for the Austrian Broadcasting Corporation (ORF), which would have caused it to lose its independence. In Britain, the right-wing government of Boris Johnson wants to decriminalise non-payment of licence fees, which could result in the end of the BBC. Johnson and his supporters have repeatedly criticised the BBC as being out of touch with the *interests of the people* and a manifestation of an urban liberal elite in London that has disregarded the majority will of the people after a Brexit. The Alternative for Germany's (AfD) media spokesperson Martin E. Renner formulates the same kind of criticism posed against the German TV channels ARD and ZDF as follows in an interview with Niemeyer (2018):

> The availability of information, broadcasts and programmes is in principle almost unlimited due to digitalisation. Conversely, everyone has the opportunity to freely disseminate information and opinions via social media or their own platforms. . . . By means of compulsory contributions guaranteed by the state, which add up to the unbelievable amount of around 8 billion euros per year, the state organises a market power in the media sector and thus interferes with competition and indirectly with the freedom of information. . . . In order to adapt the range of services offered by the existing public broadcasters to the wishes and needs of their users, all that is needed, therefore, is the complete abolition of compulsory licence fees. . . . Their intention is to casually re-educate people according to "political correctnes" which is defined by them. Currently it is all about propagating "diversity" and evoking a sense of love, peace, and harmony in a multicultural world.[9]

The AfD and other far-right actors make the case for a purely private, profit-oriented media system. The public democratic and educational mandate is dismissed as "political correctness". They want a private-sector, *völkisch* broadcasting, and a capitalist-*völkisch* internet, that is, an internet that is based on nationalist ideas.

These right-wing attacks on public service broadcasting have not yet succeeded. In the COVID crisis, public service media have reached a new heyday, as the population considers the public service combination of information, education, and entertainment to be immeasurable, especially in times of crisis. Before the start of the COVID-19 pandemic on 25 February 2020, the RTL soap opera *Gute Zeiten, schlechte Zeiten* was the most-watched TV programme among 14–49-year-olds in Germany with 1.5 million viewers and a market share of 20.2 percent (cf. DWDL, 2020a). On the 29th of March, the ARD Tagesschau (the most frequently watched news programme on German TV) reached viewing figures of 28.2 percent and a total of 3.2 million viewers among the same group (cf. 2020b). Among the total audience over three years of age, the Tagesschau even reached 11 million viewers and an audience share of 29.2 percent (cf. 2020b). Special broadcasts provided by the channels ARD and ZDF about the crisis were particularly popular. On the 25th of February, by comparison, just under 4.9 million people watched the news programme Tagesschau (cf. 2020a).

Independent, critical, non-commercial public service media are an embodiment of the democratic public sphere. A public service internet is a dimension of the democratisation of digitalisation.

Notes

1. Originally published in 1962.
2. Originally published in 1981, see Habermas, 1984, 1987 (English translations of the German original).
3. On the topicality of Marcuse's concept of technological rationality in digital capitalism, see Fuchs, 2019a.
4. For example, Jenkins, 2008. For a critique of this and similar approaches, see Fuchs 2017, Chapters 3, 5, and 8.
5. See Fuchs 2021, 2017, 2016.
6. See Fuchs, 2016, 2017, 2018, 2019b, 2020a, 2020b, 2020c, 2021.
7. For the Creative Commons licence, see https://creativecommons.org/licenses/by-nc/2.0/deed.de
8. Godwin, 1994.
9. Translated into English.

References

Alexa. (2021). Top sites. *Amazon.com*. Retrieved on 19 April 2021, from www.alexa.com/topsites

DWDL. (2020a). Die Top 20 Marktanteile von Dienstag, dem 25. February 2020. *DWDL.de*. Retrieved on 19 April 2021, from https://web.archive.org/web/20200226090231/www.dwdl.de/zahlenzentrale/

DWDL. (2020b). Die Top 20 Marktanteile von Sonntag, dem 29. März 2020. *DWDL.de*. Retrieved on 19 April 2021, from https://web.archive.org/web/20200330171813/www.dwdl.de/zahlenzentrale/

Forbes. (2020). Forbes global 2000: The world's largest public companies 2020. *Forbes*. Retrieved on 19 April 2021, from www.forbes.com/global2000/

Fuchs, C. (2008). *Internet and society: Social theory in the information age.* New York: Routledge.

Fuchs, C. (2011). *Foundations of critical media and information studies.* London: Routledge.

Fuchs, C. (2014). *Digital labour and Karl Marx.* New York: Routledge.

Fuchs, C. (2015). *Culture and economy in the age of social media.* New York: Routledge.

Fuchs, C. (2016). Social media and the public sphere. *tripleC: Communication, Capitalism & Critique, 12*(1), 57–101.

Fuchs, C. (2017). *Social media: A critical introduction* (2nd ed.). London: Sage.

Fuchs, C. (2018). *Digital demagogue: Authoritarian capitalism in the age of Trump and Twitter.* London: Pluto Press.

Fuchs, C. (2019a). Herbert Marcuse: Einige gesellschaftliche Folgen moderner Technologie. *Zeitschrift für Didaktik der Philosophie und Ethik, 41*(1), 70–74.

Fuchs, C. (2019b). *Rereading Marx in the age of digital capitalism.* London: Pluto.

Fuchs, C. (2020a). *Communication and capitalism: A critical theory.* London: University of Westminster Press. https://doi.org/10.16997/book45

Fuchs, C. (2020b). *Nationalism on the internet: Critical theory and ideology in the age of social media and fake news.* New York: Routledge.

Fuchs, C. (2020c). *Marxism: Karl Marx's fifteen key concepts for cultural & communication studies.* New York: Routledge.

Fuchs, C. (2021). *Social media: A critical introduction* (3rd ed.). London: SAGE.

Fuchs, C., & Unterberger, K. (2021). *The public service media and public service Internet manifesto.* London: University of Westminster Press. https://doi.org/10.16997/book60

Godwin, M. (1994, October). Meme, Counter-meme. *Wired.* Retrieved on 18 April 2021, from www.wired.com/1994/10/godwin-if-2/

Habermas, J. (1984). *Theory of communicative action* (T. McCarthy, Trans., Vol. 1). Boston: Beacon Press.

Habermas, J. (1987). *Theory of communicative action* (T. McCarthy, Trans., Vol. 2). Boston: Beacon Press.

Habermas, J. (1989). *The structural transformation of the public sphere: An inquiry into a category of bourgeois society* (T. Burger & F. Lawrence, Trans.). Cambridge, MA: Massachusetts Institute of Technology Press.

Habermas, J. (2008). Hat die Demokratie noch eine epistemische Dimension? Empirische Forschung und normative Theorie. In J. Habermas (Ed.), *Ach, Europa* (pp. 138–191). Frankfurt am Main: Suhrkamp.

HDR. (2020). Human development data center | Human development reports. *United Nations Development Programme.* Retrieved on 20 April 2021, from http://hdr.undp.org/en/indicators

Horkheimer, M. (2013). *Critique of instrumental reason* (M. O'Connell, Trans.). London: Verso.

Jenkins, H. (2008). *Convergence culture.* New York: New York University Press.

Lukács, G. (1971). *History and class consciousness: Studies in Marxist dialectics* (R. Livingstone, Trans.). Cambridge, MA: Massachusetts Institute of Technology Press.

Marcuse, H. (1982). Some social implications of modern technology. In A. Arato & E. Gebhardt (Eds.), *The essential Frankfurt School reader* (pp. 138–162). London; New York: Continuum Publishing.

Marx, K. (2010a). The civil war in France (F. Engels, Trans.). In *Collected works (MECW)* (Vol. 22, pp. 307–359). London: Lawrence & Wishart.

Marx, K. (2010b). The accumulation of capital (S. Moore & E. Aveling, Trans.). In F. Engels (Ed.), *Collected works (MECW)* (Vol. 35, pp. 565–703). London: Lawrence & Wishart.

Marx, K. (2010c). Economic and philosophic manuscripts of 1844 (M. Milligan & D. J. Struik, Trans.). In *Collected works (MECW)* (Vol. 3, pp. 229–346). London: Lawrence & Wishart.

Niemeyer, T. (2018). AfD: Ohne den Rundfunkbeitrag wäre alles besser. *DWDL.de*. Retrieved on 19 April 2021, from www.dwdl.de/magazin/68116/afd_ohne_den_rundfunkbeitrag_waere_alles_besser/page_1.html

Splichal, S. (2007). Does history matter? Grasping the idea of public service at its roots. In G. F. Lowe & J. Bardoel (Eds.), *From public service broadcasting to public service media* (pp. 237–256). Gothenburg: Nordicom.

United Nations. (2020). *Human development report 2020*. New York: United Nations Development Programme. Retrieved on 19 April 2021, from http://hdr.undp.org/sites/default/files/hdr2020.pdf

Wang, D. (2008). The idle and the busy: Teahouses and public life in early twentieth-century Chengdu. *Journal of Urban History*, *26*(4), 411–437.

Wikipedia. (2020). List of most-viewed YouTube videos. *Wikipedia*. Retrieved on 20 October 2020, from https://en.wikipedia.org/wiki/List_of_most-viewed_YouTube_videos

World Bank. (2020). *World Bank open data*. Retrieved on 20 April 2021, from https://data.worldbank.org/

6

SOCIAL MEDIA MODERATION

The Best-Kept Secret in Tech

Ysabel Gerrard

What is Content Moderation?

If someone had said the phrase "content moderation" a decade ago, I am willing to bet that few people outside of the tech world would have been familiar with it. Content moderation is:

> [T]he detection of, assessment of, and interventions taken on content or behaviour deemed unacceptable by platforms or other information intermediaries, including the rules they impose, the human labour and technologies required, and the institutional mechanisms of adjudication, enforcement, and appeal that support it.
>
> *(Gillespie & Aufderheide, 2020, p. 2)*

Although this chapter is about how *social media* content moderation works, I should note that this process has happened on a smaller scale in other online spaces hosting user-generated content (UGC) for decades, including online forums and bulletin boards, comment sections on news websites, commercial websites hosting buyer reviews, and dating sites. But today's content moderation landscape looks very different.

Until social media content moderation exploded as a public concern in the latter half of the 2010s, it was one of the tech world's best-kept secrets. Only a handful of writers, like Brad Stone's "Concern for Those Who Screen the Web for Barbarity" (*New York Times*, 2010), had paid attention to the hidden, mostly human labour of screening the internet for illicit content. Even internet researchers knew precious little, if anything about the work involved in "keep[ing] dick pics and beheadings out of your Facebook feed" (Chen, 2014, n.p.). Reflecting on this inattention,

DOI: 10.4324/9781003171270-6

Roberts explains that a sign of good content moderation is *invisibility*: it "leaves no trace", making it seem as though "content just magically appears on a site, rather than there being some sort of curation process and a set of logics by which content is determined to be appropriate or inappropriate" (2016, p. 148). While greater public awareness has forced tech companies to talk more openly about content moderation, its particularities are still somewhat of a mystery, but make no mistake that this is by design. Roberts calls this the "logic of opacity": social media companies' tradition of avoiding "acknowledgment that they undertake moderation at all, equivocating about who or what does the moderation work, how and under what conditions and refusing to articulate the specific policies and procedures by which their moderation practices are undertaken" (2018, n.p.).

Though clearly necessary, content moderation is also controversial: the humans undertaking this work are plagued with mental health difficulties, automated moderation technologies famously scrub the wrong things from the internet, public commentators worry about the lack of transparency from social media giants, and the rules governing online communication can create as many problems as they solve. In what follows, I lift the lid on social media content moderation, giving readers an overview of what the work entails, why we need it, how the practice works on both human and technical levels, and what the future of content moderation may hold. This chapter combines academic writing with a range of contemporary examples, including livestreamed suicides, pole-dancing and make-up tutorials, eating disorder recovery communities, and the COVID-19 pandemic (ongoing at the time of writing). It also opens up a lengthier discussion of an especially controversial case study: how images of healed self-harm scars should (or, perhaps, should not) be moderated on Instagram. Readers are advised to skip this section if they feel the content may be triggering.

But there are things about social media content moderation I do not know and wish I did. There are moments in this chapter where I pause to reflect on these knowledge gaps, frustrated by the "logic of opacity" (Roberts, 2018) and imagining a world where social media users have greater control and awareness of the governance behind their online lives.

Why Do We Need Content Moderation?

The move to a "participatory" web in the mid-2000s meant increased opportunities for ordinary internet users to share UGC like text, images, videos, emoji, and GIFs (among others, see Jenkins, 2006).[1] Participatory media differ from what we might call "traditional" media because they represent a shift in communication structures, taking us from the one-to-many communicative style of television shows, magazines, and some older websites to the many-to-many participatory dynamics we see in newer technologies like social media. The term "participation" contrasts with older notions of passive media audiences/

receivers, hence the rise of hybrid terms like "prosumer" (producer plus consumer) (Bruns, 2008). For example, people often share news stories on Twitter and Weibo; they connect with family over Messenger Video; post aesthetically pleasing pictures to their Instagram Stories; or join in with new dance trends on Douyin/TikTok.

In the mid-2000s, participatory media were widely celebrated for enabling the average, everyday media consumer to "archive, annotate, appropriate, and recirculate media content" (Jenkins, 2006, p. 1) in seemingly powerful new ways, but the reality soon kicked in that leaving people in charge of publishing their own content comes with significant risks. Also, the volume of content posted to social media quickly outpaced companies' capacity to cope: in 2017, YouTube was reported to receive "400 hours of video uploaded to its platform per minute", up fourfold from its last reported statistic in 2014 (Roberts, 2018, n.p.). These trends prompted social media companies to create new automated systems and scale up their human workforces to wash away "bad" content, ranging from the tasteless to the downright illegal.

Hosting UGC is a risky business, but "risk" means different things to different stakeholders. One interpretation of risk is a matter of brand management. As Roberts notes, companies large and small rely on content moderation to "guard against digital damage to their brand that could be caused by lewd, disturbing, or even illegal content being displayed and transmitted on their sites" (2016, p. 147). Social media companies themselves also need to minimise public relations fiascos to ensure their users – and therefore advertisers – feel safe on platforms, remaining loyal (and profitable). But another interpretation of "risk" – and the one that arguably attracts the most public debate where content moderation is concerned – is of the risk of *harm* that might befall internet users if they see distressing or triggering content, particularly children (Baym, 2015). This means social media companies need to make tough decisions about what counts as "harmful" online content and in whose interests they wish to minimise it.

What Counts as "Harmful" Online Content?

Social media platforms make important decisions about the kinds of content and behaviour they do and do not permit. Companies communicate these decisions through documents called "community guidelines" (sometimes known as "community standards" or similar). As Gillespie notes, these public-facing documents are written in "deliberately plainspoken language" (2018, p. 46) to tell users how they are allowed to behave on a site and what kinds of content are acceptable and not acceptable. But these rules have been the subject of intense debates: platforms apply them inconsistently, provide unclear explanations of community guidelines, keep the rulebooks hidden from public scrutiny, and provoke public outrage that certain rules exist to begin with. As Gerrard and Thornham (2020) note:

Some "rules" are more stable than others such as those against supporting terrorism, crime and hate groups, sharing sexual content involving minors, malicious speech and so on, mostly because they verge on or cross the threshold of illegality. But some of platforms' other rules . . . are less stable and reflect morality rather than legality.

(2020, p. 1276)

There are too many examples of harmful online content to list in one book chapter; indeed, this is precisely the problem social media companies face. While there might *seem* to be obvious examples of content that would count as harmful – slurs like racism, sexism, homophobia, transphobia, or other forms of violence like death and rape threats – platforms do not always act to take this kind of content down. Sometimes, companies cite the "public interest" to defend their inaction on rule breaking. Twitter, for example, says that Tweets posted by verified accounts or accounts with over 100,000 followers might be exempt from moderation, recognising that "sometimes it may be in the public interest to allow people to view Tweets that would otherwise be taken down" (2021, n.p.). This means that Twitter's rules are, by its own admission, unevenly applied according to the social status of the Tweeter.

There are other reasons why social media companies might choose to let seemingly harmful content stay online, and one example is a livestreamed video of a suicide. Facebook is one of several social media giants to host livestreaming services (a video broadcast in real time). The company uses a combination of content moderation tools to identify acts of self-harm and imminent threats to life in livestreamed videos, and Facebook's policy states that if a concerning livestream is brought to their attention:

a member of Facebook's Community Operations team reviews the report to determine if the person is at risk – and if so, the original poster is shown support options. . . . In serious cases, where there is an imminent danger of self-harm, Facebook may contact emergency services to conduct a wellness check. . . . We also provide resources and support to the person who flagged the troubling post, including options for them to call or message their distressed friend letting them know that they care, or contacting another friend or a trained professional at a suicide hotline for support.

(Facebook, 2021, n.p.)

Livestreamed suicides raise a series of vital, tough-to-settle questions: should the livestreams be allowed to continue as they give people's friends and family, along with emergency services, more time to intervene? Or should they be removed, given the risk of triggering other people who might see the video? And what should happen to the video after it has streamed, especially if a person has taken their own life and is no longer in control of their Facebook account? There are also legal issues at play here: Facebook is a globally dominant social network, but the implications of its policies vary according to a user's location, making them tough, probably unwise to standardise. At the time of writing, attempting suicide is considered a crime punishable by law in countries like Brunei and Malaysia (Yap, 2020), raising vital questions about the scalability of Facebook's policy to alert emergency services when a livestream suggests "imminent danger of self-harm" (Facebook, 2021, n.p.). These are just some of the many difficult questions social media companies face and which famously divide public commentators.

Online harms are also context dependent. For example, in early 2021, Academic and Activist Carolina Are had a viral pole-dancing tutorial removed from her TikTok account (Stokel-Walker, 2021). The video was viewed three million times before TikTok removed it for violating its community guidelines, claiming it displayed "adult nudity and sexual activity" (Stokel-Walker, 2021, n.p.) and therefore broke the rules. Are's account was suspended, preventing her from uploading new posts, but her original video was reinstated after she appealed. This example raises a series of questions about the definition of "harmful" online content and the operationalisation of a social media platform's rules:

- Why was the video reinstated after it supposedly broke the rules (or, a better question: Why was it ever removed if it did not break the rules)?
- What counts as "sexual activity" in TikTok's eyes, and by whose moral standards is this decision being made?
- What counts as "nudity" in TikTok's eyes (Are was wearing clothing in the video and not displaying genitalia), and by whose moral standards is this decision being made?
- Who might be "harmed" by a pole-dancing tutorial?
- In whose interests were these decisions made?

The largest social media companies typically host users from all around the world, even in countries that purport to ban them. For example, many internet users in China – which blocks several popular Western social media platforms like Facebook, Twitter, and YouTube – use circumvention tools to bypass online censorship, like simple web proxies and virtual private network (VPN) services (Mou, Wu, & Atkin, 2014). But the laws, norms, cultures, and standards for defining what counts as harmful content vary from country to country; person to person; community to community. This creates a tricky situation for social media companies to write a set of rules that all users will agree with and adhere to. Once the rules have been written, how does content moderation actually work?

How Does Content Moderation Work?

All social media companies "do" content moderation in some way, though their proficiencies vary wildly, and the answer to this question depends on the platform in question. For example, following a long online tradition, Reddit relies on volunteer moderators to enforce its content policies, "giving communities delegated power to define their own governance" (Matias, 2019, p. 2). Reddit is divided into numerous subreddits (or "subs"), which are essentially discussion boards for interest groups on topics ranging from make-up tutorials to conspiracy theories. Users mainly share text-based posts but can also contribute images, videos, GIFs and, in some subreddits, livestreamed videos (Gerrard & Squirrell, 2019). Although Reddit as a company has its own rules governing user participation – for example, "Do not post or encourage the posting of sexual or suggestive content involving minors" (Reddit, 2021, n.p.) – subreddits also enforce community-specific rules, which are displayed on the front page of each sub (Squirrell, 2019). As an example, at the time of writing, the r/MakeUpAddiction sub enforces rules like: "no photo editing" and "all makeup looks and collections must include a detailed product list" (r/MakeUpAddiction, 2021, n.p.).

This style of governance derives from older internet spaces like Usenet groups (Squirrell, 2019) and which Caplan (2018) defines as a "Community reliant approach". This style of governance differs from *artisanal approaches* ("where case-by-case governance is normally performed by between 5 and 200 workers") and *industrial approaches* ("where tens of thousands of workers are employed to enforce rules made by a separate policy team") (Caplan, 2018, p. 16). As Matias notes, although volunteer moderators have "played a fundamental role in social life online for over 40 years" (2019, p. 2), *community-reliant approaches* are relatively uncommon on large social media platforms. Also, relying on volunteer moderators does not come without its challenges: Squirrell reports that (unpaid) moderators struggle in myriad ways with their roles, facing a careful balancing act between competing pressures and acutely aware that "heavy-handed" approaches risk "resulting in a less active and engaged userbase" on a sub (2019, p. 2). As I will now explain, a more common approach to content moderation is for social media companies to take an industrial approach (Caplan, 2018), using a combination of automated and human approaches.

Automated Content Moderation

For the purposes of this chapter, I refer to automated content moderation in a broad sense, accounting for the range of systems designed to remove problematic content from social media *without direct, consistent human intervention*. As Gillespie notes, automated moderation tools tend to be "lumped under the umbrella of 'AI' [artificial intelligence]" when they might actually be "pattern matching": "comparing new content to a blacklist of already known examples (Gorwa, Binns, & Katzenbach, 2020)" (2020, p. 3). These include the use of skin filters to detect pornography and comparing new content to databases of previously banned images, text-based posts, videos, and so on (Roberts, 2017). By "automation", then, I am talking about social media companies' efforts to automatically prevent problematic content from ever reaching a platform, or to the automated removal of content that breaks the rules once it has been uploaded.

As Gillespie explains, large social media companies – Facebook, Twitter, TikTok – often point to "scale" as a justification for an industry-wide push toward automated content moderation. Platform representatives generally use the term "scale" to refer to "little more than the enormous number of users or amount of content", but scale is not the same thing as size (Gillespie, 2020, p. 2). Where content moderation is concerned, "scale" also means the ease with which a moderation process can be *scaled up*: "proceduralized such that it can be replicated in different contexts, and appear the same" (Gillespie, 2020, p. 2). As Gillespie notes, "all the major platforms dream of software that can identify hate speech, porn, or threats more quickly and more fairly than human reviewers, before the offending content is ever seen" (2020, p. 2). But the problem is that automated content moderation is not – and will never be – perfect.

In March 2019, a terrorist used Facebook Live to stream his attack on the Al Noor Mosque in Christchurch, New Zealand, murdering more than 50 people with an assault rifle. The terrorist's video was quickly reported and taken down but not before users made copies and re-posted them across the internet. "Within hours, hundreds of thousands of versions of the video (some altered with watermarks or other edits) were being re-uploaded to Facebook, as well as to YouTube and Twitter" (Gorwa et al., 2020, p. 2), and so began a cat-and-mouse game of "hashing" the videos to prevent future iterations from reaching the web. "Hashing" is the process of producing a "digital fingerprint" (Gorwa et al., 2020, p. 2) of online content and storing it in a database to prevent future uploads. Videos of the Christchurch massacre were popping up faster than they could be taken down, viewed by millions of people around the world. This example is a frank reminder that, while automation is often presented as the solution to the necessary scale of moderation for social media giants, it will never be sophisticated enough to replace the human eye.

When the COVID-19 outbreak emptied out the world's office blocks in early 2020, major social media companies turned to automation to replace a large portion of their human content moderator workforce (Gerrard, 2020). Knowing full well that "automated content moderation is not a panacea for the ills of social media" (Gillespie, 2020, p. 2), spokespeople for several social media companies offered advance apologies for the inevitable mistakes they would make during the pandemic. Twitter, for example, used its blog to explain that it would increase its "use of machine learning and automation to take a wide range of actions on potentially abusive and manipulative content" but warned that "they can sometimes lack the context that our teams bring, and this may result in us making mistakes" (Twitter, 2020, n.p.).

An especially striking aspect of Twitter's update was their commitment to not "permanently suspend[ing] any accounts based solely" on its automated enforcement systems during the pandemic, instead "look[ing] for opportunities to build in human review checks where they will be most impactful" (Twitter, 2020, n.p.). While there are times when Twitter users may welcome the automated removal of a user's account, this approach is not always the most accurate or ethical. For example, users posting supportive content about eating disorder recovery across a range of platforms often have their accounts wrongly suspended and then later reinstated (Bradley, 2021). Not only does this example highlight inconsistency and subjectivity in the application of a platform's rules, but it also reminds us that behind most social media accounts are *people*. But some of these people are very vulnerable and may suffer unduly if their accounts are removed.[2]

People belonging to marginalised groups typically bear the brunt of the problems associated with automated technologies: a minor paperwork error ends a six-year-old's life-saving medical benefits (Eubanks, 2018); predictive policing software disproportionately assigns high recidivism risk scores to Black parolees (Benjamin, 2019); Google searches for "Black girls" yield porn websites as the first hits (Noble, 2018); Amazon's recruiting engine taught itself to prefer male candidates (Dastin, 2018). These examples highlight serious limitations in how we might imagine the future of automated content moderation. This is because automated technologies rely on stereotyping and categorisation to function efficiently, but where content moderation is concerned, "Such sense-making processes are better left to the high-powered computer of the human mind" although, and as I now discuss, "not without other costs" (Roberts, 2017, n.p.).

Flagging and Human Review

Although automated moderation can prevent some illicit content from ever reaching (or remaining on) social media, some posts slip under the net. This is part of the reason why social media users are called upon to participate in platform governance by reporting (or "flagging") rule-breaking content. The flag is a common mechanism on social media for reporting "offensive" content, "allow[ing] users to express their concerns within the predetermined rubric of a platform's 'community guidelines'" (Crawford & Gillespie, 2016, p. 411). Flagging tools can be found on almost all social media platforms but, as I have already noted, content moderation is platform-specific, meaning flagging mechanisms vary. For example, on some platforms, users simply click a button and content is immediately reported, but others give users slightly more expressive vocabularies with which to make their complaints. Users often do not find out if (or why) a decision was made to either remove or retain the content they reported. As Crawford and Gillespie put it, "The process by which a flag is received, sorted, attended to, and resolved remains completely opaque to users" (2016, pp. 415–416).

Once a post has been flagged by a user, it is placed in a "queue" to be viewed by a human content moderator. This role is known as Commercial Content Moderation (CCM) and is broadly defined as: "the large-scale screening by humans of content uploaded to social-media sites – Facebook, Instagram, Twitter, YouTube, and others" (Roberts, 2017, n.p.).[3] There are different queues according to the seriousness and type of content deemed problematic: one is a priority queue where content will be viewed by an "expert" moderator (Caplan, 2018 cited in Gorwa et al., 2020, p. 6), and the other is a regular queue, through which human review takes longer. Content identified by automated tools might also be sent for human review and placed in a queue (Gorwa et al., 2020).

CCM is managed in different ways according to the size and nature of an organisation. Sometimes, it is offered in-house at large tech companies by a team of workers, or it might be outsourced via Amazon Mechanical Turk or a similar microlabour service (Roberts, 2019). At organisations taking industrial approaches to moderation (Caplan, 2018), CCM workers usually have only a few seconds to respond to flagged posts and decide whether a piece of content – an image, a video, a comment – should stay or go (Roberts, 2019). They must follow a predetermined company policy about acceptable and unacceptable content and use moderator rulebooks to learn how to handle each scenario. As Caplan notes, social media giants have faced scrutiny for "the lack of transparency into the content moderation rules and a lack of visibility into *how* platforms are developing these rules" (Caplan, 2018, p. 3). In 2017, *the Guardian* was the first press outlet to reveal Facebook's internal moderator guidelines (Hopkins, 2017). The leaked documents sparked global debate about some of the policy decisions made by Facebook, reminding us that the company's rulebooks are not going to appease all users or even its workers. During her research into the working lives of CCMs, Roberts's informants told her that they struggle to navigate biases within companies' strict content moderation guidelines. For example, one CCM worker, Max, was distressed to find that "blackface is not technically considered hate speech by default" (Roberts, 2019, p. 94) at MegaTech: his pseudonymised Silicon Valley employer.

CCM workers can be found in call centres, online on Amazon Mechanical Turk, or at the headquarters of social media and other internet companies in Silicon Valley (Roberts, 2019). But CCM work is often outsourced to places like the Philippines and India. These workers tend to be employed on temporary contracts, meaning they do not get the same level of access to healthcare that tech companies' notoriously well-paid employees do. This is a real problem: CCM workers are asked to view the worst things the internet has to offer, sometimes thousands of times per day, and they suffer a high rate of burnout (Roberts, 2019). Several investigations into the role – only recently brought to light by scholars, activists, and journalists – reveal significant mental health complaints from CCM workers.

In May 2021, *BBC News* shared the story of Facebook-based CCM worker, Isabella Plunkett, who broke her non-disclosure agreement (NDA) to tell the world about her working conditions (Criddle, 2021). Facebook contracts some of its CCM work out to a company called Covalen, based in Ireland, which recruits workers like Isabella to review "tickets", as they are known in the industry, for up to eight hours per day. Isabella was one of the CCM workers who did not work from home during the COVID-19 pandemic; this was because she was assigned to "high priority" content, reviewing Facebook's most graphic posts (Criddle, 2021). She looked at horrifying things like "graphic violence, suicide, exploitation and abuse" (Criddle, 2021, n.p.) and, like many CCM workers, Isabella has sadly developed anxiety and has been placed on antidepressants (Criddle, 2021).

A story written by Adrian Chen for the *New Yorker* tells a similar tale:

> Henry Soto worked for Microsoft's online-safety team, in Seattle, for eight years. He reviewed objectionable material on Microsoft's products – Bing, the cloud-storage service OneDrive, and Xbox Live among them – and decided whether to delete it or report it to the police. Each day, Soto looked at thousands of disturbing images and videos, which included depictions of killings and child abuse. Particularly traumatic was a video of a girl being sexually abused and then murdered. The work took a heavy toll. He developed symptoms of P.T.S.D., including insomnia, nightmares, anxiety, and auditory hallucinations. He began to have trouble spending time around his son, because it triggered traumatic memories. In February, 2015, he went on medical leave.
>
> *(2017, n.p.)*

As Roberts (2019, p. 127) notes, the problems associated with CCM work – particularly post-traumatic stress disorder (PTSD) – often take years to show up and may emerge only after a worker has left their role. While there are well-documented shortcomings of automated moderation, the scars inflicted by CCM work cannot be ignored. Will all or part of this burden ever be relieved from a human workforce? If not, how might other aspects of content moderation be enhanced to lighten the load? Before I present scholars' compelling answers to these questions, I turn to a discussion of a real-world case study of content moderation policymaking.

Case study: Should Instagram Moderate Images of Healed Self-Harm Scars?

In May 2019, artist and occupational therapist, Hannah Daisy (@make-daisychains, 2019), shared a self-designed graphic to Instagram. The text over the image reads "Instagram, please stop censoring healed self-harm scars" and is accompanied by an open letter to the platform, asking it to reconsider its policy on placing "sensitivity screens" over images of healed self-harm scars. In 2019, Instagram began placing sensitivity screens over posts that do not break its rules but that might be triggering to some users, like healed self-harm scars (Hern, 2019). This decision received mixed public responses and nodded to larger problems social media companies face when moderating mental health content.

There are many outcomes of content moderation for social media users, of which a sensitivity screen is one (Table 6.1).

TABLE 6.1 Overview and description of social media content moderation user outcomes

Moderation Outcome	Description of Outcome
Suspension or removal	If a person violates a platform's community standards, they might find that their account has been suspended or that their account or post (e.g., a comment, video, image, and so on) has been permanently removed.
Content warnings	As discussed earlier, some platforms place various kinds of warning labels on content that has a sensitive nature but does not quite break the rules. For example, as a way of limiting the spread of misinformation during the COVID-19 pandemic (ongoing at the time of writing), Instagram automatically adds links to government-approved resources when users post about the pandemic to their stories.
De-monetisation	Some platforms, like YouTube, "de-monetise" content for policy violations. YouTube Partner Program (YPP) is YouTube's "long-standing practice of sharing advertising revenue with some of their video creators" (Caplan & Gillespie, 2020, p. 2), and de-monetisation is usually "imposed as a penalty, for videos that violate YouTube's 'advertiser-friendly' content guidelines, specific to videos in the YPP" (Caplan & Gillespie, 2020, p. 2). De-monetisation means one or more of a creator's videos are excluded from the YPP, or a creator might be excluded from the YPP entirely.

Moderation Outcome	Description of Outcome
Hashtag bans	Several platforms also instigate hashtag bans: limiting the search results for certain tags or showing warnings when users search for potentially risky terms. Social media companies typically do not produce lists of banned hashtags likely to reduce the risk of people coining "workaround" tags (Chancellor, Pater, Clear, Gilbert, & Choudhury, 2016; Gerrard, 2018). While this decision may make sense in some scenarios, the opacity with which platforms ban tags is sometimes problematic. For example, in 2019, Instagram quietly restricted users' access to hashtags associated with a popular Caribbean carnival, during which "revellers from around the world parade and dance through the streets in their costumes" (Taylor, 2019). Multiple users found themselves unable to access hashtags like #trinidadcarnival2020, and an Instagram spokesperson claimed: "We apologize for the mistake. . . . it is never our intention to silence members of our community" (Taylor, 2019, n.p.).
Shadowbanning	Social media platforms are increasingly being called out for "shadowbanning" some of their users. Shadowbanning is the process of preventing certain social media accounts and/ or posts from showing up in recommendation systems. This means the content is still available on the platform, but it is more difficult to be found, and social media users are not told when their account or posts are being shadowbanned. In a recent Q&A, Head of Instagram, Adam Mosseri, strenuously denied that the platform shadowbanned its users (Cook, 2020), but his words were misleading. While this term may not be used within company walls, the act of removing certain accounts or kinds of content in recommendation systems is a proven occurrence; for example, Instagram currently does not recommend accounts where users post images of "cutting" (Hern, 2019). While Instagram is transparent about this rule, it makes less justifiable decisions about other instances of shadowbanning.

Moderation Outcome	Description of Outcome
Borderline content policies	A related but different form of moderation happens to what platforms called "borderline content": "posts that don't quite go against a platform's rules but that might not be appropriate for all members of its community" (Gerrard & McCosker, 2020, n.p.). The term gained traction in 2018, after Mark Zuckerberg wrote a blog post about Facebook's decision to limit the spread of clickbait and misinformation (Zuckerberg, 2021). Companies like Facebook aim to reduce the presence of borderline content in ways that do not fall under an outright ban or removal, and to "penalize" it so that it gets less engagement, for example, by not distributing it through recommendation algorithms (Zuckerberg, 2021, n.p.). But there are some ethical problems with the governance of borderline content, particularly for content about mental health. I would argue that users posting about mental health – whether they are in recovery, raising awareness, or doing something that might be deemed more problematic – are indicating a degree of vulnerability. To then manipulate a vulnerable person's online communication and experiences without explaining this to them should arguably be classed an online harm.

How, then, should Instagram moderate images of healed self-harm scars, if at all? Should it do nothing; send resources to users (for example, links to local charities); blur out the post using a sensitivity screen; remove the post entirely; shadowban these posts; or perhaps something else? These are real-world questions platforms like Instagram are grappling with, and they are all connected to a larger question about deciding what counts as "harmful" content, and in whose interests this classification is being made. And these decisions provoke substantive public debate:

> Why is a gay kiss more inappropriate than a straight one? Where is the line drawn between an angry political statement and a call to violence? What are the aesthetic and political judgments brought to bear on an image of a naked body – when is it "artistic" versus "offensive?"
>
> (Crawford & Gillespie, 2016, p. 413)

For many people, social media platforms are demonstrably positive spaces to talk about mental health (McCosker & Gerrard, 2020). While there are some posts that flagrantly break the rules, I would wager that a far greater number of posts are more difficult to define as harmful. When it comes to mental health, social media companies risk either stigmatising certain conditions by making rules or triggering users by allowing content to remain on a site. It can be tough to decide where the stakes are highest.

What Does the Future of Content Moderation Look Like?

Although the title of this chapter calls content moderation "the best-kept secret in tech", its processes and consequences are increasingly being brought "Out of the shadows, out from behind the screen, and into the light", as Roberts so powerfully puts it (2019, p. 222). This heightened public awareness has resulted in greater efforts to regulate content moderation, especially at large social media companies. Countries across the world are rolling out a range of regulatory models; in Germany, for example, the NetzDG Act requires companies to restrict access to unlawful content within the country's borders within 24 hours of it being reported (Heldt, 2019). The SESTA-FOSTA act in the United States, initially intended to stop sex trafficking activities online, has resulted in companies increasingly banning sexual content and nudity for fear of breaking the law (Tiidenberg & van der Nagel, 2020). In Europe, the Digital Services Act (DSA) pushes for greater transparency about content moderation outcomes and demands more opportunities for users to meaningfully challenge content moderation decisions (European Commission, 2020). And the United Kingdom's Online Harms legislation proposes holding online businesses to account for failing in their duty of care to protect people – particularly children – from harm (Department for Digital, Culture, Media and Sport, 2020). These regulatory efforts prompt a question on which I will end this chapter: *What does the future of social media content moderation look like?*

Uniting regulatory efforts seems to be a demand for greater *transparency* from social media companies. Suzor et al. explain that the lack of data on how platforms make content moderation decisions "makes it more difficult to have an informed public debate about how to regulate Internet content in a way that protects freedom of expression and other legitimate interests" (2019, p. 1527). While the authors (and I) do not dispute the need for greater transparency from social media companies, these calls tend to be vague, and there is a need for greater detail on "what information should be provided and to whom" (Suzor, Myers West, Quodling, & York, 2019, p. 1257). Pragmatic suggestions for greater transparency include, for example, listing the number of moderators working across different social media companies, telling us where they are based, and under what contracts and conditions they work. Academics like Roberts (see 2019, among other publications) have long called for better treatment of human content moderators, but it is difficult to know *what* to ask for when so many details about their work are hidden from public scrutiny. An especially compelling suggestion for improving the working lives of content moderators comes from Gillespie, who suggests strengthening automated content moderation for the most graphic content, lightening the burden on human content moderators: "Perhaps, automated tools are best used to identify the bulk of the cases, leaving the less obvious or more controversial identifications to human reviewers" (2020, p. 3).

A further suggestion for more meaningful transparency comes from Suzor et al. (2019), who argue that social media companies should provide users with a URL to the content that led to their suspension or removal from a site. The social media users surveyed in their research were frustrated to find themselves suspended or banned from a platform, without knowing which piece of content, exactly, broke the rules. Suzor et al. (2019) note that this fairly quick fix would yield significantly helpful results for social media users.

While there are, of course, several tweaks and improvements that could be made to content moderation systems, perhaps the problem is that the current industrial model (Caplan, 2018) simply does not work for everyone. It will always miss context; always make errors. As Caplan puts it:

> When global platforms grow to be the size of Facebook or YouTube, maintaining consistency in decision-making is often done at the expense of being localized or contextual. This can cause problems in the case of content like hate speech, discrimination, or disinformation when making a moderation decision depends on particular cultural and political environments. Perhaps because of this, platforms of this size tend to collapse contexts in favor of establishing global rules that make little sense when applied to content across vastly different cultural and political contexts around the world. This can, at times, have significant negative impact on marginalized groups.
>
> *(2018, p. 5)*

I am often asked by journalists if I think social media giants are "doing enough" to protect their users, particularly children. But this question is hard to answer, partly because of the "logic of opacity" (Roberts, 2017) underpinning content moderation processes but largely because I struggle to see how the current industrial model can be meaningfully improved. Yes, we can make small changes, but it sometimes feels like the current system has reached its limits. Perhaps, the time has come for social media companies to radically rethink their approach to content moderation.

Notes

1. Writers like Marwick (2013) rightly note that many of the newer technologies described as "participatory" in the mid-2000s existed before terms like this were coined and include wikis, online journals, and blogs.
2. For a detailed discussion of user responses to content moderation, see Myers West (2018) and Suzor et al. (2019).
3. See also Roberts (2019) among her other publications.

References

@makedaisychains. (2019, May 27). *Instagram*. [Online]. Retrieved on 13 May 2021, from www.instagram.com/p/Bx-UptvBF0n/

Baym, N. K. (2015). *Personal connections in the digital age* (1st ed.). Cambridge, UK; Malden, MA: Polity Press.

Benjamin, R. (2019). *Race after technology: Abolitionist tools for the new Jim Code*. London: Polity.

Bradley, S. (2021, March 17). How TikTok's recovery community is rejecting triggering pro-ana content. *Vice*. [Online]. Retrieved on 11 May 2021, from https://i-d.vice.com/en_au/article/qjpy3x/how-tiktoks-recovery-community-is-rejecting-triggering-pro-ana-content

Bruns, A. (2008). *Blogs, Wikipedia, Second Life, and beyond: From production to produsage*. New York; Oxford: Peter Lang.

Caplan, R. (2018, November 14). Content or context moderation? Artisanal, community-reliant, and industrial approaches. *Data and Society*. [Online]. Retrieved on 10 May 2021, from https://datasociety.net/library/content-or-context-moderation/

Caplan, R., & Gillespie, T. (2020). Tiered governance and demonetization: The shifting terms of labor and compensation in the platform economy. *Social Media + Society*, *6*(2), 1–13.

Chancellor, S., Pater, J. A., Clear, T., Gilbert, E., & Choudhury, M. de. (2016). #thyghgapp: Instagram content moderation and lexical variation in pro-eating disorder communities. In *Proceedings of the 19th ACM Conference on Computer – Supported Cooperative Work & Social Computing, CSCW'16*. Retrieved on 14 May 2021, from www.munmund.net/pubs/cscw16_thyghgapp.pdf

Chen, A. (2014, October 23). The laborers who keep dick pics and beheadings out of your Facebook feed. *WIRED*. [Online]. Retrieved on 19 August 2021, from www.wired.com/2014/10/content-moderation/

Chen, A. (2017, January 28). The human toll of protecting the internet from the worst of humanity. *The New Yorker*. [Online]. Retrieved on 13 May 2021, from www.newyorker.com/tech/annals-of-technology/the-human-toll-of-protecting-the-internet-from-the-worst-of-humanity

Cook, J. (2020, February 25). Instagram's CEO says shadow banning 'is not a thing': That's not true. *Huffington Post*. [Online]. Retrieved on 14 May 2021, from www.huffingtonpost.co.uk/entry/instagram-shadow-banning-is-real_n_5e555175c5b63b9c9ce434b0?ri18n=true

Crawford, K., & Gillespie, T. (2016). What is a flag for? Social media reporting tools and the vocabulary of complaint. *New Media and Society*, *18*(3), 410–428.

Criddle, C. (2021, May 12). Facebook moderator: 'Every day was a nightmare'. *BBC News*. [Online]. Retrieved on 13 May 2021, from www.bbc.co.uk/news/technology-57088382

Dastin, J. (2018, October 11). Amazon scraps secret AI recruiting tool that showed bias against women. *Reuters*. [Online]. Retrieved on 11 May 2021, from www.reuters.com/article/us-amazon-com-jobs-automation-insight/amazon-scraps-secret-ai-recruiting-tool-that-showed-bias-against-women-idUSKCN1MK08G

Department for Digital, Culture, Media and Sport. (2020, December 15). *Consultation outcome: Online Harms White Paper*. [Online]. Retrieved on 14 May 2021, from www.gov.uk/government/consultations/online-harms-white-paper/online-harms-white-paper

Eubanks, V. (2018). *Automating inequality: How high-tech tools police, profile, and punish the poor*. New York: St. Martin's Press.

European Commission. (2020, December 15). *Digital Services Act – Questions and answers*. [Online]. Retrieved on 14 May 2021, from https://ec.europa.eu/commission/presscorner/detail/en/QANDA_20_2348

Facebook. (2021). *Suicide prevention*. [Online]. Retrieved on 23 April 2021, from www.facebook.com/safety/wellbeing/suicideprevention

Gerrard, Y. (2018). Beyond the hashtag: Circumventing content moderation on social media. *New Media and Society*, *20*(12), 4492–4511.

Gerrard, Y. (2020). The COVID-19 mental health content moderation conundrum. *Social Media + Society: 2k Special Issue*, *6*(3), 1–5. https://doi.org/10.1177/2056305120948186

Gerrard, Y., & McCosker, A. (2020, November 4). The perils of moderating depression on social media. *WIRED*. [Online]. Retrieved on 12 May 2021, from www.wired.com/story/opinion-the-perils-of-moderating-depression-on-social-media/

Gerrard, Y., & Squirrell, T. (2019). The perils of livestreaming on Reddit. *VICE*. [Online]. Retrieved on 19 August 2021, from www.vice.com/en/article/zmjxge/livestreaming-live-video-reddit-feature-trial-moderators-mental-health

Gerrard, Y., & Thornham, H. (2020). Content moderation: Social media's sexist assemblages. *New Media and Society*, *22*(7), 1266–1286.

Gillespie, T. (2018). *Custodians of the internet: Platforms, content moderation, and the hidden decisions that shape social media*. New Haven, CT: Yale University Press.

Gillespie, T. (2020). Content moderation, AI, and the question of scale. *Big Data and Society*, *7*(2), 1–5.

Gillespie, T., & Aufderheide, P. (2020). Introduction. In T. Gillespie, P. Aufderheide, E. Carmi, Y. Gerrard, R. Gorwa, A. Matamoros-Fernández, S. T. Roberts, A. Sinnreich, & S. Myers West (Eds.), Expanding the debate about content moderation: Scholarly research agendas for the coming policy debates. *Internet Policy Review*, *9*(4), 1–29.

Gorwa, R., Binns, R., & Katzenbach, C. (2020). Algorithmic content moderation: Technical and political challenges in the automation of platform governance. *Big Data and Society*, *7*(1), 1–15.

Heldt, A. (2019). Reading between the lines and the numbers: An analysis of the first NetzDG reports. *Internet Policy Review*, *8*(2), 1–18.

Hern, A. (2019, February 4). Instagram to launch 'sensitivity screens' after Molly Russell's death. *The Guardian*. [Online]. Retrieved on 13 May 2021, from www.theguardian.com/technology/2019/feb/04/instagram-to-launch-sensitivity-screens-after-molly-russell-death

Hopkins, N. (2017, May 21). Revealed: Facebook's internal rulebook on sex, terrorism and violence. *The Guardian*. [Online]. Retrieved on 14 May 2021, from www.theguardian.com/news/2017/may/21/revealed-facebook-internal-rulebook-sex-terrorism-violence

Jenkins, H. (2006). *Fans, bloggers, and gamers: Exploring participatory culture*. New York; London: New York University Press.

Marwick, A. (2013). *Status Update: Celebrity, Publicity and Branding in the Social Media Age.* New Haven, CT: Yale University Press.

Matias, J. N. (2019). The civic labor of volunteer moderators online. *Social Media + Society, 5*(2), 1–12.

McCosker, A., & Gerrard, Y. (2020). Hashtagging depression on Instagram: Towards a more inclusive mental health research methodology. *New Media and Society, 23*(7), 1899–1919.

Mou, Y., Wu, K., & Atkin, D. (2014). Understanding the use of circumvention tools to bypass online censorship. *New Media and Society, 18*(5), 837–856.

Myers West, S. (2018). Censored, suspended, shadow banned: User interpretations of content moderation on social media platforms. *New Media and Society, 20*(11), 4366–4383.

Noble, S. U. (2018). *Algorithms of oppression: How search engines reinforce racism.* New York: New York University Press.

Reddit. (2021). *Content policy.* [Online]. Retrieved on 7 May 2021, from www.redditinc.com/policies/content-policy

r/MakeUpAddiction. (2021). *Reddit.* [Online]. Retrieved on 7 May 2021, from www.reddit.com/r/MakeupAddiction/

Roberts, S. T. (2016). Commercial content moderation: Digital laborers' dirty work. In S. U. Noble & B. Tynes (Eds.), *The intersectional internet: Race, sex, class and culture online* (pp. 147–159). New York: Peter Lang.

Roberts, S. T. (2017). Social media's silent filter. *The Atlantic.* Retrieved on 11 May 2021, from www.theatlantic.com/technology/archive/2017/03/commercial-content-moderation/518796/

Roberts, S. T. (2018). Digital detritus: 'Error' and the logic of opacity in social media content moderation. *First Monday, 23*(3). https://doi.org/10.5210/fm.v23i3.8283

Roberts, S. T. (2019). *Behind the screen: Content moderation in the shadows of social media.* New Haven, CT: Yale University Press.

Squirrell, T. (2019). Platform dialectics: The relationships between volunteer moderators and end users on Reddit. *New Media and Society, 21*(9), 1910–1927.

Stokel-Walker, C. (2021, February 22). TikTok censored a pole-dancing PhD who studies how social media silences women. *Impact.* [Online]. Retrieved on 23 April 2021, from www.inputmag.com/culture/tiktok-censored-banned-pole-dancer-phd-carolina-are

Stone, B. (2010, July 18). Concern for those who screen the web for barbarity. *The New York Times.* [Online]. Retrieved on 19 August 2021, from www.nytimes.com/2010/07/19/technology/19screen.html

Suzor, N. P., Myers West, S., Quodling, A., & York, J. (2019). What do we mean when we talk about transparency? Toward meaningful transparency in commercial content moderation. *International Journal of Communication, 13*, 1526–1543.

Taylor, S. (2019, July 30). Instagram apologizes for blocking Caribbean carnival content. *Vice.* [Online]. Retrieved on 13 May 2021, from www.vice.com/en/article/7xg5dd/instagram-apologizes-for-blocking-caribbean-carnival-content

Tiidenberg, K., & van der Nagel, E. (2020). *Sex and social media.* Bingley: Emerald Publishing Limited.

Twitter. (2020, March 16). *An update on our continuity strategy during COVID-19.* [Blog post]. Retrieved on 10 May 2021, from https://blog.twitter.com/en_us/topics/company/2020/An-update-on-our-continuity-strategy-during-COVID-19.html

Twitter. (2021). *About public-interest exceptions on Twitter.* [Online]. Retrieved on 12 May 2021, from https://help.twitter.com/en/rules-and-policies/public-interest

Yap, M. Y. (2020, July 29). Suicide is still treated as a crime in many Southeast Asian countries: Here are the laws. *Mashable*. [Online]. Retrieved on 23 April 2021, from https://sea.mashable.com/social-good/11598/suicide-is-still-treated-as-a-crime-in-many-southeast-asian-countries-here-are-the-laws

Zuckerberg, M. (2021, May 5). A blueprint for content governance and enforcement. *Facebook*. [Online]. Retrieved on 14 May 2021, from www.facebook.com/notes/mark-zuckerberg/a-blueprint-for-content-governance-and-enforcement/10156443129621634/

7

MAKE IT TREND! SETTING RIGHT-WING MEDIA AGENDAS USING TWITTER HASHTAGS

Gabrielle Lim, Alexei Abrahams, and Joan Donovan

Introduction

In the aftermath of the January 6, 2021 Capitol Hill riots, politicians and government employees reeling from the violent and fatal event sought to make sense of what had happened, retelling their accounts of the day, the terrors they experienced, and the fears they now face. Congresswoman Alexandra Ocasio-Cortez – known for her savvy use of technology and social media – chose to do so on February 1 via a live Instagram broadcast. Her 90-minute-long emotional testimony described hiding from the rioters in her office during the Capitol Hill siege while listening to voices of men outside her door asking where she was. "I thought I was going to die," she said on Instagram. "I have never been quieter in my entire life" (The Editors, 2021).

The response to her testimony garnered significant attention, resulting in her name trending on Twitter in the United States (Choi, 2021). By trending, we mean these hashtags appear on Twitter's publicly viewable shortlist of top trending hashtags in the sidebar or on the "explore" page, where users are recommended popular and timely content. Already a polarizing figure in US politics, Ocasio-Cortez's account of January 6 became a wedge issue with Democrats and supporters praising her for her detailed retelling of the day's events and her own experience of sexual assault, while far-right commentators and influencers accused her of overreacting, calling her testimony "hysterical" and "fiction" (Justice, 2021). As a result, two hashtags emerged on Twitter targeting Ocasio-Cortez and labeling her a liar: #AlexandriaOcasioSmollett and #AOCLied. Amplified by right-wing influencers like Candace Owens and Sebastian Gorka, these two hashtags gained traction on Twitter trending on February 3, 2020, and resulting in mainstream media coverage and further harassment of Ocasio-Cortez.

DOI: 10.4324/9781003171270-7

This series of events brings to question the role that influencers, trending algorithms, and social media has on media agenda setting. To what extent are individuals able to set media agendas by using social media to their advantage? While conventional thought has tended to relegate agenda setting power to political elites and corporate power, the third sector (e.g., civil society, activists, dissidents, independent media) has throughout history found ways to seed – if not set – narratives into mainstream public discourse (Wasow, 2020). With the advent of social media, however, nongovernmental organizations and individuals have discovered new ways of doing so albeit to varying degrees of success.

In this chapter, we explore the frequency and degree with which hashtags are deployed by right-wing influencers to amplify certain narratives and therefore drive news cycles. While it has been well documented that hashtag manipulation occurs in a diverse set of communities and countries, we chose to limit our scope to a group of right-wing influencers within the United States. While they are a decentralized set of individuals, they nonetheless play a significant role in the US information ecosystem, having found ways to plant stories in the media (Donovan & Friedberg, 2019), having engaged in multiple forms of media manipulation leading to the mainstreaming of fringe ideas (Crawford, 2020), and having been politically expedient for conservative politicians and media outlets (Davey & Ebner, 2017; Krafft & Donovan, 2020). Even with Trump out of the White House, reactionary politics and the "culture wars" continue to play out on social and mainstream media where right-wing influencers, pundits, and politicians alike engage in open information warfare (Stanton, 2021; Benkler, Faris, & Roberts, 2018). Their continual impact on the wider ecosystem therefore bears asking how and to what extent are they able to influence political discourse.

Our research questions include:

- How do right-wing influencers use hashtags on Twitter?
- Are right-wing influencers able to drive the media agenda by making hashtags trend?
- Are these hashtags then covered by the media thus amplifying their reach?
- Are right-wing influencers able to get press coverage of hashtags regardless of making a hashtag trend?

Using a mixed-methods approach of Twitter scraping, content analysis, and the Media Cloud database of news coverage, we find that some influencers are able to gain trending status with some hashtags, and that this does indeed bring about increased media coverage. However, these gains are limited, short-lived, and skewed by the type of coverage received. Further, even if a hashtag does not trend, when news media or a blog covers it, the link to the story aids in garnering more attention to the hashtag by creating fresh content for social media sharing.

We make this argument in the following sections. In the second section, we draw from media theory and recent social media studies to inform our expectations. We then provide an in-depth case study of the #AOCLied campaign to further generate our theory of agenda setting and lay out our hypotheses. In the fourth section, we test our hypotheses on 19 right-wing influencers on Twitter. Finally, we conclude with a discussion on our findings and limitations and a conclusion.

Background and Theory

While its efficacy and effects are often debated, hashtag activism continues to be a tactic within civil society groups, social movements, and activists (Jackson, Bailey, & Welles, 2020; Ofori-Parku & Moscato, 2018; Dadas, 2017). As a means for promoting change, hashtags have been a key feature of multiple insurgent movements from the Arab Spring in the early 2010s (Starbird & Palen, 2012; Donovan, 2018) to the Milk Tea Alliance that brought together pro-democracy supporters in Southeast Asia in 2020 (Strangio, 2021), to the US online-born QAnon network (Partin & Marwick, 2020). In some instances, hashtags are converted into real-life action, such as #StopTheSteal, which was used to rally pro-Trump supporters after his loss in the 2020 presidential election and was instrumental in the January 6 Capitol Hill siege (Donovan, 2021). Kate Starbird referred to the riots as "hashtags come to life" (Nguyen & Scott, 2021). Their use as a means of civic action and mobilization as well as narrative framing, identity formation, and even harassment means that they have become targets of information operations as well as information operations themselves (Friedberg & Donovan, 2019). Hashtags have been routinely hijacked, artificially amplified, and reported on as newsworthy events (Donovan & boyd, 2021). Emerging research also suggests readers react differently to news posts that include certain hashtags, eliciting anger, fear, and disgust (Rho & Mazmanian, 2020).

This is in part because information ecosystems are often self-referential and ideas, narratives, and amplification are co-constituted between its various parts both human and non-human (i.e., social media, mainstream media, independent media, and its various users, readers, and participants) (Benkler et al., 2018; Turner, 2005). In other words, what happens on social media can affect broadcast and mainstream press and vice versa. The path from online to offline and back again is not always linear. Donovan and Friedberg, for example, have illustrated how online reactionary groups have found ways to "hack" media attention by using certain online tactics for the purpose of gaining mainstream broadcast coverage (Friedberg & Donovan, 2019). Case studies, time and time again, also describe how campaign operators have used online media with the explicit goal of gaining further media coverage. For example, an Iranian influence operation that spanned multiple years created personas on Twitter posing as journalists while targeting real journalists in their tweets and direct messages in hopes of seeding false information (Lim et al., 2019). Even more innocuous forms of media manipulation, such as the use of "zoombombing" by teens and pranksters at the onset of the COVID-19 pandemic, mainstream press coverage was considered a "trophy" (Friedberg, Lim, & Donovan, 2020). More relevant to the subject of study in this chapter, right-wing groups and individuals have also organized to push fringe ideas from online spaces into mainstream press, as seen by the #AOCLied and #AlexandriaOcasioSmollett case, which we will detail later. Another example includes the "It's Okay to Be White" campaign that began on 4chan and eventually moved into real-world spaces, Tucker Carlson's nightly show, and even the Australian parliament where a motion against "anti-white racism" was debated (Donovan & Friedberg, 2020).

That social media have become salient vectors for attempts at agenda setting is not surprising as such online platforms are used by journalists and politicians not just for expression but as a means to break news, find scoops (Armstrong & Gao, 2010), and assess public opinion – however flawed this approach may be (McGregor, 2019). Shannon McGregor and Logan Molyneux's research, for example, has found that among journalists with fewer years of experience and who incorporate Twitter into their reporting tweets were considered as newsworthy as headlines appearing to be from the AP wire (McGregor & Molyneux, 2020). Twitter's influence on newsrooms has been a long time coming. A study by John Parmelee that involved in-depth interviews with political journalists in the United States during the 2012 presidential election found that Twitter was considered not only more consequential for their job than any other platform, but that it had caused significant changes to their daily reporting practices (Parmelee, 2013). Moreover, newsrooms often require their journalists to be on Twitter, resulting in almost 25% of Twitter's verified users being journalists or news organizations (the largest group) according to a 2015 report (Kamps, 2019). Twitter, likely in recognition of their ability to affect news consumption as well as news creation, has taken a more editorial approach to how it treats trending items, adding additional contextual descriptions and links to credible mainstream reporting for certain trending hashtags and topics (Perez, 2020). However, this move has been criticized as mere incremental tweaks that do not do enough to prevent the spread of misinformation or other potentially harmful information, leading some to call on Twitter to simply remove the trending feature completely as it is a vulnerable target for information operations (Ingram, 2020).

Due to this two-way relationship between social media and traditional media, we then predict that the influencers within our dataset will be able to garner media coverage outside of Twitter should they achieve trending status for their hashtags. We also predict that even if a hashtag does not achieve trending status, if it is related to an issue pertinent to certain media outlets whether due to ideological alignment or an existing relationship, they may still be able to achieve some media coverage outside of Twitter as journalists and reporters may still deem them newsworthy.

However, not all hashtags are created equal and nor do they always convert into offline change or even shifts in overall public discourse outside of Twitter.

Depending on the user's motivations, hashtags may be used to signal in-group identity, a joke, a label to aid in search results or to state the issue or topic being discussed, to engage in targeted harassment, or in some cases to rally support around a cause and make demands. These differences in motives and political environment ultimately affect user or community adoption, their reach, and ultimately their impact on the larger information ecosystem and the offline world. In India, for example, Palavi Guha argues that although hashtag activism is rampant on Indian twitter, they fail to translate into any meaningful shifts in public discourse or policy because of their failure to break into mainstream media, rendering them isolated to the platforms they originated from (Guha, 2015). One such way to do this is by making a hashtag trend. However, the mere task of attempting to make a hashtag trend is not an easy endeavor. Among multiple factors that affect whether a hashtag makes it to Twitter's coveted trending topics list are the volume and frequency of tweets using the hashtag, the participants' networks and their resulting amplification power, potential editorial oversight from within Twitter that may remove or de-index certain keywords and hashtags, as well as changes in their trending algorithm, which are unknown to users outside the company.

In light of this, we predict that while some of our influencers will be using hashtags with the intent to achieve trending status, this will be a limited number. Where hashtags are used for purposes other than a coordinated campaign, it will not achieve trending status and at best limited press coverage.

This chapter therefore tries to illustrate not only how hashtags can be used by right-wing influencers but also how they are able to gain media coverage outside of their original platform. However, these gains are often short-lived, limited in scope and reach, and may be more effective as tools of self-promotion than swaying public opinion. That being said, influence operations do not often occur as a single isolated event but are more akin to tactics of subversion, where sustained efforts occur over longer time frames (Maschmeyer, 2021). Moreover, audiences play a special role in amplifying hashtags, where coordinated behavior is a political act. While posting to Twitter is much easier to do than attending a protest, crowds move algorithms and attention in similar ways.

#AOCLied: Anatomy of a Right-Wing Hashtag Campaign

Following Donald Trump's electoral defeat of November 2020, widespread allegations of electoral fraud were advanced by right-wing social media accounts and news outlets.[1] Tensions ultimately culminated in violence on January 6, 2021, when pro-Trump rioters stormed Capitol Hill to disrupt a congressional session convened to ratify Biden's victory. In the aftermath of the riots, which left five people dead, 140 injured, and incurred millions of dollars of damage, a consensus rapidly emerged that the insurrection had incubated on social media (Frenkel, 2021; Smith, 2021; Donovan, 2021). Parler, a fringe but nascent platform that had become a cauldron of far-right disinformation, was summarily shut down by its cloud host, Amazon Web Services (Nicas & Alba, 2021). But perhaps the most significant move was made by Twitter, which took the unprecedented step of suspending Trump's account, along with a dozen other influential right-wing accounts, and purging tens of thousands accounts believed to belong to the QAnon conspiracy network (Conger, 2021). This is the largest known takedown of social media accounts in the platform's history.

In the wake of this, it would be fair to wonder whether right-wing social media influence had been substantially blunted. Events that transpired just a few weeks later, however, indicated to the contrary that the right's capacity to make hashtags trend and draw media attention (whether favorable or critical) was by no means eliminated. Among the congresspeople traumatized by the events of January 6, Representative Alexandria Ocasio-Cortez (henceforth AOC) took to Instagram on February 1 to describe her experience, revealing also that she had previously been the victim of sexual assault. As described earlier in this chapter, her revelations were met with sympathy and support on the left and center-left but with derision and disbelief on the right. Just a day later, at least two hashtags – #AOCLied and #AlexandriaOcasioSmollett – began to trend on Twitter, challenging the veracity of her post on Instagram, a platform owned by Facebook (see Figure 7.1).

We used Twitter's free-tier REST API to download a sample of tweets for each hashtag. In all, we ingested 192k tweets for #AlexandriaOcasioSmollett and 85k tweets for #AOCLied during the period February 3–11. We list some summary statistics about each of the two hashtags in Table 7.1.

Evident from Table 7.1, #AOCLied was a much smaller hashtag, with less than half the tweet volume of #AlexandriaOcasioSmollett and only about 60% as many participants (users). That said, influence within #AOCLied was relatively less skewed – only 62.73% of the #AOCLied tweets were retweets compared to 84.43% for #AlexandriaOcasioSmollett. While some users issued only retweets of others, other users posted original tweets and subsequently garnered (or failed to obtain) retweets. Sorting these "tweeters" from most retweeted to least, we can calculate how many collectively garnered 80% of all retweets, which gives a sense of the skew of influence. This turned out to be profound for both hashtags – just 57 tweeters on #AlexandriaOcasioSmollett (0.3%) garnered 80% of retweets and similarly, just 108 tweeters on #AOCLied (0.5%).

Who were these influencers? For #AlexandriaOcasioSmollett, we see that right-wing influencers @RealCandaceO, a right-wing pundit who occasionally appears on Fox News and hosts a YouTube show and podcast, single-handedly garnered 23.6% of all retweets, while @fleccas, a right-wing livestreamer, and @AndrewPollackFL, a right-wing activist whose daughter tragically died in the Parkland shooting, followed with 8.9% and 3.7%, respectively. For #AOCLied, we find that @SebGorka and @JackPoso-biec (both right-wing influencers we track later) topped the list, garnering 14.57% and 9.8% of retweets, respectively. The third most influential account,

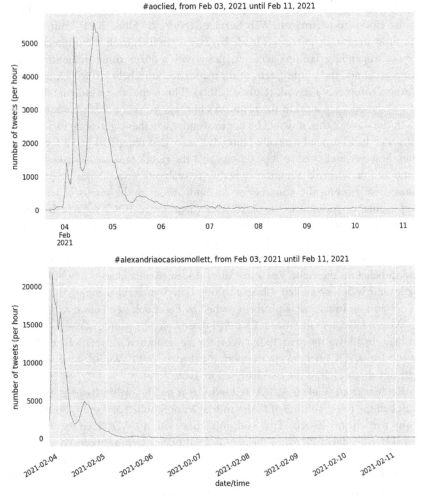

FIGURE 7.1 Time series plots of #AOCLied (top) and #AlexandriaOcasioSmollett (bottom) based on Twitter REST API captured during the first and second weeks of February 2021. According to GetDayTrends[.]com, these hashtags last trended on February 4, 2021.

however, was @DarakshanRaja (5% of retweets), whose Twitter bio suggests they are decidedly left-of-center.[2] Indeed, by plotting the retweet networks for both hashtags (Figure 7.2), it becomes clear that #AOCLied was contested by voices from the left and center-left.

Compared to the retweet network for #AlexandriaOcasioSmollett (left), we can see clear evidence of polarization on #AOCLied (right), with many accounts toward the bottom of the network (notably @DarakshanRaja, a Muslim activist) retweeting each other, but neither retweeting nor being retweeted by the clusters of accounts toward the top (led by @SebGorka). Cross-referencing all accounts in

TABLE 7.1   Summary statistics for #AOCLied and #AlexandriaOcasioSmollett

	#aoclied	#alexandriaocasiosmollett
Date range	Feb 3 - 11, 2021	Feb 3 - 11, 2021
Tweets	85,347	192,368
Users	55,360	90,847
% Retweets	62.73%	84.43%
% Tweeters obtaining 80% of retweets	0.50%	0.30%
% Anomalously born accounts	4.30%	3.90%

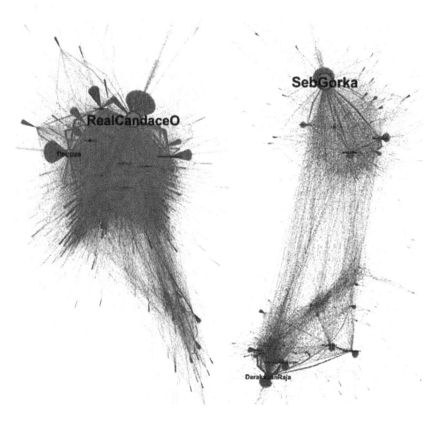

FIGURE 7.2   Twitter retweet networks for #AlexandriaOcasioSmollett (left) and #AOCLied (right). Each node is a Twitter account, each line connecting nodes is a retweet, and nodes appear larger if they garnered more retweets. Using the Force-Atlas-2 visualization algorithm, nodes tend to appear closer together if they retweeted each other.

both retweet networks with the VoterFraud2020 dataset,[3] a clear pattern emerges. While @SebGorka and other accounts toward the top of the #AOCLied retweet network had participated in hashtags amplifying allegations of electoral fraud during the October–December 2020 period, @DarakshanRaja and other accounts toward the bottom of the #AOCLied retweet network had not. As for #AlexandriaOcasioSmollett, no such polarization emerges – the hashtag is completely dominated by veterans of the electoral fraud hashtag campaigns. These patterns suggest that veterans of the 2020 electoral fraud campaign who survived the Twitter purge in early January subsequently drove both anti-AOC hashtags in early February, drawing contestation from left and center-left voices on #AOCLied but not on #AlexandriaOcasioSmollett.

The Twitter discourse on AOC quickly transcended into news coverage from across the political spectrum. Both hashtags were cited on the right, center, and left, with the *New York Post*, *Fox News*, *Newsweek*, *USA Today*, and the *Daily Kos*, all posting articles (Qamar, 2021; Jacobs, 2021; Morris, 2021; Henney, 2021; Santucci, 2021). Predictably, leftist outlets like the *Daily Kos* characterized the hashtags as an effort to "smear" AOC while also referencing those who came to her defense, such as @DarakshanRaja. On the right, the *New York Post* adopted a belittling tone to contest AOC's version, while *Fox News* drew attention to skepticism without overtly espousing it, as did *USA Today*. *Newsweek* reported directly on the Twitter conversation itself, noting that Korean pop fans "hijacked" the hashtag. In short, the anti-AOC hashtags were clearly able to achieve news coverage, whether favorable or otherwise. In some ways, this further illustrates that news outlets have come to rely on Twitter trends to gauge what audiences are interested in talking about. If the news outlet can publish quickly, they may even get a boost from the attention on social media.

Data and Methodology

Based on this background, we formulate the following research questions on the use of hashtags by right-wing influencers and their ability to achieve media coverage, thereby successfully engaging in driving the media agenda.

Research Questions

1. **Causal Question**: Are right-wing Twitter influencers effective at "agenda seeding?," that is, when coining or amplifying hashtags on Twitter, how often do they ultimately achieve coverage by media outside of Twitter?
2. **Channel/Mechanism Question**: How do these hashtags reach the attention of fringe and mainstream media? In particular, do they first "trend" or are they directly picked up by news media?

To approach our research questions, we had to collect data from Twitter and news media sources. First, to test the agenda-seeding power of right-wing Twitter influencers, we had to:

- Identify right-wing Twitter influencers, and mainstream news media outlets;

- Track all influencer tweets and news media articles;
- Identify hashtags mentioned in the tweets and filter down to those that were coined or deliberately amplified by the influencers. Coined hashtags are original hashtags whereas amplified hashtags were first coined by others but are repeatedly used in a way that suggests intentional amplification for the purposes of making them trend. We chose to include amplified hashtags because, although they may not have been initially created by the influencers themselves, they may be taken on as part of a campaign afterwards. For the purposes of this chapter we focused on hashtags that were used more than 14 times in one week. From there we identified the ones that were part of a deliberate campaign to get the hashtag trending; and
- Check if these hashtags appear in the news media shortly after their mention on Twitter.

Second, to test the channels by which agenda seeding occurs, we had to:

- Identify which hashtags trended (and *when*);
- For each hashtag, compare right-wing media coverage to mainstream (center/center-left) coverage.

Figure 7.3 helps visualize potential channels for agenda seeding. In this conception of agenda seeding, hashtags are coined or amplified by right-wing influencers. Right-wing news media outlets, or even mainstream outlets, may perhaps keep tabs on these influencers and write news articles to amplify or detract from what they are saying. For example, during the Trump presidency it was common for news outlets across the political spectrum to make direct references to Trump's tweets. While Trump's Twitter account was suspended in early January 2021, news media may continue to react to tweets by other right-wing influencers. We depict this scenario with direct lines from right-wing influencers to the news.

On the other hand, if journalists are not directly following and reacting to influencers' tweets, they may yet be keeping an eye on Twitter's shortlist of "trending" topics. In this case, right-wing influencers can still seed their agenda to the news media but must succeed in making their topics "trend," essentially gathering enough engagement over a sufficiently short period of time to break into Twitter's shortlist. We depict this indirect route in Figure 7.3 by an arrow from right-wing influencers to Twitter's trending list and a second arrow from the trending list to news media.

To identify news outlets and track their articles, we relied on MediaCloud. MediaCloud is a publicly accessible, open-source platform for tracking news published online around the world (*MediaCloud*, n.d.). The platform can be queried either in the web browser or, as we do here, programmatically via its application programming interface (API). Each query allows us to see if articles were published during a specific date range by a specific collection of news websites,

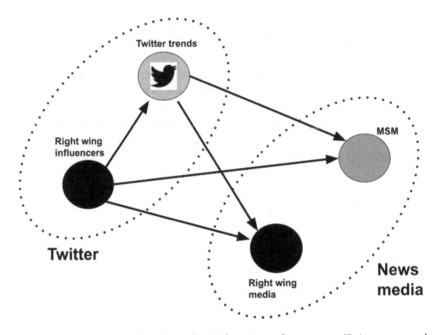

FIGURE 7.3 Agenda seeding channels. Right-wing influencers on Twitter may seed topics to media coverage by several channels, depicted by arrows. They may be directly reported on by right-wing news, directly reported on by mainstream news, or may first need to make the topics "trend" on Twitter, whereafter they rise to journalists' attention and are picked up across the political spectrum.

mentioning or failing to mention one or several keywords. Among the various curated collections available on MediaCloud are five that correspond to each of five buckets along the American political spectrum, namely left, center-left, center, center-right, and right. News websites were assigned to these five categories based on a 2018 study which tracked URL-sharing behavior among a set of American Twitter users whose political alignment was known.[4] News sites' political alignments were subsequently inferred based on the composition of Twitter users who shared them. While far from perfect, these five collections offer the best off-the-shelf solution for seeing at a glance whether a particular Twitter hashtag achieved news coverage across the political spectrum or was only advanced by partisan outlets.

To identify right-wing Twitter influencers, we relied on a list of 19 influencers curated by a data ethnographer of the American right and cross-referenced with the dataset created by Cornell Tech. This list includes notable political influencers on the right, such as Sebastian Gorka, Jack Posobiec, and James O'Keefe, who managed to keep their social media presence after the post-January 6, 2021 removals.[5] Gorka served as a deputy assistant to President Donald Trump. Posobiec continues to retain an active Twitter account despite being heavily involved in spreading the #Pizzagate conspiracy, a precursor to QAnon, and was the first person to tweet about #StopTheSteal on September 7, 2020 (DFR Lab, 2021). O'Keefe runs Project Veritas, a right-wing activist group that conducts "sting" operations against tech companies, left-wing organizations, and tech companies. O'Keefe has since been suspended by Twitter, while Gorka has lost only his YouTube channel (Donovan & Knell, 2021).

While 19 may seem like a small sample size, it is reflective of the extraordinarily skewed landscape of influence on Twitter (and social media generally), in which millions tweet but just tens or at most hundreds receive the lion's share of upvoting (likes, retweets). For comparative perspective, analyzing the VoterFraud2020 dataset of Twitter hashtags related to claims of electoral fraud during the October–December 2020 period, we find that of the 2.6 million unique Twitter accounts that participated in one or more of these hashtags, the top 158 participants (0.006%) garnered 50% of all retweets.[6] Among these top 158, Donald Trump's account was the most retweeted, single-handedly garnering 5.7% of retweets. By comparison, the 158th most influential account garnered just 0.08% of retweets – two orders of magnitude less influential than Trump. Indeed, even the 16th most influential account (@JackPosobiec, whom we tracked for this study) received ten times fewer retweets than Trump. In short, influence is extremely skewed on Twitter, and so even just 19 influencers may plausibly constitute the agenda-setting vanguard of the American right wing.

We proceeded to track these 19 influencers for two months (nine weeks), from March 15, 2021, to May 17, 2021. We used Twitter's free-tier API to check every hour for new tweets posted by any of the 19 influencers and download these new tweets to our local SQL database. This process yielded a total of 24,776 unique tweets. Of these tweets, we found 1,172 (just 4.73%) mentioned hashtags (291 unique hashtags in total).

To check if any of these hashtags reached Twitter's trending list for the United States, we queried the website GetDayTrends (n.d.). For any hashtag that has ever trended, GetDayTrends records the most recent date and time (down to the hour) and country, allowing us to check if any of the hashtags mentioned by right-wing influencers trended in the United States during our study period.

Findings

Do hashtags coined or amplified by right-wing influencers on Twitter achieve coverage by mainstream media? We broke up our dataset into nine weeks (March 15–May 17, 2020). Per week, we extracted all hashtags mentioned by right-wing influencers and identified the date/time stamp of the earliest tweet. We then ran each hashtag against MediaCloud's API to obtain the count of news media articles published the week *before* the earliest tweet and the week *after* the earliest tweet for each of the five American media collections corresponding to the political spectrum (left, center-left, center, center-right, right).

From among the total of 291 hashtags mentioned by right-wing influencers, we found that just 25 were coined while nine others were amplified. Moreover, of all the hashtags coined or amplified, it appears that only three may have been part of a deliberate hashtag campaign with the goal of achieving trending status. These three hashtags – #exposeCNN, #bodiesunderbridges, and #bidenbordercrisis – were all amplified or coined by James O'Keefe, who explicitly tweeted to his followers to share and retweet them to make them trend (e.g., "force it to trend"). Of these, only one (#exposeCNN) was successful in this regard. Note that #bidenbordercrisis, however, while amplified by O'Keefe who did encourage his followers to make it trend, was already in use; therefore, it is not entirely clear whether his participation helped drive the media coverage that ensued or if it was due to other Twitter accounts and politicians using the term.

Table 7.2 lists these hashtags by the week they were coined/amplified, along with some information about them.

TABLE 7.2 Breakdown of hashtags coined and amplified by the influencers

HASHTAG AND TRENDING ANALYSIS			
Week/Dates (all 2021)	**Hashtags coined* (by user)** bolded = trended	**hashtags amplified** by influencers** bolded = trended	**Notes**
Week 1 March 15 - March 22	#expellagentswallwell (sebgorka) #justalyinghack (sebgorka)	#antifa (28 times, mrandyngo)	#kingzuck comes in at 9 times by James O'Keefe.
Week 2 March 22 - March 29	#crowderbidensream (scrowder) #crowderbidenstream (scrowder) #crowderdebatestream (scrowder) #muhammadanwarmattered (sebgorka) #savemeeks (jackposobiec) #sayluciasname (sebgorka) #veritasarmy (jamesokeefeiii)	#bidenbordercrisis (27 times, jamesokeefeiii) #antifa (39 times, mrandyngo) #bristol (14 times, mrandyngo)	#antifanots at 12 times by Andy Ngo. James O'Keefe tried to get bidenbordercrisis trending but was not successful.
Week 3 March 29 - April 5	#bodiesunderbridges (jamesokeefeiii) #nbapayequitynow (ilmcast) #veritasarmy (jamesokeefeiii) #bodiesunderbriges (jamesokeefeiii) #bodiesunderbrides (jamesokeefeiii) #blinkenfailedalready (sebgorka) #tervurensrock (sebgorka) #bitchslappedbybeijing (sebgorka)	#antifa (34 times, mrandyngo)	James O'Keefe attempted to get #bodiesunderbridges trending. Did not succeed, but made a claim that it did.
Week 4 April 5 - April 12	#haydenthehack (sebgorka) #hutchinsonthecoward (sebgorka) #jenlikescommies (sebgorka) #justanotherdemhack (sebgorka) #iwc (scrowder) #thegorkarealitycheck (sebgorka)	#antifa (32 times, mrandyngo)	#hatehoax also used 8 times by Andy Ngo.
Week 5 April 12 - April 19	#iwc (stevencrowder) #tervurensrock (sebgorka) #veritasarmy (jamesokeefeiii)	#antifa (96 times, mrandyngo) #blm (63 times, mrandyngo) **#exposeCNN (42 times, JamesOKeefeIII)** #dauntewright (29 times, mrandyngo) #portlandriots (22 times, mrandyngo)	#exposeCNN did make trending status. However on April 15, James O'Keefe's twitter account was suspended.
Week 6 April 19 - April 26	#iwc (scrowder)	#antifa (66 times, mrandyngo) #blm (36 times, mrandyngo) #portlandriots (15 times, mrandyngo)	
Week 7 April 26 - May 3	#crowderbidenstream (scrowder)	#antifa (72 times, mrandyngo)	
Week 8 May 3 - May 10		#antifa (19 times, mrandyngo)	
Week 9 May 10 - May 17	#breaunawhite #hesdonethereading #kinzingerthekoward	#antifa (30 times, mrandyngo) **#rhod (15 times, ConceptualJames)**	#promocodeposo (possibly coined by Posobiec, though evidence others were using it earlier than him. Did not trend)

Note: Only one explicit hashtag campaign managed to hit trending status (#exposeCNN). #rhod (real housewives of Dallas) was already trending when @ConceptualJames started using it.

*coined – defined as using a hashtag that previously was not used on Twitter (i.e., an original hashtag). (Limitations: cannot check against tweets that may have been deleted/suspended.)

**amplified – defined as aggressively promoting in their tweets, not just once or twice, e.g., Andy Ngo and #antifamugshots. For the sake of analysis, we identified hashtags used over 14 times in one week. We then dug further into these hashtags to see if they were part of a deliberate campaign to make them trend.

Multiple Use Cases of Hashtags

The relatively few campaigns identified in our data collection is as expected, as not all the hashtags used were designed to be part of a deliberate campaign to game the trending algorithm. For example, @mrandyngo repeatedly tweeted about #antifa (28 times during the week of March 15–22, 39 times during March 22–29, and so on), but it is evident from the content of his tweets that he intended to disparage and detract, not to amplify, this hashtag. Others, especially Sebastian Gorka, used hashtags primarily as epithets or jokes at the expense of political or ideological opponents (e.g., #justanotherdemhack). With O'Keefe, #veritasarmy was often used as a means of in-group signaling, community building, and branding while Steven Crowder used hashtags like #crowderbidenstream as an informational label as well as a promotional tool.

To What Degree Were These 34 Hashtags Covered by the News Media?

Of the 34 hashtags that were either amplified or coined by the influencers we tracked, few received media attention, and when they did it was particularly skewed by the type of outlets that provided coverage. Table 7.3 breaks down the type of coverage across the political spectrum of media outlets. Removing hashtags that were used as informational labels or for search purposes (e.g., #BLM), only three hashtags received media coverage that could be directly attributed to the intentions and activity of the influencer in question.

Interestingly, these three were all used as part of a deliberate campaign to try and achieve trending status. In terms of agenda seeding, this could be considered a relative success. Even the ones that did not achieve trending status received some media attention. Coverage, however, was minimal and heavily skewed toward right and center-right media outlets. For example, although #exposeCNN garnered 77 stories by right-leaning media outlets, it made up only 0.08% of total stories published that week. Moreover, coverage fell off sharply after it initially

TABLE 7.3 Number of media stories mentioning each hashtag and their overall share of total stories that week

MEDIA COVERAGE OF HASHTAGS AFTER EARLIEST TWEET (story count, %)							
Hashtag	Week	Right	Center right	Center	Center left	Left	Total Stories (count only)
#bodiesunderbridges	3	7, 0.01%	1, 0%	0, 0%	0, 0%	1, 0%	9
#bidenbordercrisis	2	61, 0.05%	3, 0%	37, 0.01%	8, 0%	7, 0.01%	116
#exposeCNN	5	77, 0.08%	6, 0%	3, 0%	2, 0%	1, 0%	89

Note: Hashtags that received zero media mentions are not included in this chart, along with hashtags that were used for general information or labeling purposes, like #antifa, #bristol, #blm, #dauntewright, #lwc, #portlandriots, #rhod, or #veritasarmy.

Source: Media Cloud.

trended and as aforementioned may have backfired as it led to O'Keefe being permanently banned from Twitter.

Media Coverage can be Achieved Even Without Trending Status

While trending terms may garner relatively more media attention, this was not always the case for issues or individuals that remain pertinent to certain communities. As depicted in Table 7.3, the two other hashtag campaigns (#bidenborder-crisis and #bodiesunderbridges) did not trend and yet they achieved some media coverage. Even broader hashtags like #antifa, for example, garnered significant media mentions within the right-wing media collection at a significant 4,027 stories compared to just 600–700 stories for all other media collections. One of the influencers we were tracking, @mrandyngo, who used the hashtag extensively, was quoted frequently in the media alongside the hashtag, often embedding his tweets within the article and in some cases referring to him as an "Antifa expert" (Urbanski, 2021). During our data collection period, he was mentioned in some 147 stories about Antifa by right-wing media.[7]

Media Coverage is Heavily Skewed Across the Political Spectrum

Although several of the hashtags we tracked, whether as part of an explicit campaign like #exposeCNN or as an informational label like #antifa, did receive coverage in the media the asymmetry in stories written about them was especially pronounced. As noted during the 2016 US presidential election by Benkler, Faris, and Roberts in their book *Network Propaganda*, the information ecosystem is incredibly polarized with vastly different narratives and topics of interests between the left and right media spheres (Benkler et al., 2018). This held true again with the hashtags in our dataset. Media coverage, expectedly, skewed toward the right with the right-leaning collections providing the bulk of the stories. #exposeCNN, for example, received 83 stories from right and center-right outlets and just six from center, center-left, and left media outlets, which tended to be more critical of the campaign, reporting more on his suspension than the so-called expose.

#ExposeCNN – the Only Hashtag to Achieve Trending Status

Of the hashtags that were either coined or amplified by one of our influencers in the dataset, only one trended because of the planning, coordination, and encouragement of the individual.[8] This was #exposeCNN, which was part of a Project Veritas campaign spearheaded by its founder, James O'Keefe (@jameso-keefeiii). Project Veritas is a right-wing group that aims to reveal alleged liberal biases in the media and among public officials through the use of deceptive video editing and secret recordings (Goss, 2018). The hashtag itself had been used multiple times prior to our collection period and was part of a 2017 Project Veritas campaign as well. In the April 2021 operation, however, it was used as part of an operation to "expose" CNN as working to elect Biden over Trump (Project Veritas, 2021). This campaign primarily relied on video footage taken by a freelance satellite truck operator contracted by CNN, who O'Keefe positioned as an "insider" within the network's DC office (Ellefson, 2019). Based on data obtained through BrandWatch and GetDayTrends.com, the hashtag was used 45 times by O'Keefe but garnered 77,000 tweets between April 12 and April 20. On April 13, it achieved trending status, as did #CNNexposed and the keywords "Project Veritas."

The campaign and hashtag were a success for O'Keefe, tweeting, "#exposecnn is currently the #7 trending topic in the usa/i need the #veritasarmy to tweet #exposecnn right now to keep it moving up to #1 / share, embed, retweet this video and tweet #exposecnn." Other tweets also called attention to the fact that the hashtag was trending and urged followers to tweet at CNN to demand answers. Like many of his previous campaigns, explicit calls to action were used and may partially explain why this, over all the other hashtags that were used, hit trending status. Unlike Gorka's tweets, which tended to be used more as epithets and jokes, this was part of a deliberate campaign designed to trigger a reaction from both his followers and mainstream media. Indeed, it received the most media coverage out of all the hashtags we tracked with a total of 89 stories that week that mentioned #exposeCNN. However, as with the other hashtags, coverage was asymmetric across the political spectrum. Of the 89 stories, 83 came from right (77) or center-right (6) outlets. As a percentage of total right-wing stories published that week this amounted to 0.08%, a considerably small percentage yet still larger than all the other hashtags that managed to receive some press coverage. Furthermore, coverage quickly fell off after its initial trending status, falling to just a handful of stories after a few days (see Figure 7.4). And when the hashtag was no longer on the trending list, O'Keefe alleged that Jack Dorsey may have something to do with it, tweeting, "is @jack running interference?" and "their only hope is that @jack helps them make this story go away."

However, media outlets were not the only group to take notice. So did Twitter, which permanently banned O'Keefe from using its service on April 15 for violating its "platform manipulation and spam policy" (Bowden, 2021). Although more detailed reasons were not publicized, a representative from the company said their actions came after O'Keefe violated rules prohibiting "operating fake accounts" and attempting to "artificially amplify or disrupt conversations through the use of multiple accounts." Supporters, on the other hand, accused Twitter of buckling under pressure from CNN or as retribution for O'Keefe's #exposeCNN campaign (Coldewey, 2021). In response, O'Keefe says he is suing Twitter for defamation at the time of writing (Walsh, 2021).

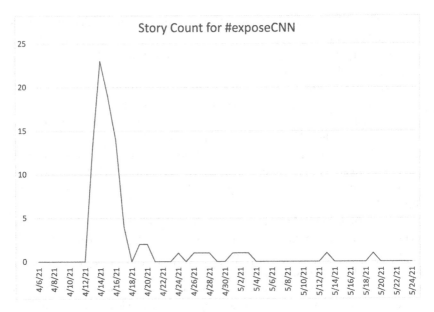

FIGURE 7.4 Number of stories published mentioning #exposeCNN among right-leaning outlets

Source: Media Cloud.

#ExposeCNN and campaigns that achieve trending status and media coverage therefore act as a double-edged sword. While they may be considered successful in terms of the attention they receive from within and beyond the platform, they also run the risk of calling attention to their attempts at gaming the system for which the platform may choose to take action.

Discussion

Our findings would seem to assuage fears of the presumptive efficacy of right-wing influencers to manipulate the agendas of news media. Right-wing influencers appear to undertake influence campaigns only a small portion of the time – just 11.7% of the hashtags they mentioned seemed to be part of a deliberate amplification effort. Moreover, 33 of 34 such efforts (97.1%) failed to trend and garnered negligible news coverage, even from right-wing outlets arguably predisposed to amplify such efforts. The single campaign (#exposecnn) that successfully breached Twitter's trending shortlist for the United States did generate greater news coverage (nearly 100 news articles) but also provoked Twitter to deplatform the primary influencer, O'Keefe, likely hobbling his ability to repeat this success. In short, the agenda seeding success of the anti-AOC hashtags in early February that prompted our investigation appear to have been the exception rather than the rule.

Why are our empirical findings so at odds with widespread fears of right-wing influence? First, it bears reflection that our study period followed in the wake of Twitter's January "purge" of right-wing influencers, chief among them Donald Trump. While not wishing to ascribe too much explanatory power to any single person, it is fair to say that Trump himself commanded a uniquely powerful influence over social and news media discourse during his presidency. Indeed, his use of Twitter to circumvent the usual institutional channels by which presidents reach their publics was unprecedented, and news media regularly engaged his tweets as talking points. Indeed, during the "Big Lie" campaign, Trump single-handedly garnered 5.7% of retweets, and when sharing news media URLs, he often dwarfed other right-wing influencers on all dimensions of upvoting. The suspension of this uniquely powerful influencer, not to mention the shifting spotlight following his departure from the Oval Office, may go some distance in explaining the right-wing's surprising inefficacy compared to agenda seeding on Twitter.

Relatedly, Twitter's decision to purge influential right-wing accounts, especially those trafficking in conspiracy theories, was met with applause and approval from centrists and left-of-center pundits and may have potentially normalized this course of action going forward. The swift suspension of O'Keefe's account in the wake of the #exposecnn campaign suggests that Twitter may be taking harsher measures to mitigate right-wing narrative entrepreneurship. However, no such punitive action was taken in response to #AOCLied and #AlexandriaOcasioS-mollett in early February, raising doubts as to what exact criteria are consulted for this decision process.

The disparity between our findings and expectations may further be explained by the many limitations of our study. What we have offered here is a novel but preliminary handling of this question. We tracked just 19 influencers over nine weeks. Moreover these nine weeks, from mid-March to mid-May 2021, may arguably have constituted a period of rebuilding for the right wing in the wake of its electoral losses. This period also overlapped with Biden's first "hundred days" in office, a period well known in American politics for favoring the incumbent. News coverage of right-wing topics, moreover, would have had to compete with positive coverage of Biden's vaccine rollout, which was handled expeditiously and accompanied by daily declining rates of COVID infections and casualties. For all these reasons, one might argue that we studied right-wing influence on Twitter at something of an operational nadir.

Among thousands of tweets captured, we focused on just those that mentioned hashtags. While hashtags are a crucial feature of Twitter that constitute points of coherence for narrative making, it remains plausible that other tweets may have raised topics that resonated with various "latent publics" and drawn news coverage independent of hashtag campaigning. To check this, we ran a few of the influencers' screen names against MediaCloud's news articles database for the March 15–May 17 period.

Figure 7.5 depicts the time series of screen name mentions for Jack Posobiec, Andy Ngo, and James O'Keefe, among US nationally scoped news outlets over

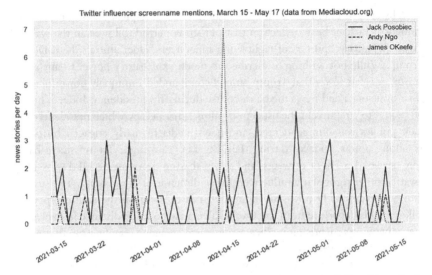

FIGURE 7.5   Daily mentions of right-wing Twitter influencers Jack Posobiec, Andy Ngo, and James O'Keefe during our study period

our study period. Mentions of O'Keefe's handle spiked immediately after his account's suspension, with several news outlets noting the suspension and his intention to sue Twitter (Wulfsohn, 2021; Robertson, 2021). Andy Ngo, on the other hand, is mentioned primarily by far-right outlets like *OAN* (*One America News Network*) or *American Free Press*, in connection with Antifa (a recurring talking point for him, as we discovered earlier) (AFP Staff, 2021). Compared to Ngo, Posobiec received greater and more consistent mentions throughout our study period but again primarily by far-right outlets like *OAN*. In short, these influencers are directly visible to news media and do not affect coverage only by way of hashtags. Moreover, they do not easily draw coverage from beyond their partisan bubble; the only exception to this was for O'Keefe and then only in connection with a trending hashtag (#exposecnn) and a controversial act of mitigation (account suspension).

Conclusion

In this chapter, we attempted to measure the efficacy with which right-wing social media influencers seed their agenda to the news media. We tracked 19 right-wing influencers on Twitter for nine weeks, intercepting over 20,000 tweets, of which over 1,000 mentioned a total of 291 unique hashtags. We found that 34 of these hashtags were either coined or deliberately amplified by these influencers, then cross-referenced each of the 34 with Twitter's trend lists and MediaCloud's news articles database for American news outlets across the political spectrum. We found that influencers succeeded in making just one of the 34 hashtags trend. The payoff of this was substantial – relative to the other 33 hashtags, the single trending hashtag (#exposecnn) garnered an order of magnitude more news articles and broke out of the right-wing media "sandbox" to draw engagement from the left and the center. This success came at considerable cost, however, as the account of the main influencer for this campaign was subsequently suspended by Twitter. Our findings therefore cast doubt on the presumptive efficiency and facility of right-wing influencers to manipulate news media agendas.

Many caveats apply to our findings, and they leave space for more expansive research in this area. We tracked only 19 influencers of potentially hundreds and only for nine weeks. Moreover these nine weeks may have fallen within a relative lull period, following closely on the heels of substantial mitigation efforts undertaken by Twitter to purge their platform of right-wing content deemed conspiratorial or misinformative. As the right wing regroups, we may observe bolder and more successful efforts to shape media discourse. Tracking a wider group of influencers for a more sustained period is a priority for future research. While we constrained our attention to hashtag campaigning, we found evidence that right-wing influencers also affect media coverage independently. Adopting a wider aperture so as not to filter out these alternative means of influence should be an ambition of further work in this area.

Notes

1. Cornell University researchers tracked Twitter hashtags alleging electoral fraud during the October–December 2020 period and shared the data publicly. See https://voterfraud2020.io.
2. They describe themselves as the "Co-Founder/Co-Director of @dcmuslimjustice" and an "[a]dvocate against Islamophobia, gender-based violence, and state [repression]."
3. The VoterFraud2020 dataset consists of a sample of all tweets posted between late October 2020 and mid-December 2020 mentioning any of over 40 hashtags related to electoral fraud allegations in connection with the American presidential elections of November 2020. The dataset was collected and generously shared by the Social Technologies Lab at Cornell University (https://voterfraud2020.io/). See Abilov, Yiqing, Matatov, Amir, and Naaman (2021) for a thorough description of the dataset and collection methodology.
4. See further details at Public Discourse in the U.S. 2020 Election: Resources & Data (Oct 20, 2020). Available at https://cyber.harvard.edu/research/2020-election-study-resources-data.
5. The 19 influencers we tracked were @cassandrarules, @jackposobiec, @cernovich, @willchamberlain, @faithgoldy, @jamesokeefeiii, @mattwalshblog, @millie__weaver, @kassydillon, @fleccas, @timcast, @markdice, @mrandyngo, @lukewearechange, @prisonplanet, @msblairewhite, @scrowder, @conceptualjames, and @sebgorka.
6. See https://voterfraud2020.io/. The skew of this dataset matches what we have seen elsewhere, both within and outside of the American context. Indeed, in our collective experience, it is not uncommon to observe roughly 1% of participants in a given thread garnering roughly 80% of upvoting.
7. Based on a MediaCloud search query for #antifa and "andy ngo" or "mrandyngo" between March 15 and May 24, 2021.

8 While O'Keefe claimed #bodiesunderbridges was trending, we did not find evidence that this was the case. #bidenbordercrisis, though amplified by O'Keefe, also did not hit trending status during this time. Furthermore, although #rhod was amplified by one of the influencers (@ConceptualJames), it was already trending at the time, making it more likely he latched onto an already existing trend. This behavior is similar for most of the other hashtags used by the influencers we tracked.

References

Abilov, A., Yiqing, H., Matatov, H., Amir, O., & Naaman, M. (n.d.). *VoterFraud2020 – A Twitter dataset of election fraud claims.* Retrieved on July 22, 2021, from https://metatags.io/

AFP Staff. (2021, March 30). Antifa violence continues to plague Oregon – American Free Press. *American Free Press.* Retrieved from https://americanfreepress.net/antifa-violence-continues-to-plague-oregon/

Armstrong, C. L., & Fangfang, Gao. (2010). Now tweet this: How news organizations use Twitter. *Electronic News,* 4(4), 218–235. https://doi.org/10.1177/1931243110389457

Benkler, Y., Faris, R., & Roberts, H. (2018). *Network propaganda: Manipulation, disinformation, and radicalization in American politics.* Oxford: Oxford University Press. https://doi.org/10.1093/oso/9780190923624.001.0001

Bowden, J. (2021, February 11). Twitter permanently suspends "Project Veritas" group. *The Hill.* Retrieved from https://thehill.com/policy/technology/538507-twitter-permanently-suspends-right-wing-project-veritas-group

Choi, M. (2021, February 1). 'I thought I was going to die': AOC personalizes insurrection, bringing up past sexual assault. *POLITICO.* Retrieved from www.politico.com/news/2021/02/01/aoc-insurrection-instagram-live-464837

Coldewey, D. (2021). Twitter bans James O'Keefe of Project Veritas over fake account policy. *TechCrunch.* Retrieved from https://social.techcrunch.com/2021/04/15/twitter-bans-james-okeefe-of-project-veritas-over-fake-account-policy/

Conger, K. (2021, January 12). Twitter, in widening crackdown, removes over 70,000 QAnon accounts. *The New York Times.* Retrieved from www.nytimes.com/2021/01/11/technology/twitter-removes-70000-qanon-accounts.html

Crawford, B. (2020, June 9). The influence of memes on far-right radicalisation – Centre for Analysis of the Radical Right. *Centre for Analysis of the Radical Right.* Retrieved from www.radicalrightanalysis.com/2020/06/09/the-influence-of-memes-on-far-right-radicalisation/

Dadas, C. (2017). Hashtag activism: The promise and risk of "attention." In D. M. Walls & S. Vie (Eds.), *Social writing/social media: Publics, presentations, and pedagogies* (pp. 17–36). Louisville, CO: The WAC Clearinghouse; University Press of Colorado. https://doi.org/10.37514/PER-B.2017.0063.2.01

Davey, J., & Ebner, J. (2017). The Fringe Insurgency – Connectivity, convergence and mainstreaming of the extreme right. *Institute for Strategic Dialogue.* Retrieved from www.isdglobal.org/isd-publications/the-fringe-insurgency-connectivity-convergence-and-mainstreaming-of-the-extreme-right/

DFR Lab. (2021, February 10). #StopTheSteal: Timeline of social media and extremist activities leading to 1/6 insurrection. *Just Security.* Retrieved from www.justsecurity.org/74622/stopthesteal-timeline-of-social-media-and-extremist-activities-leading-to-1-6-insurrection/

Donovan, J. (2018). After the #Keyword: Eliciting, sustaining, and coordinating participation across the occupy movement. *Social Media + Society, 4*(1), 2056305117750720. https://doi.org/10.1177/2056305117750720

Donovan, J. (2021, January 15). MAGA is an extreme aberration. *The Atlantic.* Retrieved from www.theatlantic.com/ideas/archive/2021/01/maga-isnt-a-normal-protest-movement/617685/

Donovan, J., & boyd, d. (2021). Stop the presses? Moving from strategic silence to strategic amplification in a networked media ecosystem. *American Behavioral Scientist, 65*(2), 333–350. https://doi.org/10.1177/0002764219878229

Donovan, J., & Friedberg, B. (2019, September 4). Source hacking: Media manipulation in practice. *Data & Society.* Data & Society Research Institute. Retrieved from https://datasociety.net/library/source-hacking-media-manipulation-in-practice/

Donovan, J., & Friedberg, B. (2020, August 11). Viral slogan: "It's ok to be white." *Media Manipulation Casebook.* Retrieved from https://mediamanipulation.org/case-studies/viral-slogan-its-ok-be-white

Donovan, J., & Knell, D. (2021, March 4). The deplatforming index: A research brief. *Media Manipulation Casebook.* Retrieved from https://mediamanipulation.org/research/deplatforming-index-research-brief

Ellefson, L. (2019, October 15). Network staffers unfazed by project Veritas' 'Expose CNN' campaign: No one 'really cares about this.' *The Wrap.* Retrieved from www.thewrap.com/network-staffers-unfazed-by-project-veritas-expose-cnn-campaign-no-one-really-cares-about-this/

Frenkel, S. (2021, January 6). The storming of Capitol Hill was organized on social media. *The New York Times.* Retrieved from www.nytimes.com/2021/01/06/us/politics/protesters-storm-capitol-hill-building.html

Friedberg, B., & Donovan, J. (2019). On the internet, nobody knows you're a bot: Pseudoanonymous influence operations and networked social movements. *Journal of Design and Science, 6.* https://doi.org/10.21428/7808da6b.45957184

Friedberg, B., Lim, G., & Donovan, J. (2020). Space invaders: The networked terrain of zoom bombing. *Technology and Social Change Research Project.* https://doi.org/10.37016/TASC-2020-02

GetDayTrends (n.d.) *Twitter Trends in United States.* Retrieved on August 3, 2021, from https://getdaytrends.com/united-states/

Goss, B. M. (2018). Veritable flak mill. *Journalism Studies, 19*(4), 548–563. https://doi.org/10.1080/1461670X.2017.1375388

Guha, P. (2015). Hash tagging but not trending: The success and failure of the news media to engage with online feminist activism in India. *Feminist Media Studies, 15*(1), 155–157. https://doi.org/10.1080/14680777.2015.987424

Henney, M. (2021, February 5). AOC addresses doubt about "terrifying" Capitol riot experience: "There was a reason I sat on my story." *Fox News.* Retrieved from www.foxnews.com/politics/alexandria-ocasio-cortez-doubt-capitol-riot-terrifying-experience

Ingram, D. (2020, September 1). Critics want Twitter to halt its trending lists: Instead, Twitter will make tweaks. *NBC News.* Retrieved from www.nbcnews.com/tech/tech-news/critics-want-twitter-halt-its-trending-lists-instead-twitter-will-n1238996

Jackson, S. J., Bailey, M., & Welles, B. F. (2020). *#HashtagActivism: Networks of race and gender justice.* Cambridge, MA: Massachusetts Institute of Technology Press.

Jacobs, E. (2021, February 4). AOC blasted for exaggerating her 'trauma' from Capitol riot experience. *New York Post.* Retrieved from https://nypost.com/2021/02/04/aoc-blasted-for-exaggerating-capitol-riot-experience/

Justice, T. (2021, March 4). #AlexandriaOcasioSmollett trends after it's revealed AOC wasn't even in Capitol during January riot. *The Federalist*. Retrieved from https://thefederalist.com/2021/02/03/alexandriaocasiosmollett-trends-after-its-revealed-aoc-wasnt-even-in-capitol-during-january-riot/

Kamps, H. J. (2019, October 13). Who are Twitter's verified users? *Medium*. Retrieved from https://haje.medium.com/who-are-twitter-s-verified-users-af976fc1b032

Krafft, P. M., & Donovan, J. (2020). Disinformation by design: The use of evidence collages and platform filtering in a media manipulation campaign. *Political Communication*, *37*(2), 194–214. https://doi.org/10.1080/10584609.2019.1686094

Lim, G., Maynier, E., Scott-Railton, J., Fittarelli, A., Moran, N., & Deibert, R. (2019, May 14). Burned after reading: Endless Mayfly's ephemeral disinformation campaign. *The Citizen Lab*. Retrieved from https://citizenlab.ca/2019/05/burned-after-reading-endless-mayflys-ephemeral-disinformation-campaign/

Maschmeyer, L. (2021). The subversive trilemma: Why cyber operations fall short of their promise. *International Security*, *46*(2), 51–90. https://doi.org/10.1162/isec_a_00418.

McGregor, S. C. (2019). Social media as public opinion: How journalists use social media to represent public opinion. *Journalism*, *20*(8), 1070–1086. https://doi.org/10.1177/1464884919845458

McGregor, S. C., & Molyneux, L. (2020). Twitter's influence on news judgment: An experiment among journalists. *Journalism*, *21*(5), 597–613. https://doi.org/10.1177/1464884918802975

Media Cloud. (n.d.). *Media Cloud*. Retrieved on 22 July 2021, from https://mediacloud.org

Morris, S. (2021, February 4). K-Pop fans hijack "AOCLied" hashtag in defense of Alexandria Ocasio-Cortez. *Newsweek*. Retrieved from www.newsweek.com/k-pop-fans-hijack-aoclied-hashtag-defense-alexandria-ocasio-cortez-1566730

Nguyen, T., & Scott, M. (2021, January 7). 'Hashtags come to life': How online extremists fueled Wednesday's Capitol Hill insurrection. *POLITICO*. Retrieved from www.politico.com/news/2021/01/07/right-wing-extremism-capitol-hill-insurrection-456184

Nicas, J., & Alba, D. (2021, January 11). How Parler, a chosen app of Trump fans, became a test of free speech. *The New York Times*. Retrieved from www.nytimes.com/2021/01/10/technology/parler-app-trump-free-speech.html

Ofori-Parku, S. S., & Moscato, D. (2018). Hashtag activism as a form of political action: A qualitative analysis of the #BringBackOurGirls Campaign in Nigerian, UK, and U.S. Press. *International Journal of Communication*, *12*, 23.

Parmelee, J. H. (2013). Political journalists and Twitter: Influences on norms and practices. *Journal of Media Practice*, *14*(4), 291–305. https://doi.org/10.1386/jmpr.14.4.291_1

Partin, W. C., & Marwick, A. E. (2020). The construction of alternative facts: Dark participation and knowledge production in the Qanon conspiracy. *AoIR Selected Papers of Internet Research*, *2020*, AoIR2020. https://doi.org/10.5210/spir.v2020i0.11302

Perez, S. (2020, September 8). Twitter begins adding headlines and descriptions to some of its 'trends.' *TechCrunch*. Retrieved from https://techcrunch.com/2020/09/08/twitter-begins-adding-headlines-and-descriptions-to-some-of-its-trends/

Project Veritas. (2021, April 13). *PART 1: CNN Director ADMITS network engaged in 'propaganda' to remove Trump from Presidency*. YouTube. Retrieved from www.youtube.com/watch?v=Dv8Zy-JwXr4

Qamar, A. (2021, February 5). Conservatives tried to smear AOC on Twitter, but users hijacked the hashtag with cuteness overload. *Daily Kos*. Retrieved from www.dailykos.com/stories/2014030

Rho, E. H. R., & Mazmanian, M. (2020). Political hashtags & the lost art of Democratic discourse. In *Proceedings of the 2020 CHI Conference on Human Factors in Computing Systems* (pp. 1–13). https://doi.org/10.1145/3313831.3376542

Robertson, K. (2021, April 15). Twitter bans the account of James O'Keefe, the founder of Project Veritas. *The New York Times*. Retrieved from www.nytimes.com/2021/04/15/business/twitter-james-okeefe.html

Santucci, J. (2021, February 5). Critics say Alexandria Ocasio-Cortez exaggerated her Capitol riot story: Here's what she said. *USA Today*. Retrieved from www.usatoday.com/story/news/politics/2021/02/05/alexandria-ocasio-cortez-capitol-riot-story-what-she-said/4411180001/

Smith, E. D. (2021, January 6). Column: It is not just Trump: Blame California social media companies for D.C. riot too. *Los Angeles Times*. Retrieved from www.latimes.com/california/story/2021-01-06/how-twitter-facebook-partly-culpable-trump-dc-riot-capitol

Stanton, Z. (2021, May 20). How the 'Culture War' could break Democracy. *POLITICO*. Retrieved from www.politico.com/news/magazine/2021/05/20/culture-war-politics-2021-democracy-analysis-489900

Starbird, K., & Palen, L. (2012). (How) will the revolution be retweeted? Information diffusion and the 2011 Egyptian uprising. *Proceedings of the ACM 2012 Conference on Computer Supported Cooperative Work (CSCW 2012)*, 7–16. https://doi.org/10.1145/2145204.2145212

Strangio, S. (2021, April 9). Twitter unveils bespoke emoji supporting Asia's 'Milk Tea Alliance.' *The Diplomat*. Retrieved from https://thediplomat.com/2021/04/twitter-unveils-bespoke-emoji-supporting-asias-milk-tea-alliance/

The Editors. (2021, February 2). *Alexandria Ocasio-Cortez gives brave Instagram Live about trauma*. Marie Claire [Magazine]. Retrieved from www.marieclaire.com/politics/a35388201/alexandria-ocasio-cortez-instagram-live-january-6/

Turner, F. (2005). Actor-networking the news. *Social Epistemology*, *19*(4), 321–324. https://doi.org/10.1080/02691720500145407

Urbanski, D. (2021, April 20). "In Defense of Looting" author tells Twitter followers to "ATTACK" police – Yet her account is still active. *TheBlaze*. Retrieved from www.theblaze.com/news/author-tells-twitter-followers-to-attack-police-account-still-active

Walsh, J. (2021, April 19). Project Veritas Founder James O'Keefe sues Twitter over ban. *Forbes*. Retrieved from www.forbes.com/sites/joewalsh/2021/04/19/project-veritas-founder-james-okeefe-sues-twitter-over-ban/?sh=683bce3b44b1

Wasow, O. (2020). Agenda seeding: How 1960s Black protests moved elites, public opinion and voting. *American Political Science Review*, *114*(3), 638–659. https://doi.org/10.1017/S000305542000009X

Wulfsohn, J. (2021, April 15). Twitter accused of protecting CNN after tech giant bans James O'Keefe: "They're all on the same team." *Fox News*. Retrieved from www.foxnews.com/media/twitter-bans-james-okeefe-accused-protecting-cnn

8

MIS/DISINFORMATION AND SOCIAL MEDIA

Melissa Zimdars

Introduction

"The Biden Family Scandal." These words have appeared across several online "news" organizations such as the Tennessee Star and the Minnesota Sun for months. Their purpose is to both spotlight and aggregate coverage of Hunter Biden's alleged foreign ties and unethical or illegal behavior. References to this scandal originated prior to the 2020 election on well-known right-leaning and far-right "news" websites, including Fox News and Breitbart, which relentlessly shared the story along with the Tennessee Star and the Minnesota Sun on social media to draw attention to the topic. These websites and their respective social media accounts did this despite the story being dismissed by most reputable news organizations for being just a smear campaign or fear-mongering political disinformation without news value (Ignatius, 2020). National Public Radio (NPR) even tweeted in October 2020 about why they were not going to "waste time" covering something that they considered to be "pure distraction." However, right-wing websites cried foul due to both the lack of news coverage and Facebook and Twitter limiting users' ability to share the story on their platforms (Dwoskin, 2020). To right-wing websites, this was further "proof," or so they told their readers and watchers, that news organizations and social media platforms were conspiring, biased toward the political left, and censorious of the political right (Lewis, 2020).

Despite the location-specific names of the Tennessee Star and the Minnesota Sun, these websites do not really function as sources of local or state news. These websites, which are part of the Star News Network or Star News Digital Media, are run by political activists with connections to the Tea Party and Breitbart. The Tennessee Star, which was the original website started in 2017,

DOI: 10.4324/9781003171270-8

publishes nearly identical content to its affiliate websites the Georgia Star, Minnesota Sun, Ohio Star, Michigan Star, and Virginia Star. These Star News websites are part of a trend of seemingly local websites popping up everywhere. Websites like Denver City Wire, and Central Colorado News, among many others, appear as local sources based on their location-based titles, but they are part of larger networks that publish identical stories regardless of their locations (Mahone & Napoli, 2020). The *Columbia Journalism Review* identified 12,000 "pink slime" websites or imposter websites that appear to be local news sources despite primarily publishing highly partisan national stories (Bengani, 2020). Of course, partisan content is not inherently a problem. The problem lies in these websites' lack of transparency in terms of their goals or mandates for circulating particular kinds of content. The problem lies also in the fact that these partisan websites regularly publish and circulate via social media misleading information for persuasive political purposes.

These websites function less as sources of local news and more as spreaders of mis/disinformation. Misinformation refers to unknowingly sharing misleading or false information, while disinformation refers to intentionally sharing information that is misleading or false, among other things, for the purposes of profit, political influence, or "to cause trouble for the sake of it" (Wardle, 2019, p. 8). Arguably, these websites circulate misinformation via both the people who engage with and share their stories and disinformation because they publish stories that regularly "frame an issue or individual" for the purposes of "partisanship, politics, and propaganda" (Wardle, 2020). Propaganda can be defined as a "deliberate attempt to persuade people to think and behave in a desired way" (Taylor, 2003, p. 6). Although propaganda can be truthful and factual, its main goal is to persuade or evoke specific responses and beliefs among people. The websites discussed in this chapter can also be viewed as propaganda or as a "vehicle of propaganda" because they regularly "withhold highly relevant news for political decision making" (Stanley, 2015, p. 55). Moreover, they regularly advance non-pertinent information irrelevant for political decision-making. Ultimately, these websites operate as mis/disinformation by combining truths and falsehoods, accuracies and distortions, for partisan and persuasive purposes.

We cannot truly understand mis/disinformation itself or how it operates without exploring the overlapping and constitutive contexts of journalism, technology, politics and government, or society and culture (Zimdars, 2020a). Understanding how social media works without considering contemporary problems in journalism, or vice versa, will get us only so far in addressing mis/disinformation. Thus, in this chapter, I look at imposter local news websites, specifically Star News websites, as mis/disinformation in relation to social media platforms and the current news context. More specifically, I show how imposter local news sources exploit a dearth of local news while using social media platforms to spread, amplify, and generate engagement with mis/disinformation.

Local News and Imposter Local News Websites

Lasswell (1971) argued that propaganda needs "favorable conditions" to be effective, and the same is true today of mis/disinformation. For websites that are part of Star News, two favorable conditions include a lack of local news around the country (Wahl-Jorgensen, 2019) and large numbers of people primarily engaging with news on social media rather than subscribing to specific sources ("Social Media Fact Sheet," 2019). Local news organizations have been closing at an alarming rate; over the last 20 years, over 1,800 local print outlets have closed ("Losing the News," 2019, p. 27). This means fewer journalists covering important issues, fewer journalists holding people in positions of power accountable, and fewer journalists contributing to a sense of connection among local community members. There are many reasons for this decline, but a major factor is that more than 70 percent of all online advertising revenue goes to Google and Facebook (Funke, 2017), with the number closer to 77 percent across local media markets (Hagey, Alpert, & Serkez, 2019).

Journalism is facing another crisis, too, which is an overall decline in public trust. Although levels of trust vary substantially based on different news organizations, most Americans trust news much less than they once did. However, there is a notable exception to this trend as overall trust for local news remains strong. In fact, over 70 percent of Americans have a "great deal" or a "fair amount" of trust in local TV news stations and newspapers (Guess, Nyhan, & Reifler, 2018, pp. 5–6). This is usually because local journalists are connected to and known in the very communities that they cover. And this local news trust tends to be high regardless of one's political ideologies or affiliations, unlike national news organizations, meaning that views on local news are less politically polarized than they are on the national level. Without sources of local news people tend to turn to social media for information which can increase their chances of being exposed to mis/disinformation (Ardia, Ringel, Smith Ekstrand, & Fox, 2020).

Imposter websites like the Tennessee Star and the Minnesota Sun superficially appear to fill the local news void while functioning more often to destabilize and undermine actual news, which could further erode public trust in journalism. Several of the Tennessee Star's stories criticize news organizations for allegedly "publishing falsehoods" (Agresti, 2021a) and "brazenly false fact-checking" (Agresti, 2021b) while inaccurately calling information added to developing news stories "retractions" (Catenacci, 2020a) and labeling other practices as "profoundly stupid" (Gockowski, 2020). Of course, journalists and news organizations are not and should not be immune to criticism. Too often, news stories are sloppy, inaccurate, and blur the lines between "real news" and "fake news" (Zimdars, 2016). But many of these issues are caused by staff reductions (from journalists to copyeditors), demands for more frequent story publishing (thanks to social media platform designs), and the need to publish stories quickly (to increase the likelihood of social media engagement and thus more digital advertising revenue).

This means that journalists these days have to do far more with far less – and they have to do it all more quickly. These less-than-ideal conditions for producing and distributing news are caused by a variety of interrelating factors, including increasingly concentrated media ownership, rising demands for profit, and monopoly over and supremacy of digital infrastructures (Pickard, 2020a).

Cloaking, Laundering, and Legitimizing Mis/Disinformation

It's important to understand more specifically how these imposter local news sources operate and how that operation is facilitated by social media. One way to think about imposter local news websites is as "cloaked websites." Daniels (2009) conceives of "cloaked sites" as a broad category that can include propaganda, astroturfing, or cyber-racism, which are "converging in new ways that make it increasingly difficult to parse facts from political spoofs and marketing ploys, and to distinguish legitimate civil rights websites from cloaked white supremacist sites" (p. 676). Daniels further argues that cloaked websites are especially problematic in a social and political context in which the lines between truths and falsehoods and news and mis/disinformation are heavily blurred. It's arguable that cloaked and imposter websites also *contribute* to destabilized notions of news and truth and to the notion that we live in a post-truth era with "scattered epistemologies and divided belief communities (Waisbord, 2018, p. 1874).

Here is just one example of how this works with Star News. The websites repeatedly ran stories about the "Big Lie," which claimed, frequently without evidence or official sources, that there was massive voter fraud in the 2020 election and that Donald Trump was the rightful winner (Blake, 2021). They parroted the same talking points as Trump's lawyers, Sydney Powell and Rudy Giuliani, and far-right news outlets like Newsmax and OANN (One America News Network). Like these other information sources, Star News websites did not advance a singular narrative articulating details of alleged voter fraud; rather, they circulated numerous narratives as they surfaced from various sources. Stories about dead voters (Catenacci, 2020b; Murdock, 2020a), lost or dumped ballots (Murdock, 2020b, 2020c), ballot harvesting (Heine, 2020a, 2020b), mail-in voter fraud (Lucas, 2020), faulty or rigged voting machine software (Heine, 2020c; Murdock, 2020d; Reynolds, 2020), people voting multiple times (Taylor, 2020), and other examples of a "massive, layered orchestration of voter fraud" (Murdock, 2020e) were heavily reported both in the months leading up to the November 2020 presidential election and in the months that followed. These stories and social media posts about the "Big Lie" are ultimately using a "throwing spaghetti at the wall to see what sticks" tactic. The overwhelming number of stories with different fraud angles involving different actors across different locations makes it incredibly difficult to parse fact from fiction. And it's designed to be that way. The goal of this content is not to create a coherent narrative or use facts to inform readers. The goal is to foster and reinforce the *feeling* among readers that fraud was rampant and unchecked and the *feeling* that mainstream news outlets and Democratic officials were ignoring the story for partisan gain. While these fraud stories tended to bubble up from various far-right sources to Star News websites, they all circulate on social media where they work collectively to engender or bolster already existing doubt about the legitimacy of the 2020 US presidential election, US democracy overall, and the news organizations that are "supposed" to be covering the story. Also, these narratives helped legitimize the 200 bills introduced across the United States after the 2020 election working to restrict access to voting (Wine, 2021).

Imposter or cloaked websites can be "difficult to distinguish from other forms of information found online because they frequently draw on legitimate sources of information to support their claims" (Daniels, 2009, pp. 676–677). Part of what makes Star News websites difficult to distinguish is their neutral and local sounding names like the Tennessee Star and the Minnesota Sun. The Minnesota Sun actually riffs off an old community newspaper called the MN Sun, or mnsun.com, which was shut down in 2009 by Sun Newspapers/American Community Newspapers (Brauer, 2009). It's the only Star News website to use "Sun" rather than "Star" as part of the name. As of February 15, 2021, the Tennessee Star describes itself by saying, "We feature articles reporting news, politics, and policy at the state level, primarily from Tennessee. We round out our daily coverage with national stories and thoughtful commentary of interest to our readers." On Facebook, the Tennessee Star is categorized as "Business," the Minnesota Sun is categorized as "Interest," and the Georgia Star is categorized as "News/Media company." The Tennessee Star's description on Facebook reads, "The Tennessee Star is your place for news and information that matters to Tennesseans! Investigative Reports, thoughtful Opinion, Sports, Lifestyle, & more." Of course, there is no mention of the website's political orientation or connections. Additionally, these websites mimic the appearance of news organizations because they are presented to us in the same way as mainstream news organizations on social media platforms like Facebook. Star News stories look the same as stories from *the Washington Post* or *the New York Times* as they all contain a headline, image, and story description. Actual news and imposter news entities alike "optimize" their "headline writing, image placement, and writing style for social media distribution" (Vaidhyanathan, 2018, p. 182). However, imposter websites and their corresponding social media pages and posts are more likely to use headlines, images, and writing styles that evoke strong emotional reactions (e.g., they're stealing the election!") by preying on readers' fears, anxieties, hopes, and desires. Recent emotionally charged headlines for the Tennessee Star include "Williamson County School System in Tennessee Won't Comment on Texas Cultural Competency Plan That Preaches All Whites Are Racist" (May 5, 2021) and "Police Refuse to Enter George Floyd Zone, Make Battered Woman Come to Them" (May 3, 2021).

Although Star News websites say in their "About Us" section that national coverage "round outs" their local coverage, national political stories comprise a vast majority of their published content. In fact, at the time of writing this chapter, the Minnesota Sun has not published a story in the "Local" category in four months, and there is a two-month gap between that story and the next most recent. Yet the front page of the Minnesota Sun is full of recent articles about Biden undermining "Middle East peace," Biden upsetting trade unions, and the prospect of impeaching Vice President Kamala Harris. All these stories also appear on Tennessee Star, Georgia Star, Virginia Star, Michigan Star, and Ohio Star websites despite their purported local news statuses. The Tennessee Star has a bit more in their local section, Georgia and Virginia have no local sections or tags, but a handful of local stories.

What these cloaked or imposter websites are doing is ultimately laundering information that's meant to persuade or reinforce political beliefs rather than inform citizens about their local communities. Klein (2012, pp. 431–432) argues that hate groups, specifically, enter into "mainstream culture by attaining legitimacy from the established media currencies of the cyber community, primarily search engines and interlinking social networks." Klein shows how racist, hate-based information travels and merges with "mainstream spaces like YouTube, Facebook, political blogs, and even occasionally news cycles" (2012, pp. 431–432). This means that p eople may be "unwittingly" engaging with racist or extremist content that has been laundered through multiple channels or across social media. Although websites that are part of the Star News group frequently publish articles full of racist dog whistles, such as a steady stream of articles lamenting "critical race theory" and diversity initiatives in education, the content they're laundering is instead in the form of highly partisan and regularly misleading information that is presented to readers as local news.

The right-wing media sphere is very interconnected, and websites tend to legitimize each other and circulate the same information across social media platforms. Websites like Breitbart, The Daily Caller, Washington Free Beacon, Campus Reform, Gateway Pundit, and many more are known entities for spreading unreliable junk. People may be less suspecting or skeptical when the Tennessee Star circulates stories originating from the Breitbart or the Daily Caller than they might be when confronted with information directly from the Breitbart or the Daily Caller. These well-known partisan websites cite what appears to be a neutral local source, presumably more in the "know" on a given topic because of their local-sounding status. This simultaneously gives stories from Breitbart or the Daily Caller more legitimacy as well as the websites being cited by Breitbart as they corroborate each other. For example, Breitbart has referenced the Minnesota Sun's story "Drag Queen Who Routinely Poses Half Nude Performed for Children in Richfield" (Berry, 2019) and another about a Minnesota state senator and "medical treatment for babies who survive botched abortions" (Berry, 2020). There are numerous examples of Breitbart, the Daily Caller, Washington Free Beacon, Campus Reform, and Gateway Pundit citing information from the Tennessee Star. The power of these websites and their circulation of stories across social media "stems from a potent mix of verifiable facts . . . familiar repeated falsehoods, paranoid logic, and consistent political orientation within a mutually-reinforcing network of like-minded sites" (Benkler, Faris, Roberts, & Zuckerman, 2017).

The legitimization and laundering happen in the opposite direction, too. Breitbart, Daily Caller, Washington Free Beacon, Campus Reform, and the Gateway Pundit are all regularly cited as sources of information in stories across Star News websites. This launders the information appearing on well-known hyperpartisan and mis/disinformation websites through the veneer of a local and politically neutral-sounding website, potentially making the cited sources appear more familiar, reputable, and even trusted over time. Here are some examples:

- "As the 2020 election draws nearer, search engine and tech giant Google is being exposed as engaging in election interference by artificially altering search results to negatively impact right-wing sites, as reported by Breitbart" (Lendrum, 2020).
- "President Joe Biden's Asia policy czar pick was a top executive at a non-profit foundation that had direct ties to the Chinese Communist Party, The Washington Free Beacon first reported Wednesday" (Catenacci, 2021).
- "YouTube deleted a pro-life news outlet's channel for 'violating our COVID-19 misinformation policy,' a spokeswoman told the Daily Caller News Foundation Wednesday" (Olohan, 2021).

In addition to citing these websites – and figures like the Gateway Pundit's Jim Hoft, who is banned from Twitter for repeatedly spreading disinformation – Star News websites also republish articles in their entirety from unreliable sources. For example, they published an identical copy of the misleading Campus Reform article, " 'All' Republicans are 'Guilty' of Capitol Attack and Should be 'Forced to Shut the Hell Up,' Louisville Professor Says" (Zeisloft, 2021).

Actual local news sources may unintentionally work to legitimize these problematic sources, too. I've found several examples of news outlets referencing information from the Tennessee Star or the Minnesota Sun, information that could actually be originating from Breitbart and other far-right websites that news organizations may be less likely to cite, without any additional details about the websites or who runs them. Here are some examples:

- "Mayor Ogles *cited a Tennessee Star article* where three former department of education employees criticized Schwinn. They accuse her of mocking the governor and knowingly giving reporters falsified records" (FOX 17 News Digital Staff, 2020).
- "We can go somewhere else with less controversy," explained Steve Gill, *editor of The Tennessee Star online media outlet*" (Wallace, 2018).

- "The ad further claims that neighboring 'DeKalb County cannot find chain of custody documents,' *citing an article from the Georgia Star News, a digital newspaper*, published on December 5" (Subramiam, 2020).
- "Fifty million dollars spent by all the eventual Republican candidates is one estimate by longtime conservative political observer Steve Gill, who is also *a columnist with the Tennessee Star website*" (Bundgaard, 2017).
- *As reported by the Minnesota Sun*, HCAO's policy states that the personal cellphone of any law enforcement officer involved in a critical incident is potentially subject to search and seizure, including phones not in the officer's possession during the incident" (Schaber, 2019).

By citing Star News websites in this manner, actual local news organizations are complicit in laundering mis/disinformation sources. These kinds of citations make these websites more familiar to people, treat them as reliable sources of information, and legitimize them as "news."

Social Media Amplification

The dominance of social media platforms for global flows of information creates another favorable condition for mis/disinformation. In the run up to the 2016 elections, studies showed that engagement with "fake news" articles on social media was often higher than with news articles produced by legacy media (Silverman, 2016). In general, "false news" tends to spread faster and farther than "true news" on social media (Vosoughi, Roy, & Aral, 2018). Although platforms like Facebook have taken modest steps to reduce 2016-era fake news stories (like the one about Pope Francis "Shocking the World" by endorsing Donald Trump for President), that does not mean that mis/disinformation is no longer a problem. In fact, imposter local news sites generate substantial engagement on Facebook. According to Nyhan (2019), "CrowdTangle data shows they are frequently linked on public pages with millions of followers and have generated more than 100,000 interactions." For example, former Donald Trump's Facebook page linked to imposter local news websites, specifically the Minnesota Sun, and other "political leaders have also created or promoted seemingly independent local websites" (Nyhan, 2019). I point out these examples not to try to make a case for the reach or effect of Star News websites or to create an exhaustive summary of the synergistic relationship between mis/disinformation sources and social media. Rather these examples demonstrate how information from these kinds of websites can sometimes generate huge engagement that amplifies strategically partisan stories.

It's arguable that one of the most favorable current conditions for mis/disinformation is social media because mis/disinformation reflects "the very nature of the platform itself" (Gillespie, 2020, p. 330). Mis/disinformation, conspiracies, fake news, clickbait, and all kinds of content that contribute to our polluted media systems spread on social media because the platforms monetize and incentivize these very kinds of content (Phillips & Milner, 2021, p. 183). Spreaders of mis/disinformation and all kinds of creators of "parasitic content" are "aware of the workings of a platform" and "take advantage of the circulation, legitimacy, and context the medium offers" (Gillespie, 2020, p. 331). Imposter websites like Star News publish content that is provocative and "eminently clickable," encouraging the very kinds of engagement that are the "economic imperative of commercial platforms," making platforms unlikely to remove the content (Gillespie, 2020, p. 332).

Star News websites – and the numerous other highly partisan, imposter local news websites – rely on the distribution, amplification, and user engagement afforded by social media platforms. These websites repeatedly amplify each other across social media through the same strategic framing of stories and talking points, which is evident by the cross-pollination between Star News websites, Breitbart, Daily Caller, Campus Reform, Gateway Pundit, and the Washington Free Beacon, among others. And while these websites amplify each other, we also individually "amplify information by publicly interacting and sharing it" and "digital platforms amplify information by algorithmically deciding which information to push and which to hide" (Phillips, 2018). Finally, the stories these websites circulate "often cycle back through the mainstream media, repeating the disinformation – amplification – reverberation (DAR) cycle" (Bennett & Livingston, 2018, p. 126).

As I briefly mentioned earlier, the kinds of content that gets amplified by individual users tend to hit "strong emotional registers, whether joy or indignation" (Vaidhyanathan, 2018, p. 5). How we *feel* about the information we're coming across online matters as much or more than what we *think* about that information (Bowman & Cohen, 2020, p. 225), particularly in terms of whether we decide to view, like, click on, or share that information. The amplification of mis/disinformation – whether by the websites themselves, algorithmically by platforms, or by individual users – helps these websites achieve their partisan goals. Several studies show that simply repeating something makes it seem truer to people (Polage, 2020, p. 236). Repeating the *same* strategic talking points across numerous social media pages and websites makes particular claims, such as the "Big Lie," familiar to readers, giving "credence to the incredible" (Benkler et al., 2017). In other words, according to Wardle (2017), "When we see multiple messages about the same topic, our brains use that as a short-cut to credibility. It must be true we say – I've seen that same claim several times today."

Addressing the Mis/Disinformation Problem

The synergistic relationship between social media and creators/distributors of mis/disinformation – as well as the detrimental relationship between social media and news – are problems that require multiple solutions. To start addressing these issues, first, we need local news sources that serve their communities and hold those with power in their local communities accountable. It's crucial to the health of democracy to reinvigorate and support local news through the public funding of journalism and/or the redistribution of funds from social media companies to news organizations. We need a "new social contract" for digital media companies that asserts "public control over communication systems" and provides funding for the "public infrastructures that democracy requires, especially journalism that can focus on local issues and hold concentrated power (like Facebook) to account" (Pickard, 2020b, p. 131).

Second, given the rise of partisan news websites circulating mis/disinformation, including imposter local news websites, it's more important than ever that news organizations need to "defend their status as impartial news-providers" (Jungherr & Schroeder, 2021). They need to also develop ethics guidelines and ongoing trainings, among other things, so journalists have a set of best practices to turn to for handling mis/disinformation (Wardle, 2020, p. 84). One ethical guideline could simply be journalists taking greater care in preventing unintentional amplification or legitimatization of imposter local news websites and other forms of mis/disinformation. For example, if websites like the Tennessee Star need to be cited in a news story, journalists should add context to those citations rather than treat them as neutral and legitimate sources of information. Here are two examples that can serve as a model of citation:

- "Gill co-founded *The Tennessee Star, a right wing, online-based media company* owned by Star News Digital Media Inc, of which Michael Patrick Leahy is the majority shareholder" (Ebert, 2019).
- "Three other political action committees have also paid Hatmaker's company, including one associated with *The Tennessee Star, a right-wing online website co-founded by conservative commentator Steve Gill*" (Ebert & Allison, 2019).

Third, bad actors on social media need to be transparently held accountable on or removed from platforms. The fact that a well-known peddler of mis/disinformation like Breitbart, which regularly violates Facebook's own terms and conditions, is still thriving on the platform demonstrates how "platforms are not just available for misuse; they are structurally implicated in it" (Gillespie, 2020, p. 333). Social media platforms need to stop allowing these websites to operate in bad faith as "news" providers. The goal of these websites isn't to inform people or to report on communities and keep citizens up to date about what's happening where they live; their function is to launder, legitimize, and amplify misleading partisan information through the veneer of local news, and social media platforms create favorable conditions for them to easily achieve that very mandate.

Phillips and Milner make a case for the importance of network ethics, which "foregrounds reciprocity, interdependence, and a shared responsibility for the whole digital ecosystem," although companies would need to be incentivized or required to do this as, typically, "ethics and guardrails aren't good for business" (2021, pp. 179–188). Thus, in addition to the changes that social media platforms need to make internally, they need to be also held accountable through regulation that challenges rather than reinforces normative assumptions that serve platforms in maintaining the current status quo (Vanacker, 2018, p. 271). One way to challenge the status quo is through regulation. The United States has a long history of allowing media companies to self-regulate and create their own rules of operation. This continues with social media and results in limited "solutions" (e.g., content flagging and labeling, the publication of news consumer guides, public service announcements) to mis/disinformation (Schulte, 2020). As a society, we must be the ones deciding what social media "social responsibilities should look like and how they should be enforced" (Pickard, 2020b, p. 130). We can no longer allow companies like Facebook to strategically position themselves in a "regulatory sweet spot" where they benefit from certain protections while rejecting responsibility or liability for the content shared on their platform (Gillespie, 2010). As Napoli and Caplan (2017) argue, we need to start thinking about social media platforms as media companies rather than as neutral platforms because these companies "engage in editorial and gatekeeping decisions related to the flow of news and information." Until regulators start acting on the fact that social media companies dominate global flows of information – not just as distributors, but also as exhibitors, as curators and creators of content experiences – it's unlikely that we'll see the much-needed policy changes.

Finally, individualized solutions like digital news literacy are important, but ultimately insufficient for addressing the problem of mis/disinformation. Any solutions that turn our attention away from fixing and supporting news, or away from requiring social media platforms to act ethically, and toward people learning how to spot bad actors or toward blaming *specific* bad actors, fail to address the mutually constitutive aspects of our mis/disinformation problem. When "fake news" started getting a lot of public attention in 2016, numerous guides were developed to help people spot mis/disinformation. My own class activity to help students assess different information sources turned into a viral "fake news" list that was framed as a way to help people avoid unreliable sources (Zimdars, 2020b). But these kinds of solutions are just Band-Aids; they may help small cuts and burns to heal, but they're not going to help treat systematic infections or diseases. Our information systems are not suffering from a few small wounds, they are systemically diseased. We need to be better news consumers, sure, but we also need to create healthy news environments that are easier for everyone to navigate and where it's easier for everyone to find or even just stumble across high-quality sources. To make digital media literacy work, we need structural solutions that begin earlier in the communication process and reduce the barriers that currently exist to being a responsible news consumer.

Right now, imposter websites and other forms of mis/disinformation are filling a void where local news sources once existed. And social media platforms are designed to prioritize the very kinds of emotionally charged, highly partisan, and provocative content that imposter websites and other forms of mis/disinformation are adept at creating and circulating. To address mis/disinformation, then, we need to more wholly think about the ways in which favorable conditions – the destruction of the news industry and how social media platforms fundamentally work – create space for websites like Star News to not only operate but also thrive. Until we start addressing multiple factors and contexts contributing to our mis/disinformation problem, we won't make a dent in solving it (Zimdars, 2020b).

References

(2019). Losing the news: The decimation of local journalism and the search for solutions. *PEN America*. Retrieved from https://pen.org/wp-content/uploads/2019/11/Losing-the-News-The-Decimation-of-Local-Journalism-and-the-Search-for-Solutions-Report.pdf

Agresti, J. D. (2021a, February 24). Analysis: The New York Times regularly publishes falsehoods that spur violent unrest and civic dysfunction. *Tennessee Star*. Retrieved from https://tennesseestar.com/2021/02/24/analysis-the-new-york-times-regularly-publishes-falsehoods-that-spur-violent-unrest-and-civic-dysfunction/

Agresti, J. D. (2021b, February 18). Analysis: The New York Times' brazenly false 'fact check' about Trump's impeachment trial. *Tennessee Star*. Retrieved from https://tennesseestar.com/2021/02/18/analysis-the-new-york-times-brazenly-false-fact-check-about-trumps-impeachment-trial/

Ardia, D., Ringel, E., Smith Ekstrand, V., & Fox, A. (2020, December). *Addressing the decline of local news, rise of platforms, and spread of mis- and disinformation online*. Chapel Hill, NC: UNC Center for Media Law and Policy University of North Carolina at Chapel Hill.

Bengani, P. (2020, August 4). As election looms, a network of mysterious 'pink slime' local news outlets nearly triples in size. *Columbia Journalism Review*. Retrieved from www.cjr.org/analysis/as-election-looms-a-network-of-mysterious-pink-slime-local-news-outlets-nearly-triples-in-size.php

Benkler, Y., Faris, R., Roberts, H., & Zuckerman, E. (2017, March 3). Study: Breitbart-led right-wing media ecosystem altered broader media agenda. *Columbia Journalism Review*. Retrieved from www.cjr.org/analysis/breitbart-media-trump-harvard-study.php

Bennett, W. L., & Livingston, S. (2018). The disinformation order: Disruptive communication and the decline of democratic institutions. *European Journal of Communication, 33*(2).

Berry, S. (2019, October 5). Drag queen reading to young children tours in adult gender fluid shows. *Breitbart*. Retrieved from www.breitbart.com/politics/2019/10/05/drag-queen-reading-to-young-children-tours-in-adult-gender-fluids-show/

Berry, S. (2020, September 22). Minnesota Democrat Tina Smith: I'm the only senator to have worked at Planned Parenthood. *Breitbart*. Retrieved from www.breitbart.com/politics/2020/09/22/minnesota-democrat-tina-smith-boasts-im-only-senator-to-have-worked-planned-parenthood/

Blake, A. (2021, February 12). Trump's 'big lie' was bigger than just a stolen election. *The Washington Post*. Retrieved from www.washingtonpost.com/politics/2021/02/12/trumps-big-lie-was-bigger-than-just-stolen-election/

Bowman, N. D., & Cohen, E. (2020). Mental shortcuts, emotion, and social rewards: The challenges of detecting and resisting fake news. In M. Zimdars & K. McLeod (Eds.), *Fake news: Understanding media and misinformation in the digital age* (pp. 223–234). Cambridge, MA: Massachusetts Institute of Technology Press.

Brauer, D. (2009, February 25). Sun chain kills South St. Paul IGH community paper. *MinnPost*. Retrieved from www.minnpost.com/braublog/2009/02/sun-chain-kills-south-st-paul-igh-community-paper/

Bundgaard, C. (2017, July 18). Governor's race could be most expensive in state history. *WKRN.com*. Retrieved from www.wjhl.com/news/tn-governors-race-could-be-most-expensive-in-state-history/

Catenacci, T. (2020a, November 14). New York Times retracts report that New Jersey Democrat won House race, Republican has gained 20,000 votes. *Tennessee Star*. Retrieved from https://tennesseestar.com/2020/11/14/new-york-times-retracts-report-that-new-jersey-democrat-won-house-race-republican-has-gained-20000-votes/

Catenacci, T. (2020b, November 7). 'Come back to haunt us': Pennsylvania lawsuit alleges 21,000 dead people still on voter rolls. *Tennessee Star*. Retrieved from https://tennesseestar.com/2020/11/07/come-back-to-haunt-pennsylvania-lawsuit-alleges-21000-dead-people-still-on-voter-rolls/

Catenacci, T. (2021, January 28). Biden's Asia policy czar was an executive of group with Chinese Communist Party ties: Report. *Tennessee Star*. Retrieved from https://tennesseestar.com/2021/01/28/bidens-asia-policy-czar-was-an-executive-of-group-with-chinese-communist-party-ties-report/

Daniels, J. (2009). Cloaked websites: Propaganda, cyber-racism and epistemology in the digital era. *New Media & Society, 11*(5).

Dwoskin, E. (2020, October 15). Facebook and Twitter take unusual steps to limit spread of New York Post story. *The Washington Post*. Retrieved from www.washingtonpost.com/technology/2020/10/15/facebook-twitter-hunter-biden/

Ebert, J. (2019, May 21). Conservative commentator Steve Gill ordered to pay $170K or face jail in child support dispute. *The Tennessean*. Retrieved from https://www.tennessean.com/story/news/politics/2019/05/21/tennessee-star-steve-gill-child-support-case/3637835002/

Ebert, J., & Allison, N. (2019, May 29). Third legislative staffer with ties to House Speaker Glenn Casada departs. *The Tennessean*. Retrieved from www.tennessean.com/story/news/politics/2019/05/29/tennessee-house-hall-monitors-speaker-glen-casada/1276708001/

FOX 17 News Digital Staff. (2020, September 10). Tennessee mayors calls for Gov. Lee to fire Education Commissioner Schwinn. *Fox17.com*. Retrieved from www.wkrn.com/news/critical-debate-tonight-at-7-p-m-for-tennessee-u-s-senate-race/

Funke, D. (2017, June 14). What's behind the recent media bloodbath? The dominance of Google and Facebook. *Poytner*. Retrieved from www.poynter.org/business-work/2017/whats-behind-the-recent-media-bloodbath-the-dominance-of-google-and-facebook/

Gillespie, T. (2010). The politics of 'platforms.' *New Media & Society, 12*(3). https://doi.org/10.1177and2F1461444809342738

Gillespie, T. (2020). Platforms throw content moderation at every problem. In M. Zimdars & K. McLeod (Eds.), *Fake news: Understanding media and misinformation in the digital age* (pp. 329–340). Cambridge, MA: Massachusetts Institute of Technology Press.

Gockowski, A. (2020, January 21). The New York Times mocked for 'profoundly stupid' endorsement of both Klobuchar and Warren. *Tennessee Star*. Retrieved from https://tennesseestar.com/2020/01/21/nyt-mocked-for-profoundly-stupid-endorsement-of-both-klobuchar-and-warren/

Guess, A., Nyhan, B., & Reifler, J. (2018). *All media trust is local? Findings from the 2018 Poynter media trust survey*. Retrieved from www.dartmouth.edu/~nyhan/media-trust-report-2018.pdf

Hagey, K., Alpert, L. I., & Serkez, Y. (2019, May 4). In news industry, a stark divide between haves and have-nots. *The Wall Street Journal*. Retrieved from wsj.com/graphics/local-newspapers-starkdivide/?ns=prod/accounts-wsj

Heine, D. (2020a, September 30). Biden's Texas political director implicated in massive mail-in ballot harvesting scheme in Harris County. *Tennessee Star*. Retrieved from https://tennesseestar.com/2020/09/30/bidens-texas-political-director-implicated-in-massive-mail-in-ballot-harvesting-scheme-in-harris-county/

Heine, D. (2020b, September 29). Rep. Ilhan Omar linked to cash-for-ballots voter fraud scheme in Minneapolis. *Tennessee Star*. Retrieved from https://tennesseestar.com/2020/09/29/rep-ilhan-omar-linked-to-cash-for-ballots-voter-fraud-scheme-in-minneapolis/

Heine, D. (2020c, December 15). After examining Michigan's Antrim County voting machines, ASOG concludes Dominion 'intentionally designed' to 'create systemic fraud.' *Tennessee Star*. Retrieved from https://tennesseestar.com/2020/12/15/after-examining-antrim-county-voting-machines-asog-concludes-dominion-intentionally-designed-to-create-systemic-fraud/

Ignatius, D. (2020, October 16). Opinion: The truth behind the Hunter Biden non-scandal. *The Washington Post*. Retrieved from www.washingtonpost.com/opinions/the-truth-behind-the-hunter-biden-non-scandal/2020/10/16/798210bc-0fd1-11eb-8074-0e943a91bf08_story.html

Jungherr, A., & Schroeder, R. (2021). Disinformation and the structural transformations of the public arena: Addressing the actual challenges to democracy. *Social Media + Society*. https://doi.org/10.1177/2056305121988928

Klein, A. (2012). Slipping racism into the mainstream: A theory of information laundering. *Communication Theory, 22*.

Lasswell, H. (1971). *Propaganda technique in the World War*. Cambridge, MA: Massachusetts Institute of Technology Press.

Lendrum, E. (2020, July 30). Google deliberately alters search results for Breitbart news. *Breitbart*. Retrieved from https://tennesseestar.com/2020/07/30/google-deliberately-alters-search-results-for-breitbart-news/

Lewis, H. (2020, June 12). The mainstream media won't tell you this. *The Atlantic*. Retrieved from www.theatlantic.com/international/archive/2020/06/conspiracy-mainstream-media-trump-farage-journalism/612628/

Lucas, F. (2020, July 9). All-mail voting threatened election security, study says. *Tennessee Star*. Retrieved from https://tennesseestar.com/2020/07/09/all-mail-voting-threatens-election-security-study-finds/

Mahone, J., & Napoli, P. M. (2020, July 13). Hundreds of hyperpartisan sites are masquerading as local news. *Nieman Lab*. Retrieved from www.niemanlab.org/2020/07/

hundreds-of-hyperpartisan-sites-are-masquerading-as-local-news-this-map-shows-if-theres-one-near-you/

Murdock, C. (2020a, November 29). Voter Integrity Project leader Matt Braynard to submit absentee vote findings to Georgia case. *Tennessee Star*. Retrieved from https://tennesseestar.com/2020/11/29/voter-integrity-project-leader-matt-braynard-to-submit-absentee-vote-findings-to-georgia-case/

Murdock, C. (2020b, November 6). A breakdown of Michigan's witching hour ballot dump from Tuesday. *Tennessee Star*. Retrieved from https://tennesseestar.com/2020/11/06/a-breakdown-of-michigans-witching-hour-ballot-dump-from-tuesday/

Murdock, C. (2020c, December 3). Organization founded by Stacey Abrams and previously chaired by Warnock under investigation for voter fraud. *Tennessee Star*. Retrieved from https://tennesseestar.com/2020/12/03/organization-founded-by-stacey-abrams-and-previously-chaired-by-warnock-under-investigation-for-voter-fraud/

Murdock, C. (2020d, November 20). Trump lawyers bombshell: We have more than enough to overturn the election. *Tennessee Star*. Retrieved from https://tennesseestar.com/2020/11/20/giuliani-powell-ellis-and-trump-lawyers-we-have-more-than-enough-to-overturn-the-election/

Murdock, C. (2020e, November 20). Lin Wood: Affidavits can expose massive Georgia vote fraud. *Tennessee Star*. Retrieved from https://tennesseestar.com/2020/11/20/attorney-lin-wood-released-telling-affidavits-ahead-of-emergency-hearing/

Napoli, P. M., & Caplan, R. (2017). Why media companies insist they're not media companies, why they're wrong, and why it matters. *First Monday*, *22*, 5. http://dx.doi.org/10.5210/fm.v22i15.7051

Nyhan, B. (2019, October 31). Americans trust local news: That belief is being exploited. *The New York Times*. Retrieved from www.nytimes.com/2019/10/31/upshot/fake-local-news.html

Olohan, M. M. (2021, February 12). Youtube deletes top pro-life news outlet's channel for 'violating our COVID-19 misinformation policy.' *Tennessee Star*. Retrieved from https://tennesseestar.com/2021/02/12/youtube-deletes-top-pro-life-news-outlets-channel-for-violating-our-covid-19-misinformation-policy/

Phillips, W. (2018). The oxygen of amplification: Better practices for reporting on extremists, antagonists, and manipulators online. *Data & Society*. Retrieved from https://datasociety.net/wp-content/uploads/2018/05/2-PART-2_Oxygen_of_Amplification_DS.pdf

Phillips, W., & Milner, R. M. (2021). *You are here: A field guide for navigating polarized speech, conspiracy theories, and our polluted media landscape*. Cambridge, MA: Massachusetts Institute of Technology Press.

Pickard, V. (2020a). *Democracy without journalism? Confronting the misinformation society*. Oxford: Oxford University Press.

Pickard, V. (2020b). Confronting the misinformation society: Facebook's "fake news" is a symptom of unaccountable monopoly power. In M. Zimdars & K. McLeod (Eds.), *Fake news: Understanding media and misinformation in the digital age* (pp. 123–132). Cambridge, MA: Massachusetts Institute of Technology Press.

Polage, D. (2020). Source credibility and belief in fake news: I'll believe you if you agree with me. In M. Zimdars & K. McLeod (Eds.), *Fake news: Understanding media and misinformation in the digital age* (pp. 235–246). Cambridge, MA: Massachusetts Institute of Technology Press.

Reynolds, J. M. (2020, November 16). Voting software was 'designed to rig elections,' Trump attorney Sidney Powell tells Maria Bartiromo. *Tennessee Star*. Retrieved from https://tennesseestar.com/2020/11/16/voting-software-was-designed-to-rig-elections-trump-attorney-sidney-powell-tells-maria-bartiromo/

Schaber, A. (2019, November 6). Prosecutors in Hennepin, Ramsey counties have turned on cops. *Star Tribune.* Retrieved from www.startribune.com/prosecutors-in-hennepin-ramsey-counties-have-turned-on-cops/564581322/

Schulte, S. R. (2020). Fixing fake news: Self-regulation and technological solutionism. In M. Zimdars & K. McLeod (Eds.), *Fake news: Understanding media and misinformation in the digital age* (pp. 361–372). Cambridge, MA: Massachusetts Institute of Technology Press.

Silverman, C. (2016, November 16). This analysis shows how viral fake election stories out-performed real news on Facebook. *BuzzFeed News.* Retrieved from www.buzzfeednews.com/article/craigsilverman/viral-fake-election-news-outperformed-real-news-on-facebook#.lowRq0BVm4

"Social Media Fact Sheet." (2019, June 12). *Pew Research Center.* Retrieved from www.pewresearch.org/internet/fact-sheet/social-media/

Stanley, J. (2015). *How propaganda works.* Princeton, NJ: Princeton University Press.

Subramiam, T. (2020, December 31). Fact-checking Trump campaign ad implying fraud in Georgia. *CNN.* Retrieved from www.cnn.com/2020/12/31/politics/trump-campaign-ga-ad-fact-check/index.html

Taylor, J. (2020, September 29). Vote fraud hits Virginia as hundreds of voters receive multiple ballots. *Tennessee Star.* Retrieved from https://tennesseestar.com/2020/09/29/vote-fraud-hits-virginia-as-hundreds-are-receiving-duplicate-ballots/

Taylor, P. M. (2003). *Munitions of the mind: A history of propaganda third edition.* Manchester: Manchester University Press.

Vaidhyanathan, S. (2018). *Anti-social media: How Facebook disconnects us and undermines democracy.* Oxford: Oxford University Press.

Vanacker, B. (2018). Concluding remarks: Digital ethics: Where to go from here? In B. Vanacker & D. Heider (Eds.), *Ethics for the digital age* (Vol. 2, pp. 215–218). New York: Peter Lang.

Vosoughi, S., Roy, D., & Aral, S. (2018). The spread of true and false news online. *Science 359*(6380), 1146–1151. doi:10.1126/science.aap9559

Wahl-Jorgensen, K. (2019). The challenge of local news provision. *Journalism, 20*(1). https://doi.org/10.1177and2F1464884918809281

Waisbord, S. (2018). Truth is what happens to news: On journalism, jake news, and posttruth. *Journalism Studies, 19*(13).

Wallace, H. (2018, December 4). Metro councilmembers to demand city employee raises in exchange for Amazon incentives. *Fox17.com.* Retrieved from https://fox17.com/news/local/metro-councilmembers-to-demand-city-employee-raises-in-exchange-for-amazon-incentives

Wardle, C. (2017, February 16). Fake news: It's complicated. *First Draft News.* Retrieved from https://firstdraftnews.org/latest/fake-news-complicated/

Wardle, C. (2019, October). Understanding information disorder. *First Draft News.* Retrieved from https://firstdraftnews.org/wp-content/uploads/2019/10/Information_Disorder_Digital_AW.pdf?x76701

Wardle, C. (2020). Journalism and the new information ecosystem: Responsibilities and challenges. In M. Zimdars & K. McLeod (Eds.), *Fake news: Understanding media and misinformation in the digital age* (pp. 71–85). Cambridge, MA: Massachusetts Institute of Technology Press.

Wine, M. (2021, February 27). In statehouses, stolen-election myth fuels a G.O.P. drive to rewrite rules. *The New York Times.* Retrieved from www.nytimes.com/2021/02/27/us/republican-voter-suppression.html

Zeisloft, B. (2021, January 18). 'All' Republicans are 'guilty' of capitol attack and should be 'forced to shut the hell up' Louisville professor says. *Tennessee Star*. Retrieved from https://tennesseestar.com/2021/01/18/all-republicans-are-guilty-of-capitol-attack-and-should-be-forced-to-shut-the-hell-up-louisville-professor-says/

Zimdars, M. (2016, December). Information infidelity: What happens when the "real" news is considered "fake" news, too? *Flow Journal*. Retrieved from www.flowjournal.org/2016/12/informational-infidelity/

Zimdars, M. (2020a). Introduction. In M. Zimdars & K. McLeod (Eds.), *Fake news: Understanding media and misinformation in the digital age* (pp. 1–12). Cambridge, MA: Massachusetts Institute of Technology Press.

Zimdars, M. (2020b). Viral "fake news" lists and the limitations of labeling and fact-checking. In M. Zimdars & K. McLeod (Eds.), *Fake news: Understanding media and misinformation in the digital age* (pp. 361–372). Cambridge, MA: Massachusetts Institute of Technology Press.

9

LOCATING SOCIAL MEDIA IN BLACK DIGITAL STUDIES

Francesca Sobande

Experiences of social media are often associated with an ability to transcend geo-cultural borders to connect and communicate with people in different parts of the world. However, social media encounters are shaped by various complex geographies, including Black geographies. Black digital studies and Black geographies work illuminates the (dis)located nature of Black people's experiences, such as how the histories of places, politics, and violence affect the daily lives of Black people. Engaging with such work is essential to critically understanding and locating social media, including in ways that eschew harmful attempts to quantify, and instead turn to approaches such as those articulated by critical geographer, cultural worker, and practitioner-scholar Naya Jones (2019, p. 1079), who poignantly writes about how "[e]mbodied or somatic inquiry has become integral to my methodology and epistemology as a geographer, with close attention to how testifiers and I mutually feel, sense, and intuit".

Therefore, this chapter focuses on the burgeoning nature of Black digital studies in Britain, to consider how such scholarship meaningfully locates and unsettles social media, and examines how social media is, at once, both bordered and borderless. This chapter highlights the importance of work that deals with regional, national, and transnational dimensions of Black people's digital and scholarly experiences. Highlighting the research of PhD and early career researchers, this work outlines how Black digital studies in Britain have been developing in ways distinctly affected by this specific geo-cultural context, as well as Black digital diasporic dynamics (e.g., discourse and delight between Black people in the US and Britain) (Sobande, 2018, 2020; Walcott, Figueroa, & Sobande, 2019). In turn, this chapter contributes to ongoing work that explores and establishes the

DOI: 10.4324/9781003171270-9

wide range of ways that Black digital studies are being undertaken with an attentiveness to the specifics of geo-cultural and sociopolitical contexts.

Relationship Between the Internet and Locations

The relationship between social media and geographies is a fraught and, sometimes, actively concealed and contested one. At times, social media is spoken about as though it is rootless, floating free from any clear connection to the parameters of places and the policies and policing practices that are part of them. The notion that social media creates borderless spaces and interactions can be a naïve one that fails to account for how people's access to, and experiences of, social media are impacted by the perceived and enforced borders of places and cultural norms, governments, and legislation contained within them. I write these words days after the distressing news of a Nigerian government directive to indefinitely suspend access to Twitter, which has been followed by reporting that "Chief legal officer orders prosecution of anyone who refuses to follow the government's block on social network" (Al Jazeera, 2021). Such somber news about the Nigerian suspension of "Twitter's activities, two days after the social media giant removed a post from President Muhammadu Buhari that threatened to punish regional secessionists" (Sotunde, 2021) exemplifies the fact that social media and people's (in)access to it is linked to geo-cultural locations and their sociopolitical environment.

Media pieces such as "The global internet is disintegrating. What comes next?" (BBC, 2019) and "China's 'splinternet' will create a state-controlled alternative cyberspace" (Kenyon, 2021) signal concerns regarding the ability of countries to police online borders and contribute to the splintering of internet experiences due to diverging national and political interests. In the words of Keith Wright (2019) for *TechCrunch*:

> There is no question that the arrival of a fragmented and divided internet is now upon us. The "splinternet", where cyberspace is controlled and regulated by different countries is no longer just a concept, but now a dangerous reality. With the future of the "World Wide Web" at stake, governments and advocates in support of a free and open internet have an obligation to stem the tide of authoritarian regimes isolating the web to control information and their populations.

Additionally, as is outlined in "Regulating behaviours on the European Union internet, the case of spam versus cookies" (Carmi, 2017, p. 289),

> [T]he internet as a new global system of networks mediated by media technologies, has enabled old and new actors to deploy strategies that draw on previous power relations while constructing new ones. The internet

stretches beyond state and regional territorial powers and therefore introduced other forms of governing that include private organizations.

As well as being about the powers of the European Union, governments, and nation-states, the relationship between social media and geographies includes online experiences and expressions of identity and the self which are influenced by locations (social, geographical, cultural, political, assumed, imagined). When accounting for this, among the many questions that arise are the following: In what ways are social media experiences located or how do such experiences involve forms of dislocation, and, perhaps, relocation? How do studies of social and digital media attend to matters regarding geography and (dis)locatedness? What are the benefits and limitations of conceptualizing the located nature of Black digital experiences?

Taking such questions into consideration, this chapter reflects on the development of Black digital studies in Britain. Although the term "Black digital studies" is used throughout this chapter, it is used with a degree of uncertainty due to awareness of the interdisciplinary, transdisciplinary, and, sometimes, anti-disciplinary nature (Bruce, 2022) of the work that is referred to as such. In other words, in writing this chapter I recognize that the term "Black digital studies" may not fully capture the different dimensions of studies of Black people's digital experiences in Britain that are discussed in the writing that follows. Accordingly, I sit with the uneasy tension between an impulse to name and acknowledge such scholarship and a desire to avoid flattening the nuanced nature of such work when attempting to make it legible to broader fields of study such as social media and digital studies.

Beyond these paragraphs, this chapter involves limited critical consideration of the (in)adequacy of the term "Black digital studies" in relation to related scholarship in Britain. However, before proceeding with this discussion of "Locating Social Media in Black Digital Studies" it seems pertinent to ruminate on both the benefits and limitations of the term "Black digital studies", including the potential for the term's use to obscure the wide range of disciplinary conventions, or lack of any disciplinary locus, at the centre of work that is referred to that way. Furthermore, prior to continuing with this writing it is imperative to clarify that despite my use of the term "Black digital studies", in Britain, currently there are no departments or degree programmes explicitly in this area. Also, there is notably scarce access to adequate supervision of Black digital doctoral studies. Thus, the existence of the scholarship that is discussed throughout this chapter should not be confused for the existence of substantial and sustained institutional support for, or recognition of, such work in academia in Britain.

As US-based practitioner–scholar Jones (2019) acknowledges in a vital article on "Black Food Geographies of Slow Violence and Resilience" which explores "reflexivity through GIF-making and autoethnography" (Jones, 2019, p. 1079), "Black geographies already exist, lived, known, and experienced by Black geographic subjects" (Jones, 2019, p. 1077). Meanings of the words associated with geographies such as "location" and "located" vary. However, typically such terms are linked to a sense of place, rootedness, and position(ing), including specific geo-cultural areas and histories. My attempt to think through "Locating Social Media in Black Digital Studies" involves ruminating on different forms of locating and locatedness, namely: 1) how critical analysis and understandings of social media that are located in Black digital studies in Britain offer valuable insights, 2) how such scholarship involves addressing the influence of geo-cultural locations (e.g., Britain) in the digital experiences discussed, 3) how Black digital studies in Britain is both located in and dislocated from a number of scholarly disciplines and areas of study. Put briefly, the understanding of locatedness that is operationalized in this work is a multidimensional one that oscillates between considerations of the characteristics of places, platforms, and the particularities of disciplines and academic fields.

Are locations and forms of locatedness tangible or imagined? To me, typically, they are both at the same time. My discussion of locatedness in this chapter is guided by an understanding of locations and locatedness as being fluid and constantly in flux. Just as the borders of geographical locations have changed over the decades, so too have the porous parameters of people's social locations and identities. For these reasons, when writing this chapter, I did so with an acute awareness of the irony of accepting the fluidity of locations and locatedness while attempting to pinpoint a clear connection between the construction and experience of specific locations and social media. I do not view the ever-changing nature of locations and locatedness as being at odds with an ability to grasp and critically analyze the relationship between them and social media, but I do note the consequential need to explore and express such a relationship in a way that does not imply that locations and locatedness are fixed.

Now, I turn to reflecting on and locating the development of Black digital studies in Britain, to concretely ground my consideration of "Locating Social Media in Black Digital Studies" and foreground this vibrant area of research which is particularly propelled by the work of Black feminists.

Development of Black Digital Studies in Britain

The area of Black digital studies in Britain has rapidly expanded in the years since work such as "Challenging the Whiteness of Britishness: Co-Creating British Social History in the Blogosphere" (Gabriel, 2015) and "Blogging While Black, British and Female: A Critical Study on Discursive Activism" (Gabriel, 2016). The development of Black digital studies in Britain has been spurred on by the work of many people and because of key events including the "Anticipating Black Futures" (2019) multidisciplinary symposium in Birmingham in 2019. Writing about another critical event on Black digital experiences, Keisha Bruce (2019) poignantly states:

What does it mean to experience digital cultures or adopt digital mediums as a Black person? How can Black creatives utilize the digital to explore the endless possibilities for Black identity? How can we conceptualize Blackness through the lens of the digital? These questions were the cornerstones of the Afrofutures_UK's event "Digital While Black" that was held at Birmingham Open Media on 23 February.

The research of PhD students and early career scholars such as Krys Osei (2018, 2019, 2021), Keisha Bruce (2019, 2022), Rianna Walcott (2020, 2022), and Kui Kihoro Mackay (2021a, 2021b) has shaped the current dynamic landscape of scholarship in Britain, which focuses on Black digital and diasporic experiences. Such work which includes collaborative writing and collective activities addresses a wide range of questions, including those that account for the specific experiences of Black women and queer people, and the significance of their creative work, visual cultural production, and knowledge creation and sharing via digital terrains.

The variety of topics examined amid Black digital studies in Britain includes Osei's (2018) unique exploration of "the aestheticisation and stylisation of Black feminist fashion communication, by highlighting the production, distribution and reception of [web-series] *An African City*, across the metropolitan diasporic locales of Accra, London and Washington, DC". Black digital studies in Britain also include work that involves a critical consideration of how hierarchical global relations and Anglocentrism affect Black people and Black scholarship. Such work includes research that contributes to "dialogue concerning the interrelated hegemony of North America, Eurocentrism, anti-Blackness, sexism and its implications in Black women's media and aesthetic practices, as well as related scholarship" (Sobande & Osei, 2020, p. 204). My own Black digital studies work in Britain officially commenced in 2015, when embarking on my PhD project "Digital Diaspora and (Re)mediating Black Women in Britain" (2015–2018, University of Dundee). This would eventually form the basis of articles such as "Watching Me Watching You: Black Women in Britain on YouTube" (Sobande, 2017), "Resisting Media Marginalisation: Black Women's Digital Content and Collectivity" (Sobande, Fearfull, & Brownlie, 2019), and my book *The Digital Lives of Black Women in Britain* (Sobande, 2020).

A key theme that runs throughout much of Black digital studies research in Britain is a focus on both differences and similarities between the contexts of Britain and the US. While Black digital studies in the US have constructively informed elements of Black digital studies in Britain, the generative dialogues between these connected yet different spaces (Black digital studies in Britain and the US) include discussions about the importance of specificity, such as avoiding framing the experiences of Black people in the US and/or Britain as universal. That said, being attentive to the specific qualities of parts of the world such as

Britain and the US does not deny the scope for also acknowledging the global existence of anti-Blackness and interconnected forms of oppression which Black people across the globe are faced with.

As the inimitable work of Moya Bailey (2021, p. 1) highlights, misogynoir which "describes the uniquely co-constitutive racialized and sexist violence that befalls Black women as a result of their simultaneous and interlocking oppression at the intersection of racial and gender marginalization" is a global phenomenon rather than one that is confined to one specific location. Thus, while the digital experiences (and studies) of Black women and Black nonbinary, agender, and gender-variant people in Britain are undoubtedly shaped by the particularities of such a place, they are often also impacted by the global nature of misogynoir and intersecting oppressions. In the words of Bailey (2021) in a section on "Misogynoir without Borders" in the brilliant book *Misogynoir Transformed: Black Women's Digital Resistance,*

> I believe that those outside the United States are best positioned to speak about misogynoir – and hopefully its transformation – in their locations. I offer an invitation to readers to see this book as the first of many that address misogynoir in several arenas and locales, where I and other writers take on the unfortunate dynamism of this noxious reality.
>
> *(p. 25)*

How do critical analyses and understandings of social media that are located in Black digital studies in Britain offer valuable insights? Such scholarship includes a wider range of approaches than those that are accounted for in this chapter. However, this piece recognizes some of the key and increasing emergent topics and perspectives within the sphere of Black digital studies in Britain which, at present, does not feel bound to a single academic discipline but is fashioned by ones such as Black studies, sociology, digital humanities, media and cultural studies, and critical studies of marketing and consumer culture.

Among topics and perspectives at the core of Black digital studies in Britain are ones which emphatically explore how the history and contemporary socio-economic status of Britain and the many regions that constitute it impact Black people's lives, including the (in)accessible nature of digital technology and the internet. For example, as part of my ongoing work I have attempted to account for how issues concerning "Regionality and Rurality" can distinctly impact the digital and media experiences of Black people in Britain (Sobande & hill, 2022), including due to lack of access to consistent internet connections and "the prevalence of high-profile media from capital cities and the comparatively constrained visibility and funding available to media outlets, practitioners, creatives and freelancers in small towns and rural areas" (Sobande, 2020, p. 53).

Scholarly efforts to locate social media experiences must be sensitive to how matters regarding material conditions, as well as regionality and rurality, can mold the details of Black people's social media encounters (or lack of them). After all, "to be Black in a capital city may be to experience life in a way that contrasts with the realities of Black people living in rural Settings" (Sobande, 2020, p. 8). Moreover, locatedness in relation to social media and digital culture can be constructed and experienced at regional, national, and transnational levels, all at once. Therefore, when "Locating Social Media in Black Studies" it seems necessary to spend time unpacking how these interconnected layers of locatedness and geographies are made manifest online.

Although it is not considered in detail in this chapter, a question that I often find myself pondering (as a Black Scottish woman) is to what extent Scottish Twitter and Black Twitter connect and overlap, if at all. Scottish Twitter and Black Twitter may be understood as being constructed in ways that involve an undeniable sense of locatedness, or at least, perceived locatedness – 1) being Scottish and/or aware of the idiosyncrasies of Scottish culture, 2. Being Black American and/or part of the Black diaspora. While Black Twitter is particularly associated with the words, work, history, and experiences of Black American people (Brock, 2020; Clark, 2014; Sharma, 2013), Black British Twitter and other location-specific aspects of the broader domain of Black Twitter have also been acknowledged even by Twitter themselves (Sobande, 2020).

The naming and conceptualizing of connections and communities on Twitter in ways that explicitly invoke ideas about nation and notions of nationality (e.g., Scottish Twitter and Black British Twitter) sparks questions such as the following: How are the social media experiences of Black people in predominantly white areas (e.g., Scotland and other parts of Britain) understood and framed in ways that involve invoking or departing from normative notions of nation, nationhood, and nationality? How does a sense of social location as a Black person in predominantly white places shape experiences of social media and/or perceptions of such experiences? What does naming these location-specific facets of Black Twitter (e.g., Black British Twitter) symbolize or suggest about the development of a Black digital diaspora? Why is Black British Twitter conceivable and perceivable, but currently, Black Scottish Twitter is not? How do various diasporic experiences (e.g., being Black and from Britain but now being located elsewhere) complicate how people experience digital spaces, including iterations of Black Twitter? These are just a few of numerous questions that may orient future Black digital studies scholarship which grapples with both the salience and troubling of the relationship between geographies, nations, nationalities, Black diaspora, and social media.

Jones (2019) has impactfully written about being "interested in how felt experiences (re)present Black food geographies as otherwise visible and very much alive – not to prove Black vitality, but to (re)claim it unapologetically" (p. 1077). Such a heartening spirit of reclaiming Black vitality is one that is also present in Black digital studies scholarship that does not seek to prove but instead seeks to sit with, and sometimes, celebrate, the Black vitality, creativity, and joy that are part of Black digital experiences and culture.

The eminent work of Jessica H. Lu and Catherine Knight Steele (2019) on "'Joy is resistance': cross-platform resilience and (re)invention of Black oral culture online" offers an incisive analysis of Black joy and its resistant qualities. Relatedly, Kui Kihoro Mackay's extensive research includes the PhD thesis "'Got on to the plane as white English and landed in London as Black Kenyan': Construction and Performance of Kenyanness Across Online and Offline Sites" which "centres the lived experiences of Facebook and Twitter users in the UK who identify as Kenyan and uses Black Feminist theory to expand the current language of identification, belonging and performance" (Mackay, 2021b). Mackay's (2021b) significant work has also addressed the topic of "Digital Black Lives: Performing (Dis)Respect and Joy Online", which involved posing powerful questions such as "How is Blackness understood in the Kenyan context? Is there room to consider a Black Kenyan Cyberculture or Black African Cyberculture?". Mackay's (2021a, 2021b) work, in addition to the scholarship of Osei, Bruce, Walcott, and others such as the forthcoming work of PhD student Temi Lasade-Anderson is carving out the direction of Black digital studies in Britain in enriching ways that deal with the workings of joy, diaspora, global power dynamics, and Black African cyberculture.

As well as being a home for critical enquiry that focuses on experiences and expressions of Black joy, kinship, intimacy, play, and pleasure in digital spaces, Black digital studies in Britain and elsewhere have shed light on the dangers and difficulties that are involved in Black people's digital experiences. Hence, the last section of this chapter which is based on a blog piece of mine for *The Sociological Review* deals with some of this when considering aspects of the digital experiences of Black women since the COVID-19 pandemic.

Politics of Digital Peace, Play, and Privacy During the COVID-19 Pandemic: Between Digital Engagement, Enclaves, and Entitlement[1]

I have been interested in digital media and people's experiences of the internet since first finding moments of enjoyment, escapism, and entertainment online at the turn of the 21st century. My memories of digital technology and internet culture back then include the myth of the millennium bug which was predicted to wreak havoc in computers with the anticipated arrival of the year 2000. Arguably, the concept of the millennium bug captures panic that is often sparked by significant digital developments, including legitimate fears regarding a potential loss of agency and autonomy. Still, not all my memories of new millennium digital discourse and dalliances are marked by feelings such as the nervousness and confusion which were invoked by the dreaded bug.

Around that same time, films including Disney Channel's *Zenon: Girl of the 21st Century* (1999) playfully imagined what digital technology (and outer space!) might be like in the future. The film left me in awe of the idea that people could be beamed into each other's homes in ways that, in hindsight, resemble many energy-draining present-day video calls. For some people, or at least, a pre-teen and teenage me, the online world of the early 2000s was a source of much excitement for many reasons. However, there was always a sense that despite some digital spaces being sites of peace, play, and personal connections, being online also involved navigating many dangers. As the years rolled on, I found myself thinking about how who people are and others' perceptions of them impact their digital experiences. Specifically, I reflected on and subsequently researched some of the intricacies of the digital lives of Black women in Britain (Sobande, 2020).

In Spring 2020, when working on the concluding chapter of my book, *The Digital Lives of Black Women in Britain*, I was struck by the distinctly different digital and daily experiences that people were dealing with during the COVID-19 (coronavirus) pandemic. Not everyone had access to the internet, a computer, or a digital device that organizations were demanding be used to access essential information and services. Assumptions about people's "home" environments and material conditions abounded, and, at times, political positions seemed to be performed via carefully curated bookshelves which perhaps revealed more about the practice of self-representation and idealized aesthetics than the person whose background they featured in. Since then, sweeping statements about the role of digital media and technology in the daily lives of "everyone" have obscured the realities of many people. Furthermore, such statements seed an unhelpful universalizing framing of life during the COVID-19 pandemic, which denies how structural factors related to race, gender, class, and intersecting oppressions have resulted in the specific circumstances that different individuals have been facing during this time of crisis.

When trying to figure out what the closing thoughts and words shared in my book would be, I ended up reflecting on the politics of digital experiences amid the COVID-19 pandemic. Questions that I sat with included the following: Who is making themselves more visible online right now, without fearing the possibility of online harassment? How will people's personal boundaries be maintained and tested? What will UK universities do to support structurally marginalized and minoritized students and staff whose online experiences may involve encountering racism, sexism, misogyny, homophobia, transphobia, colorism, Islamophobia, and other intersecting oppressions, including while learning and teaching? In the months that have followed, while some people have flippantly referred to the "pivot to online" strategies of institutions (e.g., healthcare, education, political, employers) and participated in such efforts in relatively unscathed ways, others have suddenly been expected to make themselves very visible online, without any indication of how institutions will support them if they encounter online abuse and harms.

Vital scholarship on Black cyberfeminism (Gray, 2015, 2020; McMillan Cottom, 2016), "Black women's digital resistance" (Bailey, 2021), and the oppressive nature of algorithms (Noble, 2018) are central to my understanding of the structural challenges involved in Black women's digital experiences, in addition to their creativity, collaboration, and innovation that are present too. Relatedly, although many institutions express an interest in protecting the privacy of people, including when using and storing their data online, very few institutions express an understanding of privacy that accounts for how it is shaped by inequalities and interlocking oppression such as the anti-Blackness, sexism, and misogyny (misogynoir) that Moya Bailey (2021) has extensively researched and written about. Thus, something that has stayed on my mind over the last year is the invasive expectations of institutions, and sometimes individuals, regarding access to private aspects of people's lives, especially Black women, under the guise of "digital connection and community".

As public discussions of the pandemic have surged since March 2020, so too have conversations concerning Black Lives Matter (BLM). However, few institutions appeared to join the dots between both. Crises do not exist in isolation. Institutions that were quick to issue their summer statements in support of BLM and have continually claimed to recognize that "we're" experiencing a time of crisis which is far from "business as usual", were also quick and consistent with the way that they pressured Black women to be hyper-visible online as part of their institutional response to both crises (COVID-19 and structural anti-Black racism). As such, when turning to social media and different digital spaces in pursuit of moments of play and peace in a personal capacity, some Black women have been met with the entitled messages of people who indignantly demand Black women's engagement and who represent their lack of care for Black women's boundaries as an alleged mere effort to self-educate by "reaching out".

The boundaries between public and private lives have always been blurred, but since the emergence of the COVID-19 pandemic the encroachment on people's private lives and personal spaces has been especially pronounced. Examples of this include institutions upping their monitoring of employees' social media profiles and contacting them directly there in inappropriate ways, as well as individuals instructing others to "turn your camera on" and then making scrutinizing and classist comments about what is or is not in the background of someone who appears on a video call. The personal safety and well-being of people is treated as an afterthought by institutions and individuals who insist on others making themselves visible online in ways that they are not comfortable with. There are a lot of reasons why people are cautious about becoming visible online, particularly if they are survivors of abuse and violence. Yet, I do not know of (m)any organizations that have carefully considered this when calling for people to "pivot to online" overnight, and when, assisted by digital technology, peering into the personal space of someone for whom it may not be safe to make visible.

Although digital culture can offer enriching enclaves and vital moments of connection, which are lifelines for people, such spaces can also home abusive hostility and expressions of entitlement. Digital experiences are raced, gendered, classed, and everything in between (Daniels, Gregory, & McMillan Cottom,

2016). "Zoombombing" and other iterations of online harassment that predominantly involve the targeting of racialized people, particularly Black women, signal that digital peace and digital disruption are molded by white supremacy, anti-Blackness, sexism, and misogyny. Institutions' expectations of "digital engagement" and "digital presence", not only over the last year, often necessitate shades of self-disclosure and self-exposure that involve a considerable amount of risk for those who are most marginalized in society. Moreover, interconnected inequalities influence people's experiences, or lack, of digital peace and privacy during the COVID-19 pandemic. The ascent of institutional messages that promote calls to "amplify Black women" and "listen to Black women", but without responding to the dangers that Black women face when they are hyper-visible online, reflects the surface-level and self-serving ways that many organizations engage with Black women and their work.

While digital media and spaces can involve meaningful connections and conversations, the formation of transnational solidarity, as well as joyous forms of play and ephemeral feelings of peace, part of what makes that possible is the opportunity for people to explore different ways that they feel comfortable communicating with others and sharing who they are. As institutions continue to both directly and implicitly call for the increased online visibility of people, particularly Black women, there is a need for such institutions to take seriously the extent to which they are (or are not) respecting personal boundaries and tackling online abuse and oppression.

Conclusion

This chapter's focus on "Locating Social Media in Black Digital Studies" involved an attempt to outline some of the myriad ways that Black digital studies and critical Black geographies studies provide nuanced understandings of the dynamic between locations, social media, and Black digital experiences. With an emphasis on Black digital studies in Britain, and engagement with Black digital studies and related work in the US, this writing unpacked the layered nature of locations and locatedness that affect social media experiences and scholarship on them. In considering such matters, this chapter stresses the unstable nature of the term "Black digital studies in Britain", which although being a useful way to describe and group work related to the digital experiences of Black people in Britain, may mask the details of different disciplines, critical approaches, and positions that are part of the overall fabric of what is referred to as Black digital studies in Britain. Perhaps, to be located in Black digital studies in Britain is to always be both here (situated in Black digital studies in Britain) *and* there (never bound to a single scholarly area, discipline, or field).

Although this chapter affirms the benefits of specificity when researching, writing about, and reflecting on Black digital experiences, this acknowledgement should not be confused for a denial of the global nature of anti-Blackness and interconnected forms of oppression. Furthermore, recognition of the specific digital experiences of Black people in different parts of the world should not be understood as dismissing the digitally mediated transnational nature of transformative forms of solidarity-building and support that exist between Black people across countries and continents. In sum, "Locating Social Media in Black Digital Studies" can mean being attentive to both geographically bound issues that impact the digital experiences of Black people, as well as digital activity that appears to defy borders and boundaries, even if ephemerally. Ongoing Black digital studies and feminist efforts include work that tends to "the creative, collaborative, and conjuring possibilities of digital remix culture which involves the remixing and repurposing of digital media, meanings, and messages" (Sobande & Emejulu, 2022). Related questions that future work may address include how and where do geography and forms of location show up in Black digital remixing activities.

Further still, "Locating Social Media in Black Digital Studies" entails engaging with studies of Black diaspora and diasporicity (Brown, 2009; Hesse, 2000), including those that posit that "[a]ttention to the question of place should prompt the question, where is Black Europe? Black Europe is not locatable; it is a *discourse* on location". As is suggested by the insightful words of Brown (2009) on "Black Europe and the African Diaspora: A Discourse on Location", some notions of location and locatedness that are central to Black diasporic experiences and research on them are discursive constructions that should not be mistaken for tangible spaces and places. As a result, when delineating locations and locatedness in Black digital studies scholarship, it is essential to make space for their felt, imagined, and socially constructed qualities, as well as their physical ones that are attached to certain definable contexts.

Critical analysis and understandings of social media that are located in Black digital studies in Britain offer valuable insights for a wide range of reasons that include elucidating forms of Black creativity and innovation, challenging restrictive notions of what constitutes knowledge, and undertaking the careful scrutiny of how geo-politics and British history (e.g., anti-Blackness and colonialism) contour Black experiences, including online. The future of Black digital studies in Britain is one that is yet to be determined but is sure to disrupt the often unarticulated and dominant status of whiteness that underpins many digital studies arenas in Britain and beyond. Nevertheless, it would be misguided to perceive Black digital studies in Britain as a mere response to the whiteness that permeates much of digital studies and academia in general. Black digital studies are anything but simply reactionary, nor are they about an aim to pander or prove. To return to and affirm the words of Jones (2019) on Black food geographies, maybe Black digital studies in Britain too involve an aim "to (re)claim it [Black vitality] unapologetically" (p. 1077).

The inherently colonialist, imperialist, elitist, and racist foundations of academia present a multitude of obstacles that challenge, and even attempt to prohibit, the embracement and experience of Black vitality within institutional academic environments. Put differently, the work of Black digital studies, which includes iterations of vitality and joy, is often at odds with the foundations of academia. Thus, even when Black digital studies are somewhat located in, or at least, linked to academic situations, they are never fully *of* the academy, nor should they be. Future research on the relationship between locations, locatedness, social media, and Black digital studies may include a more detailed discussion of how the institutional (dis)location of Black digital studies work (e.g., which institutions and surrounding geographies and histories are associated with it) impacts its direction and reception both within and beyond academia.

The explanation of how location and locatedness is conceptualized in my work is far from a finished one, just as the process of location-making and locating is always ongoing. Further research regarding Black digital studies in Britain may yield fruitful work that expands understandings of "Locating Social Media in Black Digital Studies". Moreover, instead of just being interpreted as sole-authored work, this chapter is best understood as being in conversation with a rich history and future of Black digital studies that involves more of an interest in provocations, ponderings, and collaborative parsing than any investment in proprietarily foreclosing discussion and debate surrounding how Black digital encounters are conceptualized, theorized, experienced, and located.

"Locating Social Media in Black Digital Studies" maybe best described as being part of continued efforts to make clear and critically analyze the geocultural embeddedness and elements of many Black social media and digital experiences. Whether you are involved in Black digital studies work or have never engaged with it before, I hope that this chapter has prompted helpful questions and considerations concerning Black digital studies constellations and their connection to different Black geographies.

Note

1. The section of this article on "The Politics of Digital Peace, Play, and Privacy During the COVID-19 Pandemic: Between Digital Engagement, Enclaves, and Entitlement" was previously published online by *The Sociological Review* on 5 May 2021. Francesca Sobande (the author) is the sole copyright holder.

References

Al Jazeera. (2021, June 5). Nigerians breaking Twitter ban rules could be prosecuted. *Al Jazeera*. Retrieved from www.aljazeera.com/news/2021/6/5/nigeria-attorney-general-warns-against-breaking-twitter-ban-rule

Anticipating Black Futures. (2019). *Anticipating Black futures: Symposium Programme.* Retrieved from https://blackfuturesuk.files.wordpress.com/2019/05/anticipating-black-futures-programme-4.pdf

Bailey, M. (2021). *Misogynoir transformed: Black Women's digital resistance.* New York: New York University Press.

BBC. (2019, May 15). The global internet is disintegrating: What comes next? *BBC.* Retrieved from www.bbc.com/future/article/20190514-the-global-internet-is-disintegrating-what-comes-next

Brock, B. (2020). *Distributed Blackness: African American cybercultures.* New York: New York University Press.

Brown, J. N. (2009). Black Europe and the African diaspora: A discourse on location. In D. C. Hine, T. D. Keaton, & S. Small (Eds.), *Black Europe and the African diaspora* (pp. 201–211). Urbana & Chicago: University of Illinois Press.

Bruce, K. (2019). Reflections: #DigitalWhileBlack. *In Search of Blackness: Digital Blackness, Ephemerality & Social Media.* Retrieved from https://digitalblacknessphd.wixsite.com/dbphd/blog/categories/black-studies

Bruce, K. (2020, October 27). Black British digital studies [Panel also featuring Francesca Sobande and Rianna Walcott]. King's College London.

Bruce, K. (2022). *Black Women and the curation of digital diasporic intimacy* (Ph.D. Thesis, University of Nottingham).

Carmi, E. (2017). Regulating behaviours on the European Union internet, the case of spam versus cookies. *International Review of Law, Computers, & Technology, 31*(3), 289–307.

Clark, M. D. (2014). *To tweet our own cause: A mixed-methods study of the online phenomenon "black Twitter".* Chapel Hill, NC: University of North Carolina at Chapel Hill Graduate School. https://doi.org/10.17615/7bfs-rp55

Daniels, J., Gregory, K., & McMillan Cottom, T. (Eds.). (2016). *Digital sociologies.* Bristol: Policy Press.

Gabriel, D. (2015, September). Challenging the whiteness of Britishness: Co-creating British social history in the blogosphere. *Online Journal of Communication and Media Technologies,* Special Issue, 1–14.

Gabriel, D. (2016). Blogging while Black, British and female: A critical study on discursive activism. *Information, Communication & Society, 19*(11), 1622–1635.

Gray, K. (2015). Race, gender, and virtual inequality: Exploring the liberatory potential of Black cyberfeminist theory. In R. A. Lind (Ed.), *Produsing theory in a digital world 2.0: The intersection of audiences and production in contemporary theory* (Vol. 2, pp. 175–192). New York: Peter Lang.

Gray, K. (2020). *Intersectional tech: Black users in digital gaming.* Baton Rouge, LA: Louisiana State University Press.

Hesse, B. (2000). Diasporicity: Black Britain's post-colonial formations. In B. Hesse (Ed.), *Un/settled multiculturalisms: Diasporas, entanglements, transruptions* (pp. 96–120). London: Zed.

Jones, N. (2019). Dying to eat? Black food geographies of slow violence and resilience. *ACME: An International Journal for Critical Geographies, 18*(5), 1076–1099.

Kenyon, F. (2021, June 3). China's 'splinternet' will create a state-controlled alternative cyberspace. *The Guardian.* Retrieved from www.theguardian.com/global-development/2021/jun/03/chinas-splinternet-blockchain-state-control-of-cyberspace

Lu, J. H., & Steele, C. K. (2019). 'Joy is resistance': Cross-platform resilience and (re)invention of Black oral culture online. *Information, Communication & Society, 22*(6), 823–837.

Mackay, K. K. (2021a). *Got on to the plane as white English and landed in London as Black Ken-yan: Construction and performance of Kenyanness across online and offline sites* (Ph.D. Thesis, Royal Holloway, University of London).

Mackay, K.K. (2021b, May 7). Digital Black lives: Performing (dis)respect and joy online. *Sociological Review.* Retrieved from www.thesociologicalreview.com/digital-black-lives-performing-disrespect-and-joy-online/

McMillan Cottom, T. (2016). Black cyberfeminism: Ways forward for intersectionality and digital sociology. In J. Daniels, K. Gregory, & T. McMillan Cottom (Eds.), *Digital sociologies* (pp. 211–232). Bristol: Policy Press.

Noble, S. U. (2018). *Algorithms of oppression: How search engines reinforce racism.* New York: New York University Press.

Osei, K. (2018, September 25). Declaration of self: Fashioning identity in an African city [Conference presentation]. *Black Feminism, Womanism, and the Politics of Women of Colour in Europe*, Berlin. Abstract Retrieved from https://woceuropeconference.files.wordpress.com/2018/09/woc-europe-programme-final-25sept18.pdf

Osei, K. (2019). Fashioning my garden of solace: A Black feminist autoethnography. *Fashion Theory, 23*(6), 733–746.

Osei, K. (2021, May 14). *Krys Osei in conversation with Tosin Adeosun* [Instagram live event]. University of the Arts, London.

Sharma, S. (2013). Black Twitter? Racial hashtags, networks and contagion. *New Formations: A Journal of Culture/Theory/Politics, 78*(2013), 46–64.

Sobande, F. (2017). Watching me watching you: Black women in Britain on YouTube. *European Journal of Cultural Studies, 20*(6), 655–671.

Sobande, F. (2018). *Digital diaspora and (re)mediating Black Women in Britain* (Ph.D. Thesis, University of Dundee).

Sobande, F. (2020). *The digital lives of Black Women in Britain.* Cham: Palgrave Macmillan.

Sobande, F., & Emejulu, A. (2022). The Black Feminism Remix Lab: On Black feminist joy, ambivalence, and futures. *Culture, Theory and Critique.*

Sobande, F., Fearfull, A., & Brownlie, D. (2019). Resisting media marginalisation: Black women's digital content and collectivity. *Consumption Markets & Culture, 23*(5), 413–428.

Sobande, F., & hill, l. r. (2022). *Black Oot here: Black lives in Scotland.* London: Bloomsbury.

Sobande, F., & Osei, K. (2020). An African city: Black Women's creativity, pleasure, diasporic (dis)connections and resistance through aesthetic and media practices and scholarship. *Communication, Culture & Critique, 13*(2), 204–221.

Sotunde, A. (2021, June 5). Nigeria says it suspends Twitter days after president's post removed. *Reuters.* Retrieved from www.reuters.com/technology/nigeria-indefinitely-suspends-twitter-operations-information-minister-2021–06–04/

Walcott, R. (2020, July 7). WhatsApp aunties and the spread of fake news. *Wellcome Collection.* Retrieved from https://wellcomecollection.org/articles/Xv3T1xQAAADN3N3r

Walcott, R. (2022). *A tweet at the table: Black British women's identity expression on social media* (Ph.D. Thesis, King's College, London).

Walcott, R., Figueroa, Y., & Sobande, F. (2019). S1/E1: Black diasporas, anglo-centrism & positionality (ASA, Hawaii) [Podcast]. *Surviving Society.* Retrieved from https://podcasts.apple.com/gb/podcast/s1-e1-black-diasporas-anglo-centrism-positionality/id1291679351?i=1000464547110

Wright, K. (2019, March 13). The 'splinternet' is already here. *TechCrunch.* Retrieved from https://techcrunch.com/2019/03/13/the-splinternet-is-already-here/

10

AN OVERVIEW OF SOCIAL MEDIA AND MENTAL HEALTH

Sarah M. Coyne, Emily Schvaneveldt, and Jane Shawcroft

Suicide and mental health issues such as depression and anxiety have risen markedly in the past few decades (e.g., American Foundation for Suicide Prevention, 2020; Heron, 2019). These statistics are concerning, and many have sought to find a cause for the increase in mental health problems worldwide. The use of mobile media (Twenge, 2017a) – social media in particular (Charles, 2019) – is often blamed in popular news reports as a primary reason for this increase, with some scholars wondering whether "smartphones [have] destroyed a generation" (Twenge, 2017a). This review will critically examine the research literature on social media and mental health and focus on both risky and protective uses of media.

Social Media and Mental Health – A Possible Link?

A host of research now links time spent using mobile media (and social media in particular) with mental health problems, such as depression or anxiety (e.g., Banjanin, Banjanin, Dimitrijevic, & Pantic, 2015; Barry, Sidoti, Briggs, Reiter, & Lindsey, 2017; Woods & Scott, 2016). Some of the most influential research in this area has been done by Jean Twenge and colleagues (e.g., Twenge, 2017b; Twenge, Martin, & Campbell, 2018). For example, one study of more than 500,000 US adolescents found that time spent engaging with new media (including social media) was associated with increased levels of mental health problems and suicide risk (Twenge, Joiner, Rogers, & Martin, 2018). Additionally, other intervention work suggests that reducing the time spent on social media to 30 minutes or less per day led to improvements in well-being, such as a decrease in loneliness or depression (Hunt, Marx, Lipson, & Young, 2018).

DOI: 10.4324/9781003171270-10

The association between social media use and mental health seems to be particularly pronounced among girls (Memon, Sharma, Mohite, & Jain, 2018; Oshima et al., 2012; Twenge, Joiner, et al., 2018; Viner et al., 2019). For example, a ten-year longitudinal study found that girls (but not boys) had a higher suicide risk in emerging adulthood if they had an early and increasing trajectory of time spent using social media starting in early adolescence (Coyne et al., 2021). Girls may be more likely to be sensitized to interpersonal stressors and are more likely to internalize these with emotional distress, often leading to depression or anxiety (Gore & Eckenrode, 1996; Rudolph, 2002). Social media provides many opportunities for interpersonal stressors, perhaps accounting for why girls experience these stressors more acutely than boys.

Theoretically, the time spent using social media and mobile devices may displace other meaningful activities that might be protective for mental health, such as face-to-face time with family or friends. This displacement might be particularly likely if social media use is more passive, with little meaningful interaction or connection with other individuals (Escobar-Viera et al., 2018). Additionally, experiences on social media might lead to feelings of thwarted belongingness or exclusion, a known factor in predicting suicide (Brunstein Klomek et al., 2019; Joiner, 2005).

Social Media and Mental Health Revisited

The previous section appears to show a clear link between social media use and mental health. However, numerous studies find no association between time spent on social media and the development of mental health issues. This group of research includes several meta-analyses that show the effects to be either nonexistent or relatively weak (Appel, Marker, & Gnambs, 2020; Huang, 2018; Meier & Reinecke, 2020; Vahedi & Zannella, 2019; Yin, de Vries, Gentile, & Wang, 2019; Yoon, Kleinman, Mertz, & Brannick, 2019). Indeed, researchers have reanalyzed the datasets used by Twenge, Joiner, et al. (2018) and have found that time spent with new media (including social media) has no impact on mental health (e.g., Kreski et al., 2020). One study found that the effect is almost nonexistent, with the effect of screen time on mental health problems being about as impactful as eating potatoes (Orben & Przybylski, 2019).

Why the mixed findings? Most research on this topic involves cross-sectional studies that use convenience samples, with few studies examining directional or individual change over time. We examined the impact of time spent using social media on both depression and anxiety over an eight-year period, examining both intra- and inter-individual change over time (Coyne, Rogers, Zurcher, Stockdale, & Booth, 2020). We found no evidence of a link between time spent using social media and individual changes in either depression or anxiety across the course of adolescence, suggesting that time is not the most important factor in this equation. This lack of evidence is likely because two individuals could spend the same exact time on social media and yet have a very different experience, depending on the context of their use. One person could hypothetically finish a session on social media feeling connected and uplifted, while another could leave feeling lonely, depressed, and excluded. In the next section, we examine some of the major contextual factors related to social media that might be risky for the development of mental health problems. The section will be followed with a discussion of protective and healthy uses of social media for mental health.

Risky Contexts Surrounding Social Media and Mental Health

There are several contexts that appear to be riskier in terms of the link between social media and mental health issues. We focus on four of these in the current chapter (though there are several more not represented here): time of day, fear of missing out, social comparisons, and pathological (or addictive) social media use.

Time of Day

Social media never stops, with new content being posted at every second of every day. However, there may be a differential effect depending on what time individuals access this content. Most adolescents use their mobile devices after "lights out," often spending many hours on social media after bedtime (Vernon, Modecki, & Barber, 2018). A consistent line of research suggests that using media right before bed or during the night tends to be most problematic in terms of predicting depression and anxiety (e.g., Shimoga, Erlyana, & Rebello, 2019; Vernon et al., 2018; Woods & Scott, 2016).

This link is important because sleep is strongly related to mental illness. The effect is likely bidirectional, with mental illness interfering with sleep and sleep disorders impacting mental health (Reynolds & O'Hara, 2013). Remember the research by Orben and Przybylski (2019), who found the impact of media on mental health was negligible and as large as the impact of eating potatoes? They also found that the largest predictor of mental health in that sample was getting adequate sleep.

Numerous mechanisms likely account for this relationship between sleep and mental health. Time spent using social media might displace the amount of time spent sleeping if individuals delay bedtime in favor of spending time on social media (Exelmans & Van den Bulck, 2017). Additionally, the content of social media might be cognitively stimulating, making it harder for individuals to wind down and fall asleep, particularly if the individual has a significant fear of missing out (FOMO) (Scott & Woods, 2019). Thus, high users of social media right before bedtime might simply be getting fewer hours of sleep each night. Social media might impact the quality of sleep also. Notifications from social media sites or messages might interrupt sleep, decreasing the amount of time spent in deep sleep or REM (Van den Bulck, 2003; Wang et al., 2017).

We recommend that individuals avoid social media in the hour before bedtime and to turn all notifications off during the nighttime hours. Instead, adolescents can use social media during daytime or early evening hours. One solution might be to store mobile phones outside the bedroom during later evening hours as opposed to a bedside cabinet (Dorrian, Centofanti, Wicking, Wicking, & Lushington, 2018). Indeed, interventions aimed at changing phone use right before bedtime have been moderately successful, increasing sleep time by an average of 21 minutes each night (Bartel, Scheeren, & Gradisar, 2019).

Fear of Missing Out

FOMO is defined as "a pervasive apprehension that others might be having regarding experiences from which one is absent" (Przybylski, Murayama, DeHaan, & Gladwell, 2013, p. 1841). Time spent on social media tends to be related to FOMO, where individuals might be crippled by feelings that they are being left out of important activities or missing out on vital experiences or information. FOMO surrounding social media tends to be related to a number of outcomes related to mental health including lack of sleep, depression, decreased psychological well-being, and anxiety (Baker, Krieger, & LeRoy, 2016; Scott & Woods, 2018). Thus, it appears that social media use might be particularly problematic when accompanied by FOMO.

Dealing with FOMO is more complicated than intervening around phone use at bedtime. FOMO tends to be strongly related to underlying factors, including personality features such as neuroticism, low self-esteem, feelings of inadequacy, and anxiety (Balta, Emirtekin, Kircaburun, & Griffiths, 2020). Thus, addressing these underlying features is likely important in diminishing FOMO around social media use. Many types of FOMO exist surrounding social media; thus, understanding which type of FOMO an individual is experiencing is vital for reducing negative experiences around social media (Altuwairiqi, Jiang, & Ali, 2019). Gaining this understanding might include addressing both technological and socioemotional issues. For example, if an individual fears that they will miss out on participating in popular interactions, research suggests they might manage this fear by setting an auto-response to inform contacts where they are or set their status to indicate when they are able to reply (Alutaybi, Al-Thani, McAlaney, & Ali, 2020). To reduce FOMO, an individual might work on improving self-esteem, managing impulsive behavior, or practice self-talk. These practices will help them be mindful of how their fear and anxiety might be interfering with the ability to have positive interactions on self-esteem. These types of targeted interventions are rare but effective in reducing social media-related FOMO.

Social Comparisons on Social Media

According to social comparison theory (Festinger, 1954), there are two types of social comparisons. An individual makes an upward social comparison when they compare themselves to someone they perceive to be "better" than them on some desired trait (e.g., attractiveness, social popularity, intelligence, athletic ability). Comparatively, an individual makes a downward social comparison when they compare themselves with those perceived to be worse on these same types of traits. Upward social comparisons, in particular, tend to be strongly related to depression (McCarthy & Morina, 2020). Upward social comparisons are common during social media use and represent one problematic context that is highly predictive of mental health issues (e.g., Robinson et al., 2019: Wang et al., 2020; Yoon et al., 2019). Unlike offline life, online life may bombard users of social media with updates, photos, and stories of hundreds of individuals every single day – the sheer frequency of interactions with others on social media might increase the likelihood of social comparisons (Harris & Bardey, 2019). Additionally, many social media users have an intent to portray their "best self," using photo-enhancing filters, embellishing stories to make themselves sound exciting, or focusing on only the good parts of life (Tiggemann & Anderberg, 2020). Thus, it is no wonder that an individual who shows high upward social comparison tends to leave social media feeling depressed and as though they cannot measure up to their peers.

It is difficult to tell someone to simply "stop comparing yourself" to others online. Indeed, some of this social comparison is evolutionary based and very difficult to modify (Festinger, 1954). However, some research has successfully intervened in reducing (as opposed to entirely eliminating) social comparisons. Simply being mindful of social media comparisons might reduce their frequency and impact (Weaver & Swank, 2019). We go into greater detail on the link between mindfulness and positive social media experiences in a later section. Additionally, an individual may be able to decrease social comparisons by having both self-compassion (Siegel, Huellemann, Hillier, & Campbell, 2020; Saeed & Sonnentag, 2018) and empathy and compassion for the individual they are comparing themselves to. For example, they can think, "What is missing from this picture? What does this person struggle with? What are their strengths and what are their weakness?" These thoughts might humanize instead of objectify the person, leading to less social comparison (Brandstätter, 2000). There are also formal media literacy programs aimed at navigating messages on social media, including ones that evoke social comparisons (Gordon et al., 2020).

Pathological Use of Social Media

Most individuals can use social media in ways that enrich and benefit their lives. However, for some, social media can become pathological in nature, interfering with the ability to function in multiple contexts. Thus, we see this type of social media use as being the most risky and problematic. This type of use is not necessarily about the content or context of social media use; rather, we view it as an unhealthy relationship that may lead to increased mental health issues.

Pathological (or addictive) social media use is characterized by addiction-like symptoms such as using media to forget about real life, feelings of withdrawal when unable to use social media, and subsequent problems in that individual's life that arise from their social media use (Lemmens, Valkenburg, & Peter, 2009). While pathological social media use is not currently recognized as a disorder (American Psychiatric Association, 2013), pathological Internet gaming is a disorder and displays symptoms similar to other behavioral addictions, such as gambling.

While pathological use of social media is not particularly common, such use tends to be strongly related to mental health problems, including depression and anxiety (Raudsepp & Kais, 2019; Stockdale & Coyne, 2020; Wartberg, Kriston, & Thomasius, 2020). However, according to the general theory of addiction, individuals with pathological tendencies typically have more unregulated behavior and are predisposed with feelings of inadequacy (Jacobs, 1986), indicating that the relationship between pathological media use and mental health may be bidirectional (Raudsepp & Kais, 2019). Pathological users of social media may be more sensitive to the effects of social comparisons (Holmgren & Coyne, 2017), and FOMO might in turn contribute to pathological social media use, encouraging impulsive and unhealthy relationships (Franchina, Vanden Abeele, Van Rooij, Lo Coco, & De Marez, 2018). Further, individuals with pathological tendencies who have poorer self-regulation skills tend to have higher levels of negative outcomes, such as depression, relational aggression, and anxiety (Holmgren & Coyne, 2017; Wartberg et al., 2020).

Because of the bidirectional relationship between emotional dysregulation and pathological social media use, many interventions focus on helping individuals increase coping skills to manage their emotional dysregulation (Pluhar, Kavanaugh, Levinson, & Rich, 2019; Raudsepp & Kais, 2019). A current popular form of therapy for pathological media use is cognitive behavior therapy (CBT), which asserts that thoughts determine feelings and aims to help individuals monitor and control their feelings by first addressing their thoughts and feelings (Dryden & Branch, 2012). While CBT is a highly suggested form of therapy, many other forms of therapy exist and may help alleviate pathological social media use and the associated negative outcomes.

Protective Contexts Surrounding Social Media and Mental Health

While some contexts of media use could be risky, other contexts are protective and seem to support a good relationship between media use and mental health.

Four of these contexts will be discussed in this chapter: active media use, reasons for getting on social media, being mindful, and prosocial behavior.

Active Social Media Use

A critical distinction when discussing the association between media use and mental health is the difference between active and passive use. Passive media use, also referred to as lurking, is characterized by simply scrolling mindlessly through social media feeds; this type of media use has been linked with increased mental health issues (Shaw, Timpano, Tran, & Joormann, 2015; Thorisdottir, Sigurvinsdottir, Asgeirsdottir, Allegrante, & Sigfusdottir, 2019; Verduyn et al., 2015). Conversely, individuals who practice active media use report having better mental health (Escobar-Viera et al., 2018; Thorisdottir et al., 2019) and social experiences, whether on media or in real life (Ng, 2019). Active media use includes commenting or liking people's posts, posting content, or purposefully checking someone's social media page for a life update. As individuals participate in active social media use, they are likely to continue in this pattern and can even develop the habit of an exploratory outlook (i.e., active use) to new social media feeds (Alloway & Alloway, 2012). Active social media use provides a protective context for media use by not only encouraging prosocial behavior on media (through comments, likes, etc.) but also safeguarding media users, since active social media users are less likely to be in risky social media situations (Ng, 2019).

Reasons for Getting on Social Media

Individuals use social media for various reasons, such as to check in on and connect with friends and family, to find information, or just because they are bored (Stockdale & Coyne, 2020). The reasons why an individual spends time using social media generally predicts their experiences. For example, social media use to alleviate boredom is associated with problematic media use – which can lead to pathological social media use (see previous section) – financial stress, anxiety, and empathy (Stockdale & Coyne, 2020). It is important to note, however, that research has not linked the reason for which someone uses social media with depression. These findings about the reasons behind social media use are likely linked to our previous discussion on active and passive media use. If someone is using social media because they are bored, it is likely that they may just endlessly scroll instead of interacting with other individuals on social media. Thus, while the reasons for why someone uses social media do not have a clear link with mental health problems, they have the potential to create either a risky or protective context for viewing media.

Being Mindful

Because of the growing body of research indicating that the way an individual uses social media significantly impacts mental health, mindfulness while using social media is also becoming an important tool to help social media users. Mindfulness is an ability that can help individuals increase their well-being by positively impacting their moment-to-moment experiences (Brown & Ryan, 2003). While anyone may get on social media for a good reason (e.g., send a message to a friend, make a quick post, active use), we all know it is easy to slip into passive use (endlessly scrolling). Mindfulness helps individuals stay aware of what they are doing and can help individuals stay active users instead of sliding into passive scrolling. For adolescents specifically, mindfulness in a variety of contexts enhances self-esteem (Tan & Martin, 2013), lowers depression (Ames et al., 2014), and helps manage anxiety (Haydicky et al., 2012).

In terms of social media, mindfulness often mediates the relationship between social media use and negative outcomes (e.g., Charoensukmongkol, 2016). As social media is often used as a mind*less* task (i.e., passive use), mindfulness can be an important tool in combating risky media contexts or problematic media use (Baker et al., 2016; Weaver & Swank, 2019). Being mindful while using social media involves consciously focusing on feelings, thoughts, and behaviors while on social media to develop increased awareness, which, in turn, helps create a protective context for viewing media (Weaver, 2019). To do this, a person could ask themselves questions such as the following: Why am I checking this site right now? What am I hoping to achieve? How am I feeling right now? How will I respond to the posts I see? (Shapiro, Carlson, Astin, & Freedman, 2006). Such questions help individuals purposefully and actively engage with social media instead of mindlessly scrolling.

Prosocial Behavior and Reaching Out

Prosocial behavior is generally described as voluntary behavior intended to benefit another person. Prosocial behavior extends not only to an individual's offline life but also to their online life. Examples of prosocial behavior on social media include users who publicly share social cause content (Chori & Seo, 2017), sign online petitions (Wilkins, Livingstone, & Levine, 2019), or establish and share fundraisers such as GoFundMe campaigns (Lavertu, Marder, Erz, & Angell, 2020). Individuals who are more prosocial in offline life are often prosocial in online life (Wright & Li, 2011). Additionally, active social media users are more likely to help family and friends on social media (Ng, 2019). Research has even determined that exposure to media with prosocial content has significant, long-term impacts on behavior because it increases the accessibility of prosocial thoughts, empathy, and helping behavior, and it decreases aggression and aggression-related cognition and affect (Coyne et al., 2018; Greitemeyer, 2011; Prot et al., 2013).

When individuals see prosocial behavior, they are more likely to in turn behave in a prosocial manner; this phenomenon also extends to social media. Thus, when social media users see or experience prosocial behavior online, they are more likely to be prosocial on social media (van Baaren, Holland, Kawakami, &

Knippenberg, 2004). Interestingly, the effects of viewing prosocial behavior on social media are linked not only to more prosocial behavior on social media but also to the individual's offline life (Lavertu et al., 2020).

Prosocial behavior on social media can create a protective context for social media users since the very act of being prosocial tends to bring about more prosocial behavior and many other positive outcomes (Coyne et al., 2018; Greitemeyer, 2011; Prot et al., 2013). Some suggestions for encouraging and increasing prosocial behavior include reaching out to friends or family you know who may be struggling (emotionally, physically, financially, etc.), creating and sharing online fundraisers for individuals in need, sharing positive and uplifting content, or even simply highlighting a loved friend or family on your social media page. These suggestions will help individuals get the "prosocial ball" rolling and help themselves and others create a positive context for social media use.

Future Directions and Limitations to the Field

There are several limitations to the existing literature on social media and mental health. Here, we focus on three major limitations and discuss possibilities for future research.

One major limitation of the field involves the methodology. Most studies use a self-report (often single item) measure to examine the time spent on social media. This measure is subject to some individual bias and tends to be only moderately accurate as a measure of social media use on the whole (Andrews, Ellis, Shaw, & Piwek, 2015; Lin et al., 2015). Additionally, most research is cross-sectional in nature, making directionality of effects difficult to identify. A few studies have started to use passive sensing apps to capture real-time social media use (Coyne et al., 2021; Radesky et al., 2020). This technology allows for an objective and accurate measure of social media use, increasing the methodological rigor of the research. However, these apps do not typically capture the content nor the context of the social media use, leading researchers to rely on self-report measures. Coding participant social media is time intensive and difficult because the context is subtle and often unknown to the researcher. Some studies have used data mining techniques to code content or general themes in social media (e.g., Husain, 2019; Seabrook, Kern, Fulcher, & Rickard, 2018), though this approach does not reach the level of complexity needed to accurately code social media experiences. Other research has utilized experience sampling methods to examine the impact of social media (Valkenburg, Beyens, Pouwels, van Driel, & Keijsers, 2021). This type of research is self-reported, so it is still subject to some bias but is often captured in the moment, leading to greater reliability. Overall, we urge researchers to recognize the bias that exists in this field and continue to innovate new ways to capture both the content and context surrounding social media experiences.

Another limitation in this field is assuming homogeneity among participants. The earlier sections examined some risky and protective factors involving social media that may move us beyond the screen time debate. While we recognize these practices as generally risky or protective, many scholars understand that media may have a differential effect on the individual user, though little research examines person-specific effects of social media use on mental health (Fikkers & Piotrowski, 2020; Valkenburg, Peter, & Walther, 2016). Theoretically, the differential susceptibility hypothesis (Valkenburg & Peter, 2013) suggests that social media may have a differential effect on adolescents or young adults given differences in personality, family background, physiology, personal history, situational factors, and so forth. Indeed, most media research on mental health shows limited effects; however, qualitative research suggests that media has a profound impact on certain individuals (Rideout & Fox, 2018). Indeed, there have been several news reports of individuals who have attempted suicide or have reported feeling extremely depressed or despondent as a result of their experiences with social media. While this type of response is not the norm, these experiences do exist and should not be minimized.

Research that focuses on group-level (or between subjects) effects may lose out on some of the individualized effects of social media. Instead, research should assume participant heterogeneity and utilize advanced statistics to understand who in particular might be at risk for having negative interactions over social media. As one example, Valkenburg et al. (2021) utilized experience sampling methods to examine daily social media use and self-esteem over a three-week period. They found that the majority of adolescents (88%) reported minimal effects of social media use on their self-esteem. This finding likely confirms much of the literature that shows very small or no effects of social media on mental health (e.g., Coyne et al., 2020). However, 4% of adolescents experienced positive effects while 8% experienced negative effects. The time spent on social media did not dramatically differ between groups; however, the experience did. It is these groups showing either positive or negative effects that researchers should continue to focus on. What types of experiences do these groups have on social media? What personal characteristics might account for the differences in experience? How might focusing on person-centered research advance our thinking about differential effects of social media on mental health? We hope that researchers continue to examine these types of person-specific effects over time to understand who is most at risk for negative outcomes with certain types of social media use.

A final limitation of the literature is the lack of media literacy programs available to parents and educators. The literature suggests that certain types of social media use might have differential effects on adolescents' mental health. However, formal media literacy programs focusing on how to educate youth on healthy social media use and empower parents to teach children good strategies are extremely rare. A few existing programs have been tested (e.g., Gordon et al., 2020); however, these programs are infrequently used in schools. Indeed, we were surprised to find that few media literacy programs focused specifically on social media and mental health, given the large amount of literature that has now explored these topics. We also note that most schools do not have formal media literacy programs focused on media and mental health. Instead, schools may have one or two lectures on the topic whereas a sustained and steady stream of media literacy education is warranted given the amount of time youth spend using media. So few formal media literacy programs exist likely because of a lack of government funding and a lack of research, training of key personnel, and implementation of programs in schools (NAMLE, 2019). We envision that these programs would focus on context and content of use instead of time, would focus on individual user characteristics, and be able to identify those youth most at risk and who would benefit from intervention efforts. We have attempted to create some free resources for parents and schools to use based on some of the research we discussed in this chapter (Coyne, 2021); however, notably, these resources have not been subjected to formal media literacy research testing on their effectiveness. We hope future researchers continue to explore ways of helping families raise media-healthy youth and recognize that formal education may play a large role in healthy media development.

Conclusion

The research on social media and mental health is mixed and filled with inconsistencies and methodological issues. However, a growing body of research suggests that certain types of social media use might be risky for the development of mental health problems for certain types of people. Conversely, social media can also be protective for some individuals, depending on the way it is used by the individual. Thus, this field is incredibly nuanced, and scholars, parents, and practitioners should pay careful attention to contextual and individual factors instead of making broad, sweeping statements about the impact of social media. Solutions suggesting that parents simply tell children to "put down their phones" or to "reduce screen time" run rampant, but they will likely not be effective in solving this particular mental health crisis. Instead, the best way forward may be a careful analysis of the ways in which youth use social media as well as particular attention to personal susceptibility.

References

Alloway, T., & Alloway, R. (2012). The impact of engagement with social networking sites (SNSs) on cognitive skills. *Computers in Human Behavior, 28*(5), 1748–1754. https://doi.org/10.1016/j.chb.2012.04.015

Altuwairiqi, M., Jiang, N., & Ali, R. (2019). Problematic attachment to social media: Five behavioural archetypes. *International Journal of Environmental Research and Public Health, 16*(12), 2136. https://doi.org/10.3390/ijerph16122136

Alutaybi, A., Al-Thani, D., McAlaney, J., & Ali, R. (2020). Combating fear of missing out (FoMO) on social media: The FoMO-R method. *International Journal of Environmental Research and Public Health, 17*(17), 6128. https://doi.org/10.3390/ijerph17176128

American Foundation for Suicide Prevention. (2020). *Suicide statistics.* Retrieved from https://afsp.org/suicide-statistics/

American Psychiatric Association. (2013). *Diagnostic and statistical manual of mental disorders* (5th ed.). https://doi.org/10.1176/appi.books.9780890425596

Ames, C. S., Richardson, J., Payne, S., Smith, P., & Leigh, E. (2014). Mindfulness-based cognitive therapy for depression in adolescents. *Child and Adolescent Mental Health, 19*(1), 74–78. https://doi.org/10.1111/camh.12034

Andrews, S., Ellis, D. A., Shaw, H., & Piwek, L. (2015). Beyond self-report: Tools to compare estimated and real-world smartphone use. *PLoS One, 10*(10), Article e0139004. https://doi.org/10.1371/journal.pone.0139004

Appel, M., Marker, C., & Gnambs, T. (2020). Are social media ruining our lives? A review of meta-analytic evidence. *Review of General Psychology, 24*(1), 60–74. https://doi.org/10.1177/1089268019880891

Baker, Z. G., Krieger, H., & LeRoy, A. S. (2016). Fear of missing out: Relationships with depression, mindfulness, and physical symptoms. *Translational Issues in Psychological Science, 2*(3), 275–282. https://psycnet.apa.org/doi/10.1037/tps0000075

Balta, S., Emirtekin, E., Kircaburun, K., & Griffiths, M. D. (2020). Neuroticism, trait fear of missing out, and phubbing: The mediating role of state fear of missing out and problematic Instagram use. *International Journal of Mental Health and Addiction, 18*(3), 628–639. https://doi.org/10.1007/s11469-018-9959-8

Banjanin, N., Banjanin, N., Dimitrijevic, I., & Pantic, I. (2015). Relationship between internet use and depression: Focus on physiological mood oscillations, social networking and online addictive behavior. *Computers in Human Behavior, 43*, 308–312. https://doi.org/10.1016/j.chb.2014.11.013

Barry, C. T., Sidoti, C. L., Briggs, S. M., Reiter, S. R., & Lindsey, R. A. (2017). Adolescent social media use and mental health from adolescent and parent perspectives. *Journal of Adolescence, 61*, 1–11. https://doi.org/10.1016/j.adolescence.2017.08.005

Bartel, K., Scheeren, R., & Gradisar, M. (2019). Altering adolescents' pre-bedtime phone use to achieve better sleep health. *Health Communication, 34*(4), 456–462. https://doi.org/10.1080/10410236.2017.1422099

Brandstätter, E. (2000). Comparison based satisfaction: Contrast and empathy. *European Journal of Social Psychology, 30*(5), 673–703. https://doi.org/10.1002/1099-0992(200009/10)30:5<673::AID-EJSP14>3.0.CO;2-D

Brown, K. W., & Ryan, R. M. (2003). The benefits of being present: Mindfulness and its role in psychological well-being. *Journal of Personality and Social Psychology, 84*, 822–848. https://doi.org/10.1037/0022-3514.84.4.822

Brunstein Klomek, A., Barzilay, S., Apter, A., Carli, V., Hoven, C. W., Sarchiapone, M., . . . Wasserman, D. (2019). Bi-directional longitudinal associations between different types of bullying victimization, suicide ideation/attempts, and depression among a large sample of European adolescents. *Journal of Child Psychology and Psychiatry, 60*(2), 209–215. https://doi.org/10.1111/jcpp.12951

Charles, S. (2019). Social media linked to rise in mental health disorders. *NBC News*. Retrieved from www.nbcnews.com/health/mental-health/social-media-linked-rise-mental-health-disorders-teens-survey-finds-n982526

Charoensukmongkol, P. (2016). Mindful Facebooking: The moderating role of mindfulness on the relationship between social media use intensity at work and burnout. *Journal of Health Psychology, 21*(9), 1966–1980. https://doi.org/10.1177/1359105315569096

Chori, J., & Seo, S. (2017). Goodwill intended for whom? Examining factors influencing conspicuous prosocial behavior on social media. *International Journal of Hospitality Management, 60*, 23–32. https://doi.org/10.1016/j.ijhm.2016.09.014

Coyne, S. M. (2021). *Social media curriculum*. Retrieved from http://sarahmcoyne.com/resources/

Coyne, S. M., Hurst, J. L., Dyer, W. J., Hunt, Q., Schvaneveldt, E., Brown, S., & Jones, G. (2021). Suicide risk in emerging adulthood: Associations with screen time over 10 years. *Journal of Youth and Adolescence*. https://doi.org/10.1007/s10964-020-01389-6

Coyne, S. M., Padilla-Walker, L., Holmgren, H., Davis, E., Collier, K., Memmott-Elison, M., & Hawkins, A. (2018). A meta-analysis of prosocial media on prosocial behavior, aggression, and empathic concern: A multidimensional approach. *Developmental Psychology*, *54*(2), 331–347. https://doi.apa.org/doi/10.1037/dev0000412

Coyne, S. M., Rogers, A. A., Zurcher, J. D., Stockdale, L., & Booth, M. (2020). Does time spent using social media impact mental health? An eight year longitudinal study. *Computers in Human Behavior*, *104*, 106160. https://doi.org/10.1016/j.chb.2019.106160

Dorrian, J., Centofanti, S., Wicking, A., Wicking, P., & Lushington, K. (2018). 0255 Smartphones in the bedroom, sleep, communication, and mental health in Australian school students. *Sleep*, *41*, A99. https://doi.org/10.1093/sleep/zsy061.254

Dryden, W., & Branch, R. (2012). *The CBT handbook*. London: SAGE Publications.

Escobar-Viera, C. G., Shensa, A., Bowman, N. D., Sidani, J. E., Knight, J., James, A. E., & Primack, B. A. (2018). Passive and active social media use and depressive symptoms among United States adults. *Cyberpsychology, Behavior, and Social Networking*, *21*(7), 437–443. https://doi.org/10.1089/cyber.2017.0668

Exelmans, L., & Van den Bulck, J. (2017). Bedtime, shut eye time and electronic media: Sleep displacement is a two-step process. *Journal of Sleep Research*, *26*(3), 364–370. https://doi.org/10.1111/jsr.12510

Festinger, L. (1954). A theory of social comparison processes. *Human Relations*, *7*(2), 117–140. https://doi.org/10.1177/001872675400700202

Fikkers, K. M., & Piotrowski, J. T. (2020). Content and person effects in media research: Studying differences in cognitive, emotional, and arousal responses to media content. *Media Psychology*, *23*(4), 493–520. https://doi.org/10.1080/15213269.2019.1608257

Franchina, V., Vanden Abeele, M., Van Rooij, A. J., Lo Coco, G., & De Marez, L. (2018). Fear of missing out as a predictor of problematic social media use and phubbing behavior among Flemish adolescents. *International Journal of Environmental Research and Public Health*, *15*(10), 2319. https://doi.org/10.3390/ijerph15102319

Gordon, C. S., Rodgers, R. F., Slater, A. E., McLean, S. A., Jarman, H. K., & Paxton, S. J. (2020). A cluster randomized controlled trial of the SoMe social media literacy body image and wellbeing program for adolescent boys and girls: Study protocol. *Body Image*, *33*, 27–37. https://doi.org/10.1016/j.bodyim.2020.02.003

Gore, S., & Eckenrode, J. (1996). Context and process in research on risk and resilience. In R. J. Haggerty, L. R. Sherrod, N. Garmezy, & M. Rutter (Eds.), *Stress, risk, and resilience in children and adolescents: Processes, mechanisms, and interventions* (pp. 19–63). Cambridge University Press.

Greitemeyer, T. (2011). Effects of prosocial media on social behavior: When and why does media exposure affect helping and aggression? *Psychological Science*, *20*(4). https://doi.org/10.1177/0963721411415229

Harris, E., & Bardey, A. C. (2019). Do Instagram profiles accurately portray personality? An investigation into idealized online self-presentation. *Frontiers in Psychology*, *10*, 871. https://doi.org/10.3389/fpsyg.2019.00871

Haydicky, J., Wiener, J., Badali, P., Milligan, K., & Ducharme, J. M. (2012). Evaluation of a mindfulness-based intervention for adolescents with learning disabilities and co-occurring ADHD and anxiety. *Mindfulness*, *3*, 151–164. https://doi.org/10.1007/s12671-012-0089-2

Heron, M. (2019, June 24). Deaths: Leading causes for 2017. *National Vital Statistics Reports*, *68*(6), 17. www.cdc.gov/nchs/data/nvsr/nvsr68/nvsr68_06-508.pdf

Holmgren, H., & Coyne, S. (2017). Can't stop scrolling! Pathological use of social networking sites in emerging adulthood. *Addiction Research & Theory*, *25*(5), 375–382. https://doi.org/10.1080/16066359.2017.1294164

Huang, C. (2018). Time spent on social networking sites and psychological well-being: A meta-analysis. *Cyberpsychology, Behavior, and Social Networking*, *20*, 346–354. https://doi.org/10.1089/cyber.2016.0758

Hunt, M. G., Marx, R., Lipson, C., & Young, J. (2018). No more FOMO: Limiting social media decreases loneliness and depression. *Journal of Social and Clinical Psychology*, *37*(10), 751–768. https://doi.org/10.1521/jscp.2018.37.10.751

Husain, M. S. (2019). Social media analytics to predict depression level in the users. In S. Paul, P. Bhattacharya, & A. Bit (Eds.), *Early detection of neurological disorders using machine learning systems* (pp. 199–215). Medical Information Science Reference/IGI Global. https://doi.org/10.4018/978-1-5225-8567-1.ch011

Jacobs, D. F. (1986). A general theory of addictions: A new theoretical model. *Journal of Gambling Behavior*, *2*(15), 15–31. https://doi.org/10.1007/BF01019931

Joiner, T. E. (2005). *Why people die by suicide*. Cambridge, MA: Harvard University Press.

Kreski, N., Platt, J., Rutherford, C., Odgers, C., Schulenberg, J., & Keyes, K. (2020). Social media use and depressive symptoms among United States adolescents. *Journal of Adolescent Health*, *68*(3), 572–579. https://doi.org/10.1016/j.jadohealth.2020.07.006

Lavertu, L., Marder, B., Erz, A., & Angell, R. (2020). The extended warming effect of social media: Examining whether the cognition of online audiences offline drives prosocial behavior in 'real life.' *Computers in Human Behavior*, *110*. https://doi.org/10.1016/j.chb.2020.106389

Lemmens, J. S., Valkenburg, P. M., & Peter, J. (2009). Development and validation of a game addiction scale for adolescents. *Media Psychology*, *12*(1), 77–95. https://doi.org/10.1080/15213260802669458

Lin, Y.-H., Lin, Y.-C., Lee, Y.-H., Lin, P.-H., Lin, S.-H., Chang, L.-R., . . . Kuo, T. B. J. (2015). Time distortion associated with smartphone addiction: Identifying smartphone addiction via a mobile application (app). *Journal of Psychiatric Research*, *65*, 139–145. https://doi.org/10.1016/j.jpsychires.2015.04.003

McCarthy, P. A., & Morina, N. (2020). Exploring the association of social comparison with depression and anxiety: A systematic review and meta-analysis. *Clinical Psychology & Psychotherapy*, *27*, 640–671. https://doi.org/10.1002/cpp.2452

Meier, A., & Reinecke, L. (2020). Computer-mediated communication, social media, and mental health: A conceptual and empirical meta-review. *Communication Research*, 1–28. https://doi.org/10.1177/0093650220958224

Memon, A., Sharma, S., Mohite, S., & Jain, S. (2018). The role of online social networking on deliberate self-harm and suicide risk in adolescents: A systemized review of literature. *Indian Journal of Psychiatry*, *60*(4), 384–392. https://pubmed.ncbi.nlm.nih.gov/30581202/

NAMLE. (2019). *State of media literacy report*. Retrieved from https://namle.net/state-of-media-literacy-report/

Ng, Y. (2019). Active and passive Facebook use and associated costly off-line helping behavior. *Psychology Reports*, *123*(6), 2562–2581. https://doi.org/10.1177/0033294119860262

Orben, A., & Przybylski, A. (2019). The association between adolescent well-being and digital technology use. *Nature Human Behavior, 3*, 173–182. https://doi.org/10.1038/s41562-018-0506-1

Oshima, N., Nishida, A., Shimodera, S., Tochigi, M., Ando, S., Yamasaki, S., . . . Sasaki, T. (2012). The suicidal feelings, self-injury, and mobile phone use after lights out in adolescents. *Journal of Pediatric Psychology, 37*(9), 1023–1030. https://doi.org/10.1093/jpepsy/jss072

Pluhar, E., Kavanaugh, J., Levinson, J., & Rich, M. (2019). Problematic interactive media use in teens: Comorbidities, assessment, and treatment. *Psychology Research and Behavior Management, 12*, 447–455. https://doi.org/10.2147/PRBM.S208968

Prot, S., Gentile, D., Anderson, C., Suzuki, K., Swing, E., Lim, K. M., . . . Lam, B. C. P. (2013). Long-term relations among prosocial-media use, empathy, and prosocial behavior. *Psychological Science, 25*(2), 358–368. https://doi.org/10.1177/0956797613503854

Przybylski, A. K., Murayama, K., DeHaan, C. R., & Gladwell, V. (2013). Motivational, emotional, and behavioral correlates of fear of missing out. *Computers in Human Behavior, 29*(4), 1841–1848. https://doi.org/10.1016/j.chb.2013.02.014

Radesky, J., Weeks, H. M., Ball, R., Schaller, A., Yeo, S., Durnez, J., . . . Barr, R. (2020). Young children's use of smartphones and tablets. *Pediatrics, 146*, Article e20193518. https://doi.org/10.1542/peds.2019-3518

Raudsepp, L., & Kais, K. (2019). Longitudinal associations between problematic social media use and depressive symptoms in adolescent girls. *Preventive Medicine Reports, 15*, 100925. https://doi.org/10.1016/j.pmedr.2019.100925

Reynolds, C. F., III, & O'Hara, R. (2013). DSM-5 sleep-wake disorders classification: Overview for use in clinical practice. *American Journal of Psychiatry, 170*(10), 1099–1101. https://doi.org/10.1176/appi.ajp.2013.13010058

Rideout, V., & Fox, S. (2018). Digital health practices, social media use, and mental well-being among teens and young adults in the U.S. *Articles, Abstracts, and Reports*, 1093. Retrieved from https://digitalcommons.psjhealth.org/publications/1093

Robinson, A., Bonnette, A., Howard, K., Ceballos, N., Dailey, S., Lu, Y., & Grimes, T. (2019). Social comparisons, social media addiction, and social interaction: An examination of specific social media behaviors related to major depressive disorder in a millennial population. *Journal of Applied Biobehavioral Research, 24*(1), Article e12158. https://doi.org/10.1111/jabr.12158

Rudolph, K. D. (2002). Gender differences in emotional responses to interpersonal stress during adolescence. *Journal of Adolescent Health, 30*(4), 3–13. https://doi.org/10.1016/s1054-139x(01)00383-4

Saeed, Z., & Sonnentag, T. L. (2018). Role of self-compassion on college students' social self-evaluations and affect across two domains [Special issue]. *Psi Chi Journal of Psychological Research, 23*(2), 132–141. https://doi.org/10.24839/2325-7342.JN23.2.132

Scott, H., & Woods, H. C. (2018). Fear of missing out and sleep: Cognitive behavioural factors in adolescents' nighttime social media use. *Journal of Adolescence, 68*, 61–65. https://doi.org/10.1016/j.adolescence.2018.07.009

Scott, H., & Woods, H. C. (2019). Understanding links between social media use, sleep and mental health: Recent progress and current challenges. *Current Sleep Medicine Reports, 5*(3), 141–149. https://doi.org/10.1007/s40675-019-00148-9

Seabrook, E. M., Kern, M. L., Fulcher, B. D., & Rickard, N. S. (2018). Predicting depression from language-based emotion dynamics: Longitudinal analysis of Facebook and Twitter status updates. *Journal of Medical Internet Research, 20*(5), Article e168. https://doi.org/10.2196/jmir.9267

Shapiro, S. L., Carlson, L. E., Astin, J. A., & Freedman, B. (2006). Mechanisms of mindfulness. *Journal of Clinical Psychology*, *62*, 373–386. doi:10.1037/11885-007

Shaw, A., Timpano, K., Tran, T., & Joormann, J. (2015). Correlates of Facebook usage patterns: The relationship between passive Facebook use, social anxiety symptoms, and brooding. *Computers in Human Behavior*, *48*, 575–580. https://doi.org/10.1016/j.chb.2015.02.003

Shimoga, S. V., Erlyana, E., & Rebello, V. (2019). Associations of social media use with physical activity and sleep adequacy among adolescents: Cross-sectional survey. *Journal of Medical Internet Research*, *21*(6), Article e14290. https://doi.org/10.2196/14290

Siegel, J. A., Huellemann, K. L., Hillier, C. C., & Campbell, L. (2020). The protective role of self-compassion for women's positive body image: An open replication and extension. *Body Image*, *32*, 136 144. https://doi.org/10.1016/j.bodyim.2019.12.003

Stockdale, L. A., & Coyne, S. M. (2020). Bored and online: Reasons for using social media, problematic social networking site use, and behavioral outcomes across the transition from adolescence to emerging adulthood. *Journal of Adolescence*, *79*, 173–183. https://doi.org/10.1016/j.adolescence.2020.01.010

Tan, L., & Martin, G. (2013). Taming the adolescent mind: Preliminary report of a mindfulness-based psychological intervention for adolescents with clinical heterogeneous mental health diagnoses. *Clinical Child Psychology and Psychiatry*, *18*, 300–312. https://doi.org/10.1177/1359104512455182

Thorisdottir, I., Sigurvinsdottir, R., Asgeirsdottir, B., Allegrante, J., & Sigfusdottir, I. (2019). Active and passive social media use and symptoms of anxiety and depressed mood among Icelandic adolescents. *Cyberpsychology, Behavior, and Social Networking*, *22*(6), 535–542. https://doi.org/10.1089/cyber.2019.0079

Tiggemann, M., & Anderberg, I. (2020). Social media is not real: The effect of 'Instagram vs reality' images on women's social comparison and body image. *New Media & Society*, *22*(12), 2183–2199. https://doi.org/10.1177/1461444819888720

Twenge, J. M. (2017a, September). Have smartphones destroyed a generation? *The Atlantic*. Retrieved from www.theatlantic.com/magazine/archive/2017/09/has-the-smartphone-destroyed-a-generation/534198/

Twenge, J. M. (2017b). *IGen: Why today's super-connected kids are growing up less rebellious, more tolerant, less happy – and completely unprepared for adulthood – and what that means for the rest of us*. New York: Simon and Schuster.

Twenge, J. M., Joiner, T. E., Rogers, M. L., & Martin, G. N. (2018). Increases in depressive symptoms, suicide-related outcomes, and suicide rates among US adolescents after 2010 and links to increased new media screen time. *Clinical Psychological Science*, *6*(1), 3–17. https://doi.org/10.1177/2167702617723376

Twenge, J. M., Martin, G. N., & Campbell, W. K. (2018). Decreases in psychological well-being among American adolescents after 2012 and links to screen time during the rise of smartphone technology. *Emotion*, *18*(6), 765–780. https://doi.org/10.1037/emo0000403

Vahedi, Z., & Zannella, L. (2019). The association between self-reported depressive symptoms and the use of social networking sites (SNS): A meta-analysis. *Current Psychology*, 1–16. https://doi.org/10.1007/s12144-019-0150-6

Valkenburg, P. M., Beyens, I., Pouwels, J. L., van Driel, I. I., & Keijsers, L. (2021). *Social media use and adolescents' self-esteem: Heading for a person-specific media effects paradigm* (Unpublished manuscript).

Valkenburg, P. M., & Peter, J. (2013). The differential susceptibility to media effects model. *Journal of Communication*, *63*(2), 221–243. https://doi.org/10.1111/jcom.12024

Valkenburg, P. M., Peter, J., & Walther, J. B. (2016). Media effects: Theory and research. *Annual Review of Psychology*, *67*, 315–338. https://doi.org/10.1146/annurev-psych-122414-033608

van Baaren, R., Holland, R., Kawakami, K., & Knippenberg, A. (2004). Mimicry and prosocial behavior. *Psychological Science*, *15*(1), 71–74. https://doi.org/10.1111/j.0963-7214.2004.01501012.x

Van den Bulck, J. (2003). Text messaging as a cause of sleep interruption in adolescents, evidence from a cross-sectional study. *Journal of Sleep Research*, *12*(3), 263–263. https://doi.org/10.1046/j.1365-2869.2003.00362.x

Verduyn, P., Lee, D., Park, J., Shablack, H., Orvell, A., Bayer, J., . . . Kross, E. (2015). Passive Facebook usage undermines affective well-being: Experimental and longitudinal evidence. *Journal of Experimental Psychology*, *144*(2), 480–488. http://dx.doi.org/10.1037/xge0000057480

Vernon, L., Modecki, K. L., & Barber, B. L. (2018). Mobile phones in the bedroom: Trajectories of sleep habits and subsequent adolescent psychosocial development. *Child Development*, *89*(1), 66–77. https://doi.org/10.1111/cdev.12836

Viner, R. M., Aswathikutty-Gireesh, A., Stiglic, N., Hudson, L. D., Goddings, A. L., Ward, J. L., & Nicholls, D. E. (2019). Roles of cyberbullying, sleep, and physical activity in mediating the effects of social media use on mental health and wellbeing among young people in England: A secondary analysis of longitudinal data. *The Lancet Child & Adolescent Health*, *3*(10), 685–696. https://doi.org/10.1016/s2352-4642(19)30186-5

Wang, W., Wang, M., Hu, Q., Wang, P., Lei, L., & Jiang, S. (2020). Upward social comparison on mobile social media and depression: The mediating role of envy and the moderating role of marital quality. *Journal of Affective Disorders*, *270*, 143–149. https://doi.org/10.1016/j.jad.2020.03.173

Wang, X. T., Yi, Z., Kang, V., Xue, B., Kang, N., Brewer, G., & Ming, X. (2017). Messaging affects sleep and school performance in Chinese adolescents. *Health Behavior and Policy Review*, *4*, 60–66. https://doi.org/10.14485/HBPR.4.1.7

Wartberg, L., Kriston, L., & Thomasius, R. (2020). Internet gaming disorder and problematic social media use in a representative sample of German adolescents: Prevalence estimates, comorbid depressive symptoms and related psychosocial aspects. *Computers in Human Behavior*, *103*, 31–36. https://doi.org/10.1016/j.chb.2019.09.014

Weaver, J. L., & Swank, J. M. (2019). Mindful connections: A mindfulness-based intervention for adolescent social media users. *Journal of Child and Adolescent Counseling*, *5*(2), 103–112. https://doi.org/10.1080/23727810.2019.1586419

Wilkins, D., Livingstone, A., & Levine, M. (2019). All click, no action? Online action, efficacy perceptions, and prior experience combine to affect future collective action. *Computers in Human Behavior*, *91*, 97–105. https://doi.org/10.1016/j.chb.2018.09.007

Woods, H. C., & Scott, H. (2016). #Sleepyteens: Social media use in adolescence is associated with poor sleep quality, anxiety, depression and low self-esteem. *Journal of Adolescence*, *51*, 41–49. https://doi.org/10.1016/j.adolescence.2016.05.008

Wright, M., & Li, Y. (2011). The associations between young adults' face-to-face prosocial behaviors and their online prosocial behaviors. *Computers in Human Behavior*, *27*(5), 1959–1962. https://doi.org/10.1177/0963721411415229

Yin, X. Q., de Vries, D. A., Gentile, D. A., & Wang, J. L. (2019). Cultural background and measurement of usage moderate the association between social networking sites

(SNSs) usage and mental health: A meta-analysis. *Social Science Computer Review, 37*(5), 631–648. https://doi.org/10.1177/0894439318784908

Yoon, S., Kleinman, M., Mertz, J., & Brannick, M. (2019). Is social network site usage related to depression? A meta-analysis of Facebook – depression relations. *Journal of Affective Disorders, 248*, 65–72. https://doi.org/10.1016/j.jad.2019.01.026

11

ADOLESCENT SOCIAL MEDIA USE AND MENTAL HEALTH

A Personal Social Media Use Framework

Drew P. Cingel, Michael C. Carter,
and Lauren B. Taylor

The impact of social media on the health and development of young people has been a primary area of interest and concern among adolescents, parents, clinicians, health practitioners, and policy makers alike since their widespread development and adoption in the past two decades. Although many studies consider samples of young adults and older adults, researchers have focused specifically on adolescents due to their unique stage of development and because anxiety, depression, and stress are prevalent among this group (Mojtabai, Olfson, & Han, 2016). Although there exists a large body of research considering the relationships between adolescent social media use and well-being, research pursuits remain ongoing. Indeed, as social media as a phenomenon have changed over time, efforts to study social media have changed as well, albeit more slowly (see Beyens, Pouwels, van Driel, Keijsers, & Valkenburg, 2020). For instance, it is still largely unknown how, if, when, and for whom social media benefits or harms adolescent users' psychological health (Odgers & Jensen, 2020; Prinstein, Nesi, & Telzer, 2020). This is due to near-constant changes in the social media landscape, similarities and differences between social media platforms, individual differences among users, and varying measurement of social media use by researchers. Nevertheless, a great deal of progress has been made in recent years, and a strong foundation exists for the study of social media and adolescent mental health.

While social media's rapid maturation and proliferation have subverted clear distinctions between what is and is not social media (boyd & Ellison, 2013), recent conceptual perspectives have begun to view social media in terms of a digital ecosystem or ecology (Bayer, Triệu, & Ellison, 2020; Nesi, Choukas-Bradley, & Prinstein, 2018) that is user-centric (DeVito, Walker, & Birnholtz, 2018), made up of a variety of ubiquitous elements (e.g., profiles, networks; Bayer et al., 2020), and is embedded within technological systems (e.g., devices; Meier & Reinecke,

DOI: 10.4324/9781003171270-11

2020) and individuals' broader offline environments (Valkenburg & Peters, 2013). Such conceptual advancements have led to shifts in the measure of social media use (e.g., multiple vs. single platform studies; a focus on social media elements to generalize effects to later iterations of social media) and can serve as an organizing structure to evaluate social media's influence among adolescents. This is particularly important, given the breadth and depth of research pertaining to the association between social media and adolescent mental health and well-being. For instance, when reviewing this research domain, scholars often note different patterns of relationships between the same variables across studies (e.g., Cingel & Olsen, 2018) which may come as a function of changes in the social media landscape across time or due to differences in social media measurement and its conceptualization (e.g., overall time spent on social media; time spent specifically on Instagram; active compared to passive use). Indeed, the varying conceptual and operational definition of social media across studies has been noted as a significant limitation toward assessing social media use's impact on adolescents' mental health in a number of recent reviews (Valkenburg, Beyens, van Driel, & Keijsers, 2021).

The Personal Social Media Ecosystem Framework

As a result, one way to sort and contextualize the existing literature is to organize social media use and mental health effects research among adolescents in line with the Personal Social Media Ecosystem Framework (PSMEF), which we extend here from an initial conceptualization of personal social media ecosystems (PSMEs) (DeVito et al., 2018). DeVito and colleagues (2018) originally defined PSMEs as user-specific digital ecosystems made up of unique audiences, norms, features, and affordances spread across the social media apps people use. To build on the concept, the PSMEF re-explicates PSMEs as a set of interrelated, networked, and nested *digital settings* (i.e., user interfaces on live social media apps) that are embedded within a broader ecology of environmental systems (e.g., the Internet). In this way, this framework assumes that audiences, norms, features, affordances, and social media effects can exist at different levels of social media as an environmental system but fundamentally at the level of digital settings (e.g., specific profiles). Further, it proposes that *social media elements*, or contextually transcendent components over social media applications (Bayer et al., 2020), serve as particular types of digital setting themselves (e.g., profiles generally). In this way, the PSMEF formally integrates the concept of social media elements to PSMEs and proposes that PSMEs represent a user-centric set of nested and networked digital environments that can span across multiple social media applications. Thus, all the digital settings youth navigate to and/or engage in over social media applications collectively constitute their PSME.

The general structure of the PSMEF provides a way to organize literature on social media effects as they map onto particular dimensions of adolescents' social media environment based on how social media use is assessed by a given study (e.g., averaged social media use metrics at the platform level). Organizing extant social media use and effects research as it relates to adolescents' health and development in this way should then help to highlight current findings as they provide insight into the role of social media in the lives of contemporary adolescents in a generalizable way. Focusing on social media elements will help to map social media effects to later iterations of social media environments in their use of particular social media elements (Bayer et al., 2020). Thus, there is a theoretical rationale to compare seemingly ubiquitous social media elements and a means to study other ubiquitous social media components.

For instance, since posts inter-networked in users' For You Page and Following Page on TikTok (two different *user-generated content streams* embedded in the *TikTok Home page*) share the same underlying features and affordances, it is possible to make theoretically valid comparisons across these content streams as a type of social media element on the application. Further, conceptualizing social media in terms of digital sub-settings subordinate to the application and superordinate to features accommodates platforms' adoption of seemingly ubiquitous social media content environments (e.g., *tiktoks* on TikTok, *reels* on Instagram, and *shorts* on YouTube) because, as digital settings, they largely share the same core underlying structural components (e.g., user-generated short videos [i.e., shorts]). They, among other groupings of digital settings (e.g., stories), represent a type of generalizable social media environment that can extend on the concept of social media elements.

In the following section, we review the importance of studying mental health outcomes among adolescents during a critical developmental period. Later, we examine literature assessing the impact of social media use, as assessed by measures mapping onto particular facets of social media as an environment, on adolescents' mental disorders to complement recent reviews focusing on the topic more generally (e.g., self-esteem; Valkenburg et al., 2021). Also, we focus our review on research pertaining to participants aged 10–18 to be able to draw conclusions on adolescents and not emerging adults due to differences in development. We then conclude by highlighting key work in this literature more broadly (e.g., problematic social media use, person-specific social media effects). Given the breadth of this research area, and the number of individual variables that could relate to an individual's mental health, we focus this review on clinical mental disorders, including depression, anxiety, and eating disorders.

Adolescent Development, Mental Disorders, and Social Media Use

Adolescence is a stage of development that begins with puberty and ends when individuals make the transition into adult roles – often thought of as beginning around the age of ten and lasting until the late teens/early twenties (Steinberg, 2016), although other scholars consider the late teens and early twenties to be the developmental period of emerging adulthood (ages 18–25; Arnett, 2000, 2007). During this time, adolescents enter a phase of secondary socialization and begin to explore interpersonal relationships beyond those with family members. This individuation process also occurs during this pivotal time to encourage exploration of interpersonal relationships and how to act in society at large (e.g., Levine, Green, & Millon, 1986; Allison & Sabatelli, 1988). The individuation process centers on the idea that adolescents must move away from childhood notions of the parent–child relationship in order to assert a separate identity and foster relationships beyond those with their parents (Blos, 1967; Kroger, 1985). Concomitant with this development, adolescence is also associated with the emergence of mental health concerns and mental disorders.

Mental health refers to the "successful performance of mental function, resulting in productive activities, fulfilling relationships with other people, and the ability to change and to cope with adversity" (U.S. Department of Health and Human Services, 1999, p. 21). Common mental disorders include depression, anxiety, and disordered eating. Scholars have long investigated mental disorders during the developmental period of adolescence. This is because research has suggested that at least half of mental disorders diagnosed during adulthood begin during adolescence (Knopf, Park, & Mulye, 2008), and this increase over the course of adolescence (e.g., Green & Horton, 1982; Petersen & Hamburg, 1986), although it is important to note that large percentages of adolescents do not experience mental health concerns during this time.

One aspect of adolescent development clearly tied to an individual's mental health is social connection and interaction. Indeed, researchers have identified adolescence as a critical period for social interaction, particularly with peers (Blakemore & Mills, 2014). It is not just time spent with peers that is of vital importance, however, as multiple research studies show that social approval is increasingly important (de Goede, Branje, & Meeus, 2009). Thus, it is perhaps not surprising that a lack of social approval, or the experience of social rejection, is associated with mental disorders among adolescence, including depression (Arseneault, 2018).

In addition to the emergence of mental health concerns and mental disorders, adolescence serves also as a period for the emergence of social media use behaviors. Adolescents have long been among the earliest adopters of emerging media, particularly social media (Auxier & Anderson, 2021), and most adolescents currently have at least one active social media account and spend multiple hours each day using social media (Rideout & Robb, 2019). The majority of this use is social in nature (Anderson & Jiang, 2018), which is not surprising given the importance of social connections to normative and healthy adolescent development.

Thus, some researchers have theorized that social media use among adolescents may be beneficial to their mental health via increasing opportunities for social interaction. For example, Valkenburg and Peter (2009a) forwarded the Internet-enhanced self-disclosure hypothesis, arguing that online communication promotes self-disclosure, which relates positively to adolescents' friendship quality and their subsequent well-being. Other work suggested that online communication associated with adolescent friendship quality over a six-month period, supporting this hypothesis (Valkenburg & Peter, 2009b), and systematic reviews indicate that these gains in friendship quality can support mental health (Best, Manktelow, & Taylor, 2014). Other researchers have argued that social media accounts can provide a repository of many of the positive events in an adolescent's life and thus can serve as a space of positive self-affirmation (Cingel & Olsen, 2018). Therefore, under this view, social media have the potential to support adolescent mental health and well-being through fostering connections, self-disclosure, and self-affirmation, all of which are important during adolescent development.

Conversely, however, researchers have worried that at least some adolescents may not have developed the self-regulation to use social media in a healthy way, and thus, may experience negative impacts on mental health. These researchers have measured obsessive, dependent, or addictive social media use, loosely conceptualized as use that alters one's mood, makes one preoccupied, causes withdrawal symptoms or anxiety, or causes interpersonal conflict (Bányai et al., 2017). This type of use is related to negative mental health and the experience of mental disorders among adolescents (Bányai et al., 2017).

In summary, as adolescents individuate themselves from their parents and establish closer ties with peers, social interaction and connection becomes vitally important. Appropriate and healthy social interaction is generally associated with better mental health among adolescents (Pachucki, Ozer, Barrat, & Cattuto, 2015), while a lack of interaction or social rejection is associated with negative mental health outcomes (Arseneault, 2018). Given this, it is not surprising that adolescents turn to social media as a means to build and maintain connection with peers. Research, however, suggests that social media use can both contribute to and mitigate against adolescent mental health (e.g., Best et al., 2014). Therefore, in the remaining sections of this chapter, we sort existing studies based on how they operationalize social media use to provide a nuanced view on how adolescents' unique PSMEs relate to their mental health.

Social Media Use and Mental Disorders

Much of the literature examining the relationship between social media use and mental disorders among adolescents has operationalized social media use broadly, most commonly as a measure of overall frequency of use (Schønning, Hjetland, Aarø, & Skogen, 2020), with the majority of research suggesting a positive relationship between social media use and mental disorder symptomatology (e.g., Keles, McCrae, & Grealish, 2020; Vidal, Lhaksampa, Miller, & Platt, 2020). It is important to note that depression is the most studied mental disorder in relation to social media use (Schønning et al., 2020), as increases in depression diagnoses and suicide rates among adolescent populations are often attributed to increasing rates of social media use (Twenge, 2019; Vidal et al., 2020) and is commonly studied in conjunction with anxiety, as the two disorders are comorbid and the most prevalent disorders in adolescents (Keles et al., 2020). For example, among a sample of British 14-year-olds (N = 10,904), the number of hours spent using social media daily was related to higher depressive symptoms (Kelly, Zilanawala, Booker, & Sacker, 2018). Similarly, a study among Chinese adolescents (N = 2,625, M_{age} = 15.1 years) found that the number of hours spent on social media was associated with increased anxiety (Yan et al., 2017). Frequency of social media use and increases in both depression and anxiety have been demonstrated in a sample of adolescents from six diverse European countries (Spain, the Netherlands, Poland, Iceland, Romania, and Greece; N = 10,930, M_{age} = 15.8 years (Tsitsika et al., 2014); as well as in a sample of 467 Scottish adolescents aged 11–17 (Woods & Scott, 2016). Additionally, the number of social media accounts owned (i.e., Facebook, Twitter, and Instagram) was linked to increased anxiety, depression, and other externalizing problems (i.e., ADHD and CD) among a sample of US adolescents (N = 226, M_{age} = 15.3 years) (Barry, Sidoti, Briggs, Reiter, & Lindsey, 2017). Thus, when measured at an aggregate level, several studies have linked social media use to increases in depression and anxiety among adolescents around the world, including a diverse set of both high- and low-income countries.

While the majority of research finds a positive relationship between frequency of social media use and mental disorders, it is important to note that some studies have found no relationship with depression (Blomfield Neira & Barber, 2014 in Australia; Kreski et al., 2021 in the United States; Puentes & Parra, 2014 in Colombia) or even opposite relationships suggesting that social media use in some cases may improve mental disorder symptomatology through mediators such as increased social support and connectedness (Erfani & Abedin, 2018; Keles et al., 2020). Additionally, longitudinal studies have found inconsistent support for a direct association between the frequency of social media use and depression (Coyne, Padilla-Walker, & Holmgren, 2018; Heffer, Good, Daly, MacDonell, & Willoughby, 2019; Houghton et al., 2018). However, these studies did find an effect for certain groups of individuals. Among a sample of 457 US adolescents (M_{age} = 13.5 years at Time 1), increasing hours spent on social media across time points predicted greater depression at the final data collection point (six years later; Coyne et al., 2018). Additionally, for adolescents who reported increases in daily use of social media that peaked and then declined until final data collection also showed greater depression, whereas adolescents who reported consistent moderate use (30–60 minutes per day) had significantly lower depression. Similarly, Houghton and colleagues (2018) found no association between daily hours spent on social media and depression in a sample of Australian adolescents (N = 1,749, 10–15 years old at Time 1); however, when grouping the sample by gender, they found small, positive effects on depression among males at subsequent time points. In summary, when measuring general social media use, researchers have found a mixture of relationships with depression, anxiety, and disordered eating symptomatology. When considering certain moderators such as gender, however, even those studies that do not find a direct effect of social media use on mental disorders do find an effect among certain individuals within the sample, suggesting that the relationship between social media use and mental disorders is complex and nuanced.

Indeed, these mixed findings regarding the relationship between frequency of social media use and mental disorder symptomatology in adolescents illustrate the need for both more nuanced measures of social media use and for the importance of examining adolescents' unique characteristics. Additionally, discrepant measures of frequency, which range from self-reported hours spent on social media to broad categorizations rated on five-point scales ranging "never" to "always" or "almost every day" lack variation and further contribute to the mixed results (Twenge, 2019), further emphasizing the need for more specific measures of social media use. Though longitudinal studies suggest that over time there are little to no effects of frequent social media use on mental disorder symptomatology in young adulthood, the cross-sectional studies examining adolescents provide do generally indicate that there are immediate or short-term effects of use on symptomatology. In fact, longitudinal surveys with shorter time periods between data collection points (i.e., six months rather than six years) find that increases in frequency of social media use are directly related to increases in depression (Brunborg & Andreas, 2019). If the effects of frequency tend to even out over time for most adolescents, understanding the short-term effects of social media use is significant as it may be another metric for identifying adolescents at risk for developing mental disorders. Furthermore, while understanding the relationship between time spent online and mental disorders can be useful, this type of general measurement does not address *how* adolescents are using social media or *where* their activity is taking place.

Platform-Specific Use and Mental Disorders

In attempt to generate a more nuanced understanding of the complex relationship between social media use and mental disorders in adolescents, some researchers have taken a platform-specific approach to examine the unique effects of social media platforms on mental disorder symptomatology. As a function of its ubiquity, Facebook has been the most studied platform (Erfani & Abedin, 2018; Schønning et al., 2020); however, research attention is shifting to highly visual platforms like Instagram and Snapchat that are more commonly used among adolescent populations who show declining preference for less visual platforms such as Facebook and Twitter (Robb, 2020). This is particularly important to note, as adolescents have differential preferences for certain social media sites. Thus, understanding how the use of each relates to mental disorders is important for a more general understanding of how an individual's PSME makes them more or less susceptible to experiencing negative effects on mental health. For that reason, the following discussion will first focus on studies on Facebook and then a grouped discussion of studies on Instagram and Snapchat.

Facebook

Similar to operationalizations of general social media use, platform-specific social media use is also frequently assessed through measuring the frequency of use. Studies suggest that the frequency of Facebook's use is associated with increased mental disorder symptomatology. For example, several studies by Frison and Eggermont (2015a, 2016) and Frison, Subrahmanyam, and Eggermont (2016) have documented links between daily time spent on Facebook, as well as various specific activities on Facebook, and depression among Belgian adolescents. They find that different types of use (mainly active or passive) by male and female adolescents differentially relate to depression, but both groups still do show increases in depression (Frison & Eggermont, 2016). Furthermore, adolescents engaging in social comparison (Appel, Gerlach, & Crusius, 2016) or experiencing fear of missing out (FOMO) (Burnell, George, Vollet, Ehrenreich, & Underwood, 2019) when using Facebook experience increased depression in comparison to individuals using the platform for other motivations, such as support-seeking (Frison & Eggermont, 2015b).

In addition to depression, Facebook use has been associated with clinical body image concerns and eating disorders. For example, a longitudinal survey of 438 Australian females (M_{age} = 13.6 years at Time 1) found that daily time spent on Facebook was associated with increased body image concerns including body-consciousness and eating disorder symptomatology (Tiggemann & Slater, 2017). Similarly, Meier and Gray (2014) found that time spent on Facebook, as well as photo-related activity on Facebook, was linked to increased body image disturbance, including self-objectification and drive for thinness, for a sample of 103 female adolescents (ages 12–18) in the United States. Therefore, similar to research that measures general social media use, research focusing on Facebook detects significant relations between use, depression, anxiety, and disordered eating among adolescent participants.

Instagram and Snapchat

As highly visual social media platforms like Instagram and Snapchat have increased in popularity among adolescents, so too have concerns about the mental disorder outcomes of exposure to image-dominated platforms. However, very few studies have considered the unique use of these platforms among adolescents, but those that did have found positive relationships between exposure to visual platforms and mental disorder symptomatology. For example, among a sample of

523 Italian adolescents (M_{age} = 13.6, 53.5% female), frequency of use of Instagram and Snapchat was associated with increased body image concern and internalization whereas there was no relationship for frequency of Facebook use with either outcome (Marengo, Longobardi, Fabris, & Settanni, 2018). Similarly, frequency of use of both Snapchat and Instagram was positively related to a clinical measure of disordered eating in a sample of Australian adolescents (N = 996; M_{age} = 13.08, 53.6% female; Wilksch, O'Shea, Ho, Byrne, & Wade, 2020). In addition to eating disorders and related concerns, Frison and Eggermont (2017) found that the frequency of exposure to images on Instagram was related to increases in depression over time for Flemish adolescents (N = 440, M_{age} = 14.96 years, 39% male).

While this platform-specific approach provides insight into the effects of use of various social media platforms, and suggests that Facebook, Instagram, and Snapchat use are all linked to mental disorders among adolescents, social media use does not exist in a vacuum and the observed effects may fluctuate when considering how various platforms are used in conjunction with one another. Recent reports suggest that the majority of US adolescents aged 13–18 use four or more social media platforms, compared to only 7% who use only one platform (Robb, 2020), further emphasizing the importance of measures that are more generalizable across adolescents' PMSEs that focus on how individuals engage differentially with social media.

Within-Platform Studies Investigating Mental Disorders

To our knowledge, no studies have specifically investigated how engagement in particular digital settings over social media relate to the maintenance or development of mental disorders among adolescents. However, emerging evidence supports the importance of such efforts by suggesting that *how* adolescents interact across particular sub-facets of social media may differentially affect their mental health (e.g., Frison, Bastin, Bijttebier, & Eggermont, 2019; Lonergan et al., 2020), thus providing evidence for the importance of considering adolescents' unique social media ecosystems. For instance, among an Australian adolescent sample (N = 4,209; 53% females), the avoidance of posting selfies, engagement in photo manipulation (i.e., editing selfies), photo investment (e.g., anticipatory anxiety toward the posting of selfies), and scrutinization of others' selfies over social media positively associated with a greater odds of meeting clinical thresholds for an array of eating disorders while controlling for age and body-mass-index (Lonergan et al., 2020). Further, there were few differences as a function of participants' gender. When abstracting across specific measures (e.g., investment in others' selfies, photo manipulation), these results would imply that specific facets of image-based social media platforms that facilitate the enactment of appearance-related online behaviors (e.g., posting and adding locations over Instagram, etc.) or offer access to others' selfies (e.g., digital locales housing user-generated content feeds [e.g., Instagram Home Page] or other users' Instagram profiles) could serve as key classes of digital settings that could potentially contribute to the maintenance of eating disorders among adolescents. Taken together with more general measures of social media use, as detailed earlier, this would suggest that it might not be social media use that relates to disordered eating, per se, but rather, unique and differential engagement in specific practices brought about by features unique to certain segments of adolescents' PSMEs.

This notion is further supported by evidenced associations between adolescents' chat activities over social media and their mental health. For instance, a longitudinal study conducted among a sample of Belgian adolescents ($N = 1,235$; 52% males) demonstrated that the frequency of adolescents' private Facebook interactions influences their later severity of depressive symptom (controlling for age, gender, and time spent on Facebook). The process, however, occurs indirectly and differentially depending on gender and the underlying mechanisms under investigation. For example, whereas online co-rumination (i.e., problem discussion with their closest same-sex friend) did not significantly predict depression symptoms over time, perceived online social support at Time 1 had a significant negative effect on depression symptoms at Time 2, but only among girls. This would suggest that private messaging over social media generally, which itself is facilitated within particular digital settings that exist in social media applications (e.g., messages, DMs), could serve to support adolescents' mental health. In this case, private Facebook communication may have a protective effect against depression among adolescent girls via increasing perceptions of online social support (Frison et al., 2019). It is unclear whether this effect is additive or persists when considering adolescent girls' level of perceived offline social support, however.

Despite providing valuable indication of the importance of going beyond generalized social media measures (e.g., time spent using social media or image-based social media), these studies did not consider social media as a system of digital settings in line with the PSMEF. On the one hand, platform-specific studies (e.g., Frison et al., 2019) suffer from an omission bias (Odgers & Jensen, 2020; Prinstein et al., 2020) making it unclear if findings from Frison and colleagues (2019) would generalize when assessing chat-based activities across adolescent girls' PSMEs more comprehensively (e.g., private messaging/group messaging behaviors across the applications they use). Similarly, generalized social media use measures (e.g., Lonergan et al., 2020) fail to map their effects to social media elements existing across adolescents' PSMEs, a necessary step to generalize findings to later iterations of social media platforms (Bayer et al., 2020). Understanding how social media effects map onto specific digital settings (in providing access to certain social media elements [e.g., user-generated content feed]) or classes of digital settings would also help to inform on their nature.

For instance, if a preoccupation with others' self-depictions via visual images over social media serves to maintain disordered eating beliefs or behaviors, does this association vary when it occurs via viewing social media profiles, posts in particular types of social media content environments (e.g., stories, shorts), or across certain user-generated content feeds? Understanding these nuances could help pave ways for technological intervention and help to inform on how to design future platforms in ways that could better support users' mental health. Indeed, it is not unreasonable to presume that future iterations of social media may take on the shape of dynamic user interfaces that include tailored displays with varying constellations of social media elements or features, and thus may differ across users, similar to the notion of multiple user interface designs (e.g., Seffah, Forbridg, & Javahery, 2004). Altogether, although these studies advance our theoretical understanding of how certain types of digital settings may relate to the maintenance or the development of particular mental disorders among adolescents, they also underscore the need for more robust operationalization of social media in consideration of social media as a user-centric digital environment in line with the PSMEF.

Summary and Conclusions

While it is clear that social media serves as a key environmental context that can serve to facilitate adolescent development (Nesi et al., 2018), how social media use is studied has limited our current understanding of how it relates to adolescents' mental health and how it may generalize to later iterations of social media as an evolving digital landscape. The findings cited here illustrate that a great deal of insight has been produced about the nature of this association since social media's widespread adoption amongst the public, despite challenges to its study (e.g., rapid maturation). For example, researchers leveraging an array of methodological approaches and conceptual frameworks have greatly helped to progress our understanding of social media effects in ways that have been evidenced to associate with adolescents' mental health. Beyond the work reviewed, the study of problematic social media use (Marino, Gini, Vieno, & Spada, 2018; Banyai et al., 2017), general screen time effects (Houghton et al., 2018; Woods & Scott, 2016), and person-specific effects of social media use among adolescents (e.g., self-esteem, state happiness; Valkenburg et al., 2021; Beyens et al., 2020) have all provided key insights into how social media can relate to adolescents' mental well-being. It is apparent that adolescents who maintain an addictive or maladaptive relationship with social media platforms (e.g., Facebook) express poorer mental health (Marino et al., 2018); that adolescents who use social media later at night may suffer from impaired sleep due to blue light exposure and, as a result, decreased mental health (Woods & Scott, 2016; Hale, Li, Hartstein, & LeBourgeois, 2019); and that some social media effects themselves are dependent on users' individual differences, expressing positive, negative, and nonsignificant effects from adolescent to adolescent that can also differ in variability and direction by platform

(Beyens et al., 2020). The latter finding particularly endorses the need for more specific social media measures to help disentangle such effects, which could be addressed via the PSMEF and the study of social media elements (see Bayer et al., 2020). Altogether, social media effects on adolescents' mental health appear heterogeneous across different adolescents, multidimensional (occurring indirectly at the level of the device and directly via engagement within platforms), and may very well depend on how youth engage across their unique social media environment.

What conclusions can we draw then from this consideration of the relations between adolescent social media use and mental disorders as they pertain to the PSMEF? First, general measures of social media use are mixed in whether they suggest a positive or null relationship between social media use and mental disorder symptomatology, although we note that even those that demonstrate generally null effects also suggest positive effects of social media on mental disorder symptomatology for certain demographics within the sample (e.g., Coyne et al., 2018, Houghton et al., 2018). Even more nuanced considerations generally detect relations between user engagement in specific activities within a certain platform and mental disorder symptomatology (e.g., Frison et al., 2019). Taken together, these studies and extant findings have built a foundation of knowledge that suggests that the effects of social media on mental disorders among adolescents are complex, nuanced, and likely idiosyncratic. Very recent work suggests that for the large majority of adolescents, there are no associations between social media use and a key indicator of mental health (i.e., self-esteem, state happiness), yet a minority of the sample experiences a negative effect of social media on mental health (Beyens et al., 2020; Valkenburg et al., 2021).

Such findings offer the next step for research in this research domain as they raise important questions. Who are these individuals who do experience negative effects of social media on their mental health, and does their PSME differ from those who experience null effects? Through the social media platforms they use, the content with which they engage, the audience with which they interact, and the specific ways they use each platform, have certain adolescents created a unique digital ecosystem that makes them more susceptible to negative effects, while the majority of adolescents have created one that makes them less susceptible? Do these patterns of effects result from other person–environment interactions? By working to provide more concrete answers to these questions, researchers can help parents, educators, and other practitioners understand how to help adolescents to derive benefits from their social media use and mitigate against negative outcomes. This is especially important, again considering that approximately half of mental disorders diagnosed during adulthood begin in adolescence (Knopf et al., 2008). An even more nuanced understanding of how social media contributes to and mitigates against mental health will provide key information that can help to address this public health concern.

References

Allison, M. D., & Sabatelli, R. M. (1988). Differentiation and individuation as mediators of identity and intimacy in adolescence. *Journal of Adolescent Research, 3*(1), 1–16. https://doi.org/10.1177/074355488831002

Anderson, M., & Jiang, J. (2018). Teens, social media, & technology 2018. *Pew Research Center.* Retrieved from https://www.pewresearch.org/internet/2018/05/31/teens-social-media-technology-2018/

Appel, H., Gerlach, A. L., & Crusius, J. (2016). The interplay between Facebook use, social comparison, envy, and depression. *Current Opinion in Psychology, 9,* 44–49. https://doi.org/10.1016/j.copsyc.2015.10.006

Arnett, J. J. (2000). Emerging adulthood: A theory of development from the late teens through the twenties. *American Psychologist, 55*(5), 469–480. https://doi.org/10.1037/0003 066X.55.5.469

Arnett, J. J. (2007). Emerging adulthood: What is it, and what is it good for? *Child Development Perspectives, 1*(2), 68–73. https://doi.org/10.1111/j.1750-8606.2007.00016.x

Arseneault, L. (2018). The persistent and pervasive impact of being bullied in childhood and adolescence: Implications for policy and practice. *Journal of Child Psychology and Psychiatry, 59*(4), 405–421. https://doi.org/10.1111/jcpp.12841

Auxier, B., & Anderson, M. (2021). Social media use in 2021. *Pew Research Center.* Retrieved from https://www.pewresearch.org/internet/2021/04/07/social-media-use-in-2021/

Bányai, F., Zsila, Á., Király, O., Maraz, A., Elekes, Z., Griffiths, M. D., . . . Demetrovics, Z. (2017). Problematic social media use: Results from a large-scale nationally representative adolescent sample. *PLoS One, 12*(1). https://doi.org/10.1371/journal.pone.0169839

Barry, C. T., Sidoti, C. L., Briggs, S. M., Reiter, S. R., & Lindsey, R. A. (2017). Adolescent social media use and mental health from adolescent and parent perspectives. *Journal of Adolescence, 61,* 1–11. https://doi.org/10.1016/j.adolescence.2017.08.005

Bayer, J. B., Triệu, P., & Ellison, N. B. (2020). Social media elements, ecologies, and effects. *Annual Review of Psychology, 71,* 471–497. https://doi.org/10.1146/annurev-psych 010419–050944

Best, P., Manktelow, R., & Taylor, B. (2014). Online communication, social media, and adolescent wellbeing: A systematic narrative review. *Children and Youth Services Review, 41,* 27–36. https://doi.org/10.1016/j.childyouth.2014.03.001

Beyens, I., Pouwels, J. L., van Driel, I. I., Keijsers, L., & Valkenburg, P. M. (2020). The effect of social media on well-being differs from adolescent to adolescent. *Scientific Reports, 10,* 1–11. https://doi.org/10.1038/s41598-020-67727-7

Blakemore, S.-J., & Mills, K. L. (2014). Is adolescence a sensitive period for socio-cultural processing? *Annual Review of Psychology, 65,* 187–207. https://doi.org/10.1146/annurevpsych-010213-115202

Blomfield Neira, C. J., & Barber, B. L. (2014). Social networking site use: Linked to adolescents' social self-concept, self-esteem, and depressed mood. *Australian Journal of Psychology, 66*(1), 56–64. https://doi.org/10.1111/ajpy.12034

Blos, P. (1967). The second individuation process of adolescence. *The Psychoanalytic Study of the Child, 22*(1), 162–186. https://doi.org/10.1080/00797308.1967.11822595

boyd, D. M., & Ellison, N. B. (2013). *Sociality through social network sites.* Oxford: Oxford University Press.

Brunborg, G. S., & Andreas, J. B. (2019). Increase in time spent on social media is associated with modest increase in depression, conduct problems, and episodic heavy drinking. *Journal of Adolescence, 74,* 201–209. https://doi.org/10.1016/j.adolescence.2019.06.013

Burnell, K., George, M. J., Vollet, J. W., Ehrenreich, S. E., & Underwood, M. K. (2019). Passive social networking site use and well-being: The mediating roles of social comparison and the fear of missing out. *Cyberpsychology: Journal of Psychosocial Research on Cyberspace, 13*(3), article 5. http://dx.doi.org/10.5817/CP2019-3-5

Cingel, D. P., & Olsen, M. K. (2018). Getting over the hump: Examining curvilinear relationships between adolescent self-esteem and Facebook use. *Journal of Broadcasting and Electronic Media, 62*(2), 215–231. https://doi.org/10.1080/08838151.2018.1451860

Coyne, S. M., Padilla-Walker, L. M., & Holmgren, H G. (2018). A six-year longitudinal study of texting trajectories during adolescence. *Child Development, 89*(1), 58–65. https://doi.org/10.1111/cdev.12823

de Goede, I. H. A., Branje, S. J. T., & Meeus, W. H. J. (2009). Developmental changes and gender differences in adolescents' perceptions of friendships. *Journal of Adolescence, 32*(5), 1105–1123. https://doi.org/10.1016/j.adolescence.2009.03.002

DeVito, M. A., Walker, A. M., & Birnholtz, J. (2018). "Too gay for Facebook": Presenting LGBTQ+ identity throughout the Personal Social Media Ecosystem. *PACM HCI CSCW, 2*(44). 1–23. https://doi.org/10.1145/3274313

Erfani, S. S., & Abedin, B. (2018). Impacts of the use of social network sites on users' psychological well-being: A systematic review. *Journal of the Association for Information Science and Technology, 69*(7), 900–912. https://doi.org/10.1002/asi.24015

Frison, E., Bastin, M., Bijttebier, P., & Eggermont, S. (2019). Helpful or harmful? The different relationships between private Facebook interactions and adolescents' depressive symptoms. *Media Psychology, 22*(2), 244–272. https://doi.org/10.1080/15213269.2018.1429933

Frison, E., & Eggermont, S. (2015a). The impact of daily stress on adolescents' depressed mood: The role of social support seeking through Facebook. *Computers in Human Behavior, 44,* 315–325. https://doi.org/10.1016/j.chb.2014.11.070

Frison, E., & Eggermont, S. (2015b). Toward an integrated and differential approach to the relationships between loneliness, different types of Facebook use, and adolescents' depressed mood. *Communication Research, 47*(5), 701–728. https://doi.org/10.1177/0093650215617506

Frison, E., & Eggermont, S. (2016). Exploring the relationships between different types of Facebook use, perceived online social support, and adolescents' depressed mood. *Social Science Computer Review, 34*(2), 153–171. https://doi.org/10.1177/0894439314567449

Frison, E., & Eggermont, S. (2017). Browsing, posting, and liking on Instagram: The reciprocal relationships between different types of Instagram use and adolescents' depressed mood. *Cyberpsychology, Behavior, and Social Networking, 20*(10), 603–609. https://doi.org/10.1089/cyber.2017.0156

Frison, E., Subrahmanyam, K., & Eggermont, S. (2016). The short-term longitudinal and reciprocal relations between peer victimization on Facebook and adolescents' well-being. *Journal of Youth and Adolescence, 45*(9), 1755–1771. https://doi.org/10.1007/s10964-016-0436-z

Green, L. W., & Horton, D. (1982). Adolescent health: Issues and challenges. In T. J. Coates, A. C. Peterson, & C. Perry (Eds.), *Promoting adolescent health* (pp. 23–43). New York: Academic Press. https://doi.org/10.1016/B978-0-12-177380-9.50008-6

Hale, L., Li, X., Hartstein, L. E., & LeBourgeois, M. K. (2019). Media use and sleep in teenagers: What do we know? *Current Sleep Medicine Reports, 5*, 128–134. https://doi.org/10.1007/s40675-019-00146-x

Heffer, T., Good, M., Daly, O., MacDonell, E., & Willoughby, T. (2019). The longitudinal association between social-media use and depressive symptoms among adolescents and young adults: An empirical reply to Twenge et al. (2018). *Clinical Psychological Science, 7*(3), 462–470. https://doi.org/10.1177/2167702618812727

Houghton, S., Lawrence, D., Hunter, S. C., Rosenberg, M., Zadow, C., Wood, L., & Shilton, T. (2018). Reciprocal relationships between trajectories of depressive symptoms and screen media use during adolescence. *Journal of Youth and Adolescence, 47*(11), 2453–2467. https://doi.org/10.1007/s10964-018-0901-y

Keles, B., McCrae, N., & Grealish, A. (2020). A systematic review: the influence of social media on depression, anxiety and psychological distress in adolescents. *International Journal of Adolescence and Youth, 25*(1), 79–93. https://doi.org/10.1080/02673843.2019.1590851

Kelly, Y., Zilanawala, A., Booker, C., & Sacker, A. (2018). Social media use and adolescent mental health: Findings from the UK Millennium Cohort Study. *EClinical Medicine, 6*, 59–68. https://doi.org/10.1016/j.eclinm.2018.12.005

Knopf, D., Park, M. J., & Mulye, T. P. (2008). *The mental health of adolescents: A national profile, 2008*. San Francisco, CA: National Adolescent Health Information Center.

Kreski, N., Platt, J., Rutherford, C., Olfson, M., Odgers, C., Schulenberg, J., & Keyes, K. M. (2021). Social media use and depressive symptoms among United States adolescents. *Journal of Adolescent Health, 68*(3), 572–579. https://doi.org/10.1016/j.jadohealth.2020.07.006

Kroger, J. (1985). Separation-individuation and ego identity status in New Zealand university students. *Journal of Youth and Adolescence, 14*, 133–147. https://doi.org/10.1007/BFO2098653

Levine, J. B., Green, C. J., & Millon, T. (1986). The separation-individuation test of adolescence. *Journal of Personality Assessment, 50*(1), 123–139. https://doi.org/10.1207/s15327752jpa5001_14

Lonergan, A. R., Bussey, K., Fardouly, J., Griffiths, S., Murray, S. B., Hay, P., . . . Mitchison, D. (2020). Protect me from my selfie: Examining the association between photo-based social media behaviors and self-reported eating disorders in adolescence. *International Journal of Eating Disorders, 53*, 755–766. https://doi.org/10.1002/eat.23256

Marengo, D., Longobardi, C., Fabris, M. A., & Settanni, M. (2018). Highly-visual social media and internalizing symptoms in adolescence: The mediating role of body image concerns. *Computers in Human Behavior, 82*, 63–69. https://doi.org/10.1016/j.chb.2018.01.003

Marino, C., Gini, G., Vieno, A., & Spada, M. M. (2018). A comprehensive meta-analysis on problematic Facebook use. *Computers in Human Behavior, 83*, 262–277. https://doi.org/10.1016/j.chb.2018.02.009

Meier, A., & Reinecke, L. (2020). Computer-mediated communication, social media, and mental health: A conceptual and empirical meta-review. *Communication Research.* Online publication. https://doi.org/10.1177/0093650220958224

Meier, E. P., & Gray, J. (2014). Facebook photo activity associated with body image disturbance in adolescent girls. *Cyberpsychology, Behavior, and Social Networking, 17*, 199–206. https://doi.org/10.1089/cyber.2013.0305

Mojtabai, R., Olfson, M., & Han, B. (2016). National trends in the prevalence and treatment of depression in adolescents and young adults. *Pediatrics, 138*(6), e20161878. https://doi.org/10.1542/peds.2016-1878

Nesi, J., Choukas-Bradley, S., & Prinstein, M. J. (2018). Transformation of adolescent peer relations in the social media context: Part 1—A theoretical framework and application to dyadic peer relationships. *Clinical Child and Family Psychology Review, 21*(3), 267–294. https://doi.org/10.1007/s10567-018-0261-x

Odgers, C. L., & Jensen, M. R. J. (2020). Annual research review: Adolescent mental health in the digital age: Facts, fears, and future directions. *Journal of Child Psychology and Psychiatry, 61*(3), 336–348. https://doi.org/ 10.1111/jcpp.13190

Pachucki, M. C., Ozer, E. J., Barrat, A., & Cattuto, C. (2015). Mental health and social networks in early adolescence: A dynamic study of objectively-measured social interaction behaviors. *Social Science & Medicine, 125,* 40–50.

Petersen, A. C., & Hamburg, B. A. (1986). Adolescence: A developmental approach to problems and psychopathology. *Behavior Therapy, 17*(5), 480–499. https://doi.org/10.1016/S00057894(86)80090-9

Prinstein, M. J., Nesi, J., & Telzer, E. H. (2020). Commentary: An updated agenda for the study of digital media use and adolescent development – future directions following Odgers & Jensen (2020). *Journal of Child Psychology and Psychiatry, 61*(3), 349–352. https://doi.org/10.1111/jcpp.13219

Puentes, A. P. R., & Parra, A. F. (2014). Relationship between the time of use of social networks on the internet and mental health in Colombian adolescents. *Colombian Psychology ACTA, 17*(1), 131–140. https://doi.org/10.14718/ACP.2014.17.1.13

Rideout, V. J., & Robb, M. B. (2019). *The common sense census: Media use by Tweens and Teens, 2019.* San Francisco, CA: Common Sense Media.

Robb, M. B. (2020). *Teens and the news: The influencers, celebrities, and platforms they say matter most, 2020.* San Francisco, CA: Common Sense Media.

Schønning, V., Hjetland, G. J., Aarø, L. E., & Skogen, J. C. (2020). Social media use and mental health and well-being among adolescents – A scoping review. *Frontiers in Psychology, 11.* https://doi.org/10.3389/fpsyg.2020.01949

Seffah, A., Forbridg, P., & Javahery, H. (2004). Multi-devices 'Multiple' user interfaces: Development models and research opportunities. *The Journal of Systems and Software, 73,* 287–300. https://doi.org/10.1016/j.jss.2003.09.017

Steinberg, L. (2016). *Adolescence* (8th ed.). Boston, MA: McGraw Hill.

Tiggemann, M., & Slater, A. (2017). Facebook and body image concern in adolescent girls: A prospective study. *International Journal of Eating Disorders, 50*(1), 80–83. https://doi.org/10.1002/eat.22640

Tsitsika, A. K., Tzavela, E. C., Janikian, M., Ólafsson, K., Iordache, A., Schoenmakers, T. M., . . . Richardson, C. (2014). Online social networking in adolescence: Patterns of use in six European countries and links with psychosocial functioning. *Journal of Adolescent Health, 55*(1), 141–147. https://doi.org/10.1016/j.jadohealth.2013.11.010

Twenge, J. M. (2019). More time on technology, less happiness? Associations between digital media use and psychological well-being. *Current Directions in Psychological Science, 28*(4), 372–379. https://doi.org/10.1177/0963721419838244

U.S. Department of Health and Human Services. (1999). *Mental health: A report of the surgeon general.* Rockville, MD: U.S. Department of Health and Human Services, Substance Abuse and Mental Health Services Administration, Center for Mental Health Services, National Institutes of Health, National Institute of Mental Health.

Valkenburg, P. M., Beyens, I., van Driel, I. I., & Keijsers, L. (2021). Social media use and adolescents' self-esteem: Heading for a person-specific media effects paradigm. *Journal of Communication, 71*(1), 56–78. https://doi.org/10.1093/joc/jqaa039

Valkenburg, P. M., & Peter, J. (2009a). Social consequences of the Internet for adolescents: A decade of research. *Current Directions in Psychological Science, 18*(1), 1–5. https://doi.org/10.1111/j.1467-8721.2009.01595.x

Valkenburg, P. M., & Peter, J. (2009b). The effects of instant messaging on the quality of adolescents' existing friendships: A longitudinal study. *Journal of Communication, 59*(1), 79–97. https://doi.org/10.1111/j.1460-2466.2008.01405.x

Valkenburg, P. M., & Peter, J. (2013). The differential susceptibility to media effects model. *Journal of Communication, 63*, 221–243. https://doi.org/ doi:10.1111/jcom.12024

Vidal, C., Lhaksampa, T., Miller, L., & Platt, R. (2020). Social media use and depression in adolescents: A scoping review. *International Review of Psychiatry, 32*(3), 235–253. https://doi.org/10.1080/09540261.2020.1720623

Wilksch, S. M., O'Shea, A., Ho, P., Byrne, S., & Wade, T. D. (2020). The relationship between social media use and disordered eating in young adolescents. *International Journal of Eating Disorders, 53*(1), 96–106. https://doi.org/10.1002/eat.23198

Woods, H. C., & Scott, H. (2016). # Sleepyteens: Social media use in adolescence is associated with poor sleep quality, anxiety, depression and low self-esteem. *Journal of Adolescence, 51*, 41–49. https://doi.org/10.1016/j.adolescence.2016.05.008

Yan, H., Zhang, R., Oniffrey, T. M., Chen, G., Wang, Y., Wu, Y., . . . Moore, J. B. (2017). Associations among screen time and unhealthy behaviors, academic performance, and well-being in Chinese adolescents. *International Journal of Environmental Research and Public Health, 14*(6), 596. https://doi.org/10.3390/ijerph14060596

12

THERE IS NO EASY ANSWER

How the Interaction of Content, Situation, and Person Shapes the Effects of Social Media Use on Well-Being

Philipp K. Masur, Jolanda Veldhuis, and Nadia Bij de Vaate

Social media have become an essential part of children's and young adolescents' lives. They grow up and mature with smartphones, tablets, and computers that render access to social media platforms ubiquitous. As using Facebook, Instagram, or TikTok intensifies, it is no wonder that scholars, parents, and policy makers voice concerns about potential negative effects on children's and adolescents' physical and mental health. Whereas some scholars argue that we are "in the middle of a full-blown mental health crisis for adolescents and young adults" (Twenge as cited in Brody, 2019) and claim that social media are one of the core reasons for increases in depression and suicides in the younger generation (Twenge, Joiner, Rogers, & Martin, 2018), others counter that evidence for such claims is weak and largely based on oversimplifying, cross-sectional survey investigations (Orben & Przybylski, 2019; Schemer, Masur, Geiss, Müller, & Schäfer, 2021). The proliferation of particularly screen-based activities has led to an overdrawn focus on the amount of "screentime", a comparatively broad measure of an individual's engagement with electronic media as a singular factor shaping young adolescents' well-being (Dienlin & Johannes, 2020; Whitlock & Masur, 2019). Despite advances in related, but more specific areas (e.g., research on cyberbullying, self-presentation and body image, social media use, and social support) that engage more deeply with the activities, contents, or practices within social media, scholars continue to grapple with contradicting findings from studies with too broad measures and cross-sectional designs. It seems that there is a generally misplaced confidence in the ability to find a simple answer to a rather complex problem. This is even more surprising as longitudinal, large-scale, and meta-analytic evidence suggests that overall net effects of social media use are at best small (Meier & Reinecke, 2020; Orben, Dienlin, & Przybylski, 2019).

DOI: 10.4324/9781003171270-12

Many scholars (e.g., Beyens, Pouwels, van Driel, Keijsers, & Valkenburg, 2020; Orben, 2020; Vanden Abeele, 2020; Whitlock & Masur, 2019) have thus called for a more in-depth analysis of social media's influences on well-being that disentangles *what* (e.g., different platforms, different types of content, different online interactions) affects *whom* (e.g., males vs. females, personality types, experiences, mental health history) under *which circumstances* (e.g., time of day, presence of others, mood, motivation) and with *what effect* (positive vs. negative, supportive vs. detrimental, short-term vs. long-term) and with regard to *which type of well-being* (e.g., trait vs. state, cognitive vs. affective). In this chapter, we propose a holistic framework that takes different theoretical advances toward understanding and identifying specific boundary conditions of detrimental and beneficial media use effects into account.

Toward a Holistic Model of Social Media Use Effects on Well-being

Recently, scholars have pushed toward a person-specific media use paradigm (Beyens et al., 2020) emphasizing that we should not expect media use effects to be similar for all people. Instead, we should identify relevant personal characteristics (e.g., socio-demographics, prior mental health history, literacy) that help explain why social media effects on well-being vary from person to person. However, by focusing only on between-person differences, we may commit the *fundamental attribution error* (Ross & Nisbett, 2011) and overestimate dispositional factors' power in explaining our behaviors. Others have thus highlighted the importance of distinguishing the type of content individuals consume to explain variances in effects on well-being (Whitlock & Masur, 2019). From this point of view, watching a funny YouTube video may be less detrimental than comparing, for example, yourself with others on Instagram.

Focusing only on individual differences or only on content characteristics will nonetheless fall short of grasping the entire picture. Individuals use and experience social media within a total environment that forms a complex system of interrelated and interacting factors, which can be placed on a continuum from the micro- to the macro-level (cf. Magnusson, 1981). It would be impossible to investigate the entirety of factors that influence human behaviors, thoughts, or feelings at a given point in time. But attempting to explain variation in individuals' well-being does require us to identify more systematically where the variance stems from. Taking a situational perspective (cf. Masur, 2018, chapter 7.1) and asking what influences a person's well-being at a *given time* can help to identify relevant "groups" of factors that we should at least expect to account for some variance in well-being. In line with a long-standing tradition in psychology (Rauthmann, Sherman, & Funder, 2015), such factors can be differentiated into personal and environmental factors (see Table 12.1).

TABLE 12.1 Overview of influences on well-being at a given time

	Personal Factors	*Environmental Factors*
Non-situational (comparatively stable)	Traits, dispositional tendencies, trait-like qualities (e.g., personality)	Structural settings (e.g., culture, socio-technological environment)
Contextual (fluctuating, but recurring)	Internal perceptions (e.g., perceived duties, context-related goals)	Device- or platform-related characteristics (e.g., content, norms and practices, addictive design) and other contextual factors (e.g., typical audiences)
Situational (highly fluctuating)	Internal perceptions (e.g., feelings, situational goals, stress, mindfulness, level of energy)	Interpersonal perceptions (e.g., perceptions of others) and external perceptions (e.g., perceptions of place, location, physical cues)

Personal factors include, on the one hand, comparatively stable traits (e.g., personality, impulsivity, trait anxiety) and dispositional tendencies (e.g., opinions, attitudes, skills, long-term goals, habitual behaviors). On the other hand, they include fluctuating internal factors such as contextually activated role perceptions, situationally activated goals, and feelings (e.g., perceived stress, fear-of-missing-out). *Environmental factors* include, on the one hand, comparatively stable characteristics of the larger structural settings in which individuals find themselves in (e.g., culture, tradition, political system, economy) as well as contextual (e.g., perceptions of norms and rules), device- or platform-specific (e.g., characteristics of platforms, perceptions of practices and norms), and situationally perceived cues of the physico-social environment (e.g., other people, physical cues, place and location). Such a classification allows to characterize these factors with regard to their stability, that is, whether they remain stable and thus constant influences over longer periods of time (e.g., personality) or whether they fluctuate considerably across contexts (e.g., practices, types of content), or even situations (e.g., moods, goals). It further forces us to clearly indicate whether such a factor is a direct antecedent of individuals' well-being (e.g., negative content) or rather a moderator of such direct effects (e.g., self-esteem, mood, energy level).

Adopting such a situational perspective sharpens our ability to uncover boundary conditions for social media use effects on well-being. Also, acknowledging the interactional nature of influences on individuals' well-being reveals that social media use itself may not always be the cause for less (or more) well-being. At times, more (or less) well-being may be caused by other factors (e.g., a predisposition for depression, a generally low self-esteem) and social media use instead increases or buffers against such effects.

In the following, we will use this framework to identify *what* aspect of social media (what conceptualizations of social media are useful to study effects on well-being?) affects *whom* (what are relevant stable person-related moderators?) under *which circumstances* (what are relevant contextual, device-specific, or situational moderators?) with regard to *which type of well-being* (do we need to focus on trait or state of well-being?).

Conceptualizing Social Media

The first question is: What exactly exerts an effect on individuals' well-being? Social media must be regarded as a form of computer-mediated communication (CMC) that focuses on connecting users and facilitating social interaction. Yet, social media is likewise an umbrella term for certain platforms (e.g., Facebook, Instagram, Twitter, or TikTok) or a broader type of media that is defined by five typical characteristics (Bayer, Trieu, & Ellison, 2020; Carr & Hayes, 2015): Social media are Internet-based (i.e., online), disentrained (i.e., supporting asynchronous social interaction), interactive (i.e., social in nature), based primarily on user-generated content, and mass personal (i.e., involving broadcasting of interpersonal communication to larger audiences). Individuals use social media for various purposes ranging from active contribution to passive consumptions (Escobar-Viera et al., 2018; Thorisdottir, Sigurvinsdottir, Asgeirsdottir, Allegrante, & Sigfusdottir, 2019): active uses include communicating with other users (e.g., through status updates or dyadic channels), interacting with content (e.g., liking, commenting, and tagging), engaging in self-presentation and self-exposure (e.g., status updates and posting photos), and seeking entertainment (e.g., playing games). Passive uses include browsing content without interacting, watching videos, and looking at pictures.

Meier and Reinecke (2020) propose a taxonomy that distinguishes two overarching approaches to conceptualizing social media use: the *channel*-centered approach and the *communication*-centered approach. When using the former, scholars create "methodological buckets" by focusing on devices, platforms, or applications instead of engaging with the specific contents, activities, message characteristics that define them. The channel-centered approach thus treats social media as a "black box" and differences in how people use these media are ignored. In the literature, we nonetheless find different levels of analysis within the channel-centered approach depending on whether scholars focused on certain devices (e.g., smartphones, tablets, or generally screen-based technologies), types of applications (e.g., email, messenger, SNS), branded applications (e.g., Facebook vs. Instagram), or specific features (e.g., status updates, chat functions, games, profiles).

The communication-centered approach, in contrast, focuses on possible communication processes and message exchanges on social media. It thus opens the "black-box" of the channel-centered approach (Meier & Reinecke, 2020). Within this approach, we can further distinguish analyses on the interaction level (e.g., relationship between the communicators, directionality of interaction, characteristics of particular audiences) and the message level (e.g., content characteristics, valence, communication mode, accessibility).

Inconsistencies in published findings on the effects of social media use on well-being may be in part explainable by differences in such levels of analyses. A large part of the literature has adopted a channel-centered approach by focusing on devices or branded applications. Such analyses treat social media use as a trait-like quality and are limited to measuring comparatively stable between-person differences in aggregated behavioral patterns (e.g., overall smartphone use, screentime, frequency of Facebook use). It is hardly surprising that such analyses are aimed at predicting rather stable indicators of well-being (e.g., life satisfaction, loneliness, depression). Newer studies have started to investigate how certain features or activities of social media shape well-being outcomes. For example, experience sampling studies showed that using media for different purposes (e.g., recovery vs. procrastination) also had varying influences on well-being (Reinecke & Hofmann, 2016). Similarly, active posting on Facebook had positive, yet fleeting impacts on subsequent mood (Bayer, Ellison, Schoenebeck, Brady, & Falk, 2018).

Focusing on the type of interactions that users engage in and the messages they are exposed to provides an important avenue for future research. Moving beyond methodological buckets such as devices or applications and focusing on the intricate relationships between different types of social media uses, content- and person-related characteristics, as well as contextual and situational factors will provide a nuanced insight into how social media use affects well-being. Such a paradigm shift also changes the perspective from trying to explain differences *between* people to trying to understand differences in social media use *within* people. It sounds trivial to assume that not all social media use is bad or good. Yet, current research tends to ignore this by flattening the heterogeneity of social media use into broad and artificial measures.

Who is Susceptible?

In a second step, we need to ask for *whom* certain types of social media use actually affect well-being. Valkenburg, Beyens, Pouwels, van Driel, and Keijsers (2021) have recently argued that one should not expect social media use effects to be uniform across individuals and propose a "personalized media effects paradigm". Although, we believe that a too-strong emphasis on between-person differences may not be helpful (cf. fundamental attribution error) and a paradigm shift toward "N = 1 type of analyses" (p. 74) may even be problematic as it could devalue our goal to make inferences about populations, we nonetheless agree that a better understanding of the susceptibility of certain individuals is important and a logical extension of prior work.

When we talk about person-specific susceptibility, we aim at identifying traits, dispositional tendencies, or trait-like qualities that account for variation in the effect of social media use on well-being. For example, several studies have shown that gender might matter in explaining differences in the between-person relationships of social media use and well-being indicators such as life satisfaction (Frison & Eggermont, 2016; Orben et al., 2019). Similarly, older people seem to benefit more from actively using social networking sites (SNS) than younger people (Kim & Shen, 2020; Reinecke & Hofmann, 2016).

However, many potential trait-like moderators have not yet been studied systematically. Research suggests, for example, that impulsivity (Billieux, Linden, & Rochat, 2008), trait anxiety (Elhai, Levine, Dvorak, & Hall, 2016), or the fear of missing out (Blackwell, Leaman, Tramposch, Osborne, & Liss, 2017) are positively related to higher smartphone or social media use or even problematic social media use. Trait self-esteem is likewise related to certain types of social media use (e.g., frequency of reacting to profiles) and subjective well-being (Valkenburg, Peter, & Schouten, 2006) and thus a potentially important covariate in explaining social media effects on well-being. Identifying stable person-related characteristics that explain variance in social media effects on well-being will be pivotal for understanding person-specific susceptibility in future research.

However, it is important to clearly indicate whether such stable personal factors moderate between-person relationships between overall social media use and stable indicators of well-being (e.g., life satisfaction) or whether they moderate within-person relationships between different types of social media use, content consumption, or use behaviors and more fleeting indicators of well-being (e.g., affect). Disentangling interactions between stable person characteristics and varying contextual or situational factors may be particularly fruitful. For example, being exposed to a certain body ideal on Instagram may be particularly detrimental for people with a low self-esteem or younger individuals who were recently bullied for their physical appearance at school. Similarly, talking extensively to a close friend via social media could increase affective well-being after a person has had a negative experience. The context and situation matter for understanding person-specific susceptibility. An isolated focus on person-specific characteristics may hence again be oversimplifying.

Under What Circumstances Does the Effect Occur?

The third question asks what device- or platform-specific, contextual, or situational factors moderate social media use effects on well-being. By using primarily survey-based designs, we have flattened situational variance in people's social media use experiences into somewhat artificial, aggregated measures of overall use and well-being. To describe circumstances, we need to identify both personal and environmental factors related to context, device or applications, and the situation (cf. also Vanden Abeele, 2020). The goal should be to find factors that are amenable to empirical investigation and that are present (i.e., measurable) across all situations.

First, *contexts* refer to structured social settings characterized by canonical activities, norms and rules, relationships and internal values (e.g., Nissenbaum, 2010). Contexts are thus related to social spheres related to, for example, friends, family, work, or school. Contexts vary, but their characteristics nonetheless remain comparatively stable. From this, it follows that experiences within a context will be similar (although not the same) even if dispersed in time. On social media, people likewise act in contexts. Their experiences – and thus also whether or not using social media will be a pleasant or negative experience – will also be determined by their perceptions about audiences (e.g., their friends or followers) and the norms and practices this social network prescribes or endorses. However, the types of practices and norms are also determined by *device-* or *application-specific characteristics*. Each platform allows or emphasizes certain types of interactions (e.g., liking, commenting, sharing posts) and thus leads to specific social dynamics (e.g., disclosing selfies on Instagram, sharing work-related information on Facebook, sharing private information on SnapChat) that, in turn, shape potential impacts of content, notifications, or message type on well-being. For example, whereas an Instagram user may engage in sharing a lot of photos to receive likes and comments from his or her friends or followers, assessing whether this contributes or reduces well-being is not as clear. Receiving likes on a post may be a positive experience, but posting a photo that one really likes and not receiving any likes can be a very unpleasant experience. Overall, various contextual factors including competing goals, attentional demands, and obligations (Hofmann, Reinecke, & Meier, 2016), pressure to connect and be available (Licoppe, 2004), the imagined audience (Litt, 2012), as well as application features and perceived behavioral options (cf. Vanden Abeele, 2020) could be important moderators of social media effects on well-being.

Next to contextual factors, there are *situational personal and environmental factors* that need to be considered. Situationally activated personal factors relate to internal perceptions of motives, goals, feelings, or moods. For example, a recent study has found that situational autonomy dissatisfaction moderates the within-person relationship between online vigilance and momentary perceived stress (Gilbert, Baumgartner, & Reinecke, 2021). Being mindful during instant messaging was also related to less stress and positive affect (Bauer, Loy, Masur, & Schneider, 2017). Situational goal conflict, for example, using social media to procrastinate, likewise predicts situational well-being (Reinecke & Hofmann, 2016). Situational environmental factors refer to interpersonal perceptions of others and their behaviors, as well as external perception of place, time, locations, and other physical cues. For example, where an individual is using social media might matter (e.g., at home, at work, or while on transportation) for how content is perceived. If social media are used together with other persons (e.g., friends, partner, family), this may further change how an individual reacts to social media content, practices, or certain experiences. Dogruel and Schnauber-Stockmann (2021), for example, found that the responsiveness norms (measured as a trait-like quality) and the type of sender (e.g., close friends or family members vs. other persons) interacted in predicting the probability to respond to instant messenger messages and may thus explain momentary stress or anxiety.

In sum, we believe that identifying relevant contextual, device- or platform-specific characteristics as well as situational factors presents an important challenge for future research. Also, adopting a situational lens helps to scrutinize whether social media are indeed the cause or whether they are rather a contributing force that increases already existing downward or upward spirals related to situational well-being.

What Type of Well-Being is Affected?

Finally, we need to scrutinize what type or component of well-being is actually affected. In the previous sections, we already implicitly mentioned that we can differentiate stable (e.g., life satisfaction) and more fleeting components of well-being (e.g., positive or negative affect, moods). However, disentangling effects of the various factors described earlier on well-being requires us to differentiate indicators of well-being in more detail.

Well-being is a subcategory of mental health, which can be divided into two parts: psychopathology and psychological well-being (Meier & Reinecke, 2020). This is known as the two continua model of mental health. Psychopathology can be referred to as negative mental health, reflecting disturbance or personal distress in one's life (Lahey, Krueger, Rathouz, Waldman, & Zald, 2017; Meier & Reinecke, 2020). Psychological well-being, on the other hand, can be referred to as positive mental health and reflects a person's quality of life and overall functioning (Diener, Lucas, & Oishi, 2018). It is important to note that, psychological well-being is not the absence of psychopathology, just as psychopathology is not just the absence of psychological well-being (Meier & Reinecke, 2020). Psychopathology is usually seen as the presence or absence of specific symptoms or disorders. Symptoms, or a set of symptoms, form the basis for the absence or presence of a disorder (i.e., depressive symptoms can form the basis of a depressive disorder). In the context of social media effects research, psychopathology is distinguished in two dimensions: internalizing and externalizing dimensions of psychopathology (Meier & Reinecke, 2020). Internalizing psychopathology refers to inward-directed behaviors, cognitions, and emotions such as anxiety and depression whereas externalizing psychopathology refers to outward-directed behavior, cognitions, and emotions such as aggression and substance abuse. Risk factors that may increase individuals' vulnerability to develop psychopathology can include, for example, loneliness, social isolation, and low sleep quality (Meier & Reinecke, 2020).

Psychological well-being includes two dimensions: hedonic and eudaimonic well-being. Hedonic well-being generally represents "feeling well" and is defined as subjective experiences of pleasure and pain at a given point in time (Huta, 2017; Ryan & Deci, 2001). Within the hedonic approach, three subcomponents of subjective well-being can be distinguished: positive affect, negative affect, and life satisfaction. Positive and negative affect tap upon the affective dimension of hedonic well-being, whereas life satisfaction taps upon the cognitive dimension of hedonic well-being. Eudaimonic well-being generally represents "doing well" and is defined as the degree to which a person is fully functioning. Eudaimonic well-being is often reflected by meaning and relevance to a broader context, personal growth, excellence, and authenticity/autonomy (Huta & Waterman, 2014).

This overview on concepts of well-being shows that simply asking whether social media use (negatively) affects well-being is oversimplifying. We have to further specify whether we mean that higher social media use leads to less (or more) psychological well-being (e.g., life satisfaction) or actually to certain psychopathologies (e.g., depression). Moreover, we have to specify whether we indeed assume that social media use has an influence on stable, person-related concepts of well-being or whether it rather affects more fleeting, state components of well-being (e.g., positive or negative affect, mood, feelings). Some components of well-being are clearly determined by many different things in an individual's life (e.g., overall life satisfaction) and may thus be less likely to be fundamentally influenced by social media use. Momentary feelings, however, could be strongly affected by particular types of uses, messages, or contents. As mentioned earlier, using an experience sampling study, Bayer and colleagues (2018) have shown that active posting on Facebook leads to positive emotional experiences right after posting but not to any long-term changes in trait mood across two weeks. We should not expect social media use to uniformly affect all types of well-being.

Effect Heterogeneity in Research on Social Media and Body Image

Studies that explicitly try to answer the question whether or not social media use affects adolescents' well-being often remain oversimplifying and neglect the various factors we outlined earlier. More specific research areas such as studies focusing on the impact of cyberbullying, self-presentation, body image representation, or online gaming provide a more nuanced picture of boundary conditions of social media use effect. In what follows, we will discuss some findings from research on idealized image presentation on social media platforms and its effects on adolescents' body (dis)satisfaction. This research area exemplifies quite vividly how acknowledging different personal and environmental factors as well as different levels of analysis contribute to a nuanced understanding about when exposure to certain types of content or specific behaviors become detrimental for individuals' well-being.

Social media play a major role in distributing and reinforcing beauty ideals. Affordances of social media allow easy and ample access to idealized self-presentations for young adolescents (Holland & Tiggemann, 2016). Social media allow users to not only consume media content but also create and upload pictures and react to others' posts (Perloff, 2014), which seems to contribute to a more dispersed picture of various body sizes and appearances nowadays, the so-called body positivity trend (Lazuka, Wick, Keel, & Harriger, 2020). However, specific stereotypical portrayals of body ideals (e.g., being thin and ultra-fit for women and ultra-muscular and toned for men) and facial-ideals (e.g., having a smooth skin) are still pervading the social media landscape, often being reinforced by positive comments and likes (e.g., Holland & Tiggemann, 2016). Aligning with our rationale presented earlier, however, social media users seem to respond differently to these idealized appearance depictions: abundant research has shown both detrimental effects and beneficial effects from such exposure on, for example, body (dis)satisfaction (e.g., Bij de Vaate, Veldhuis, & Konijn, 2020). Adopting the situational lens outlined earlier can help to understand differences in respective findings. Taking into account both stable and situational personal and environmental factors in fact paints a clearer picture for whom and when exposure to body ideals negatively affects well-being.

When Exposure to Body Ideals Becomes Detrimental

Many studies have shown unfavorable effects of social media use on body image perceptions (Holland & Tiggemann, 2016). Although more intensive use of SNS like Instagram and Facebook seemed to instigate a greater body dissatisfaction and body concerns, not all studies found such negative effects from general SNS use. Various studies have shown that specifically appearance-focused activities and engagement in appearance-related content (e.g., posting pictures of oneself and inspecting those of others) contributed to inducing body image disturbances (Holland & Tiggemann, 2016; Mingoia, Hutchinson, Wilson, & Gleaves, 2017). Relatedly, research into selfies as a specific form of appearance-focused online self-presentation indicated that active engagement in selfie-behaviors, such as selecting and editing selfies, was associated with increased feelings of body dissatisfaction (McLean, Paxton, Wertheim, & Masters, 2015).

Social comparison tendencies play a major role in internalizing and processing idealized body portrayals in either direction (e.g., Holland & Tiggemann, 2016). On social media, comparison processes are largely *upward* in nature (Fardouly, Pinkus, & Vartanian, 2017). Studies have underpinned that online appearance comparisons with others who are considered to have a better appearance might lead to a more negative body image and dissatisfaction (Bij de Vaate et al., 2020;

Fardouly et al., 2017). However, previous studies revealed the importance to distinguish between *motives of self-evaluation* and *self-improvement* (Veldhuis, Konijn, & Knobloch-Westerwick, 2017). Both motives may lead to upward comparison, but comparison with ideal-body media figures to evaluate oneself generally leads to more negative body perceptions compared to looking at others as an inspiration for self-improvement.

These outcomes indicate that *environmental factors* such as type of content (i.e., idealized and appearance-focused visuals, selfies), practices on specifically photo-based platforms (e.g., liking and commenting Instagram, social comparison), and situational personal factors (e.g., motive) need to be considered to explain negative effects on well-being.

When Exposure to Body Ideals is Beneficial

Studies have found positive effects of exposure to body ideals. With current digital applications, people can easily create, select, and edit appearance-focused content before they show themselves online. Feeling in control of posting idealized pictures might enhance people's self-evaluations (cf. Tiidenberg & Gómez Cruz, 2015), which in turn may motivate people to engage in online self-presentation and reinforce their positive self-evaluations. Experiencing higher body appreciation and self-objectification was found to be associated with greater engagement in selecting, editing, and posting selfies (Veldhuis, Alleva, Bij de Vaate, Keijer, & Konijn, 2020).

Comparing oneself with idealized media figures (upward comparison) can also instigate a higher body satisfaction (Veldhuis et al., 2017). If a person is highly motivated to "improve the self", seeing idealized bodies might rather inspire and spark feelings of attainability of having a better body. Differentiating underlying social comparison motives thus is an important *situational personal factor* that explains how users *cognitively process* idealized media fare and whether social media's impact on body image is harmful or beneficial.

Downward comparison may also explain positive effects on well-being. It occurs when people evaluate themselves against somebody who they think is worse off, that is, looks worse than they do. The *motive of self-enhancement* often underlies this process and leads to positive appraisals of one's own appearance. The literature review by Bij de Vaate et al. (2020) has indeed found such positive effects from downward social comparisons on body image.

Individual and Situational Susceptibility

Predispositions like self-esteem and appearance schematicity play a role in explaining the divergent reactions to ideal body fare, rendering those with lowered self-esteem and those who attribute more importance and meaning to one's appearance more susceptible to adverse effects (Veldhuis, 2020). *Person-related stable factors* like age, gender, and ethnicity seem to have a guiding impact in processing ideal body media fare (e.g., Holland & Tiggemann, 2016; López-Guimerà, Levine, Sánchez-carracedo, & Fauquet, 2010). For example, especially young girls are in a developmental stage in which they undergo bodily changes, are developing their own identity, and are more open to peer influences, while also being avid consumers of media.

On a situational level, the context in which an image is presented matters as well. Particularly on social media, visual posts are contextualized by captions, comments, and likes (Perloff, 2014; Veldhuis, 2020). Empirical studies have shown that texts elucidating on ultrathin bodies as being "normal" increased viewers' body dissatisfaction whereas texts that confirmed the underweight status of such bodies decreased their body dissatisfaction (Veldhuis, Konijn, & Seidell, 2012). Likewise, ideal body depictions accompanied by self-improvement texts that the reader also could attain such a body increased feelings of body satisfaction (Veldhuis et al., 2017). Furthermore, likes are interpreted as social support expressed by peers and therefore lead to a feeling of being accepted (in case of ample likes) or rejected (in case of few likes; Rosenthal-von der Pütten et al., 2019). Hence, given the active interplay between media users in newer digital and social media formats, it is vital to further investigate social media's impact on body image perceptions in light of the *contextual and situational factors* formed by peer and verbal contexts (Perloff, 2014; Veldhuis, 2020).

Conclusion and Future Perspectives

As previous research has shown, scholars and policy makers often try to find easy answers to rather complex problems. The question of whether or not social media negatively impacts young adolescents' mental or physical health is no exception in this regard. In this chapter, we argued that social media effects on well-being vary across individuals, contexts, and situations. We urge future research to investigate the intricate combination of personal and environmental factors in explaining heterogeneity in social media use effects. We believe that taking a situational perspective to identify relevant factors on various levels of analysis and with various levels of stability is a useful starting point that helps to identify interactions between, for example, stable person characteristics (such as gender, age, literacy) and more fleeting contextual (e.g., perceptions of audiences, norms, and practices) and varying situational factors (e.g., momentary motives, goals, feelings) and how their combination affects different components of subjective well-being. Methodologically, this will require novel approaches that allow for more granular assessments of social media use behaviors as well as highly repetitive assessments of individuals' momentary well-being. Collaboration between disciplines that spurs combinations of computational assessment approaches (e.g., behavioral observation via logging), situational assessment (e.g., via experience sampling), and more traditional questionnaire designs will allow for more precision in assessing the various factors that may explain heterogeneity in social media use effects.

Understanding specific boundary conditions of such effects, however, is not just a purely academic endeavor. For example, the fact that individuals respond in very different ways to social media content in terms of their body perceptions also holds practical implications for redirecting negative media effects through media-based body image interventions. Being such popular and pervasive venues for providing information and setting social standards, social media should be considered as effective means to (re)negotiate such standards. A one-size-fits-all approach seems generally ineffective, but considering a holistic view on social media influences, social media-based interventions can work if tailored to individual user's needs.

References

Bauer, A. A., Loy, L. S., Masur, P. K., & Schneider, F. M. (2017). Mindful instant messaging: Mindfulness and autonomous motivation as predictors of well-being in smartphone communication. *Journal of Media Psychology: Theories, Methods, and Applications*, 29(3), 159–165. https://doi.org/10.1027/1864-1105/a000225

Bayer, J. B., Ellison, N., Schoenebeck, S., Brady, E., & Falk, E. B. (2018). Facebook in context(s): Measuring emotional responses across time and space. *New Media & Society*, 20(3), 1047–1067. https://doi.org/10.1177/1461444816681522

Bayer, J. B., Trieu, P., & Ellison, N. B. (2020). Social media elements, ecologies, and effects. *Annual Review of Psychology*, 71(1), 471–497. https://doi.org/10.1146/annurev-psych-010419-050944

Beyens, I., Pouwels, J. L., van Driel, I. I., Keijsers, L., & Valkenburg, P. M. (2020). The effect of social media on well-being differs from adolescent to adolescent. *Scientific Reports*, 10(1), 10763. https://doi.org/10.1038/s41598-020-67727-7

Bij de Vaate, N., Veldhuis, J., & Konijn, E. (2020). How online self-presentation affects well-being and body image: A systematic review. *Telematics and Informatics*, 47. https://doi.org/10.1016/j.tele.2019.101316

Billieux, J., Linden, M. V. der, & Rochat, L. (2008). The role of impulsivity in actual and problematic use of the mobile phone. *Applied Cognitive Psychology*, 22(9), 1195–1210. https://doi.org/10.1002/acp.1429

Blackwell, D., Leaman, C., Tramposch, R., Osborne, C., & Liss, M. (2017). Extraversion, neuroticism, attachment style and fear of missing out as predictors of social media use and addiction. *Personality and Individual Differences*, 116, 69–72. https://doi.org/10.1016/j.paid.2017.04.039

Brody, J. E. (2019). The crisis in youth suicide. *The New York Times*. Retrieved from www.nytimes.com/2019/12/02/well/mind/the-crisis-in-youth-suicide.html

Carr, C. T., & Hayes, R. A. (2015). Social media: Defining, developing, and divining. *Atlantic Journal of Communication*, 23(1), 46–65. https://doi.org/10.1080/15456870.2015.972282

Diener, E., Lucas, R. E., & Oishi, S. (2018). Advances and open questions in the science of subjective well-being. *Collabra: Psychology*, 4(1), 15. https://doi.org/10.1525/collabra.115

Dienlin, T., & Johannes, N. (2020). The impact of digital technology use on adolescent well-being. *Dialogues in Clinical Neuroscience*, *22*(2), 135–142. https://doi.org/10.31887/DCNS.2020.22.2/tdienlin

Dogruel, L., & Schnauber-Stockmann, A. (2021). What determines instant messaging communication? Examining the impact of person- and situation-level factors on IM responsiveness. *Mobile Media & Communication*, *9*(2), 210–228. https://doi.org/10.1177/2050157920943926

Elhai, J. D., Levine, J. C., Dvorak, R. D., & Hall, B. J. (2016). Fear of missing out, need for touch, anxiety and depression are related to problematic smartphone use. *Computers in Human Behavior*, *63*, 509–516. https://doi.org/10.1016/j.chb.2016.05.079

Escobar-Viera, C. G., Shensa, A., Bowman, N. D., Sidani, J. E., Knight, J., James, A. E., & Primack, B. A. (2018). Passive and active social media use and depressive symptoms among United States adults. *Cyberpsychology, Behavior and Social Networking*, *21*(7), 437–443. https://doi.org/10.1089/cyber.2017.0668

Fardouly, J., Pinkus, R. T., & Vartanian, L. R. (2017). The impact of appearance comparisons made through social media, traditional media, and in person in women's everyday lives. *Body Image*, *20*, 31–39. https://doi.org/10.1016/j.bodyim.2016.11.002

Frison, E., & Eggermont, S. (2016). Exploring the relationships between different types of Facebook use, perceived online social support, and adolescents' depressed mood. *Social Science Computer Review*, *34*(2), 153–171. https://doi.org/10.1177/0894439314567449

Gilbert, A., Baumgartner, S., & Reinecke, L. (2021). *Situational boundary conditions of digital stress: Goal conflict and autonomy frustration make smartphone use more stressful.* PsyArXiv. https://doi.org/10.31234/osf.io/fzct9

Hofmann, W., Reinecke, L., & Meier, A. (2016). Of sweet temptations and bitter aftertaste: Self-control as a moderator of the effects of media use on well-being. In L. Reinecke & M. B. Oliver (Eds.), *The routledge handbook of media use and well-being* (pp. 211–222). New York: Routledge.

Holland, G., & Tiggemann, M. (2016). A systematic review of the impact of the use of social networking sites on body image and disordered eating outcomes. *Body Image*, *17*, 100–110. https://doi.org/10.1016/j.bodyim.2016.02.008

Huta, V. (2017). An overview of hedonic and eudaimonic well-being concepts. In *The Routledge handbook of media use and well-being: International perspectives on theory and research on positive media effects* (pp. 14–33). London: Routledge/Taylor & Francis Group.

Huta, V., & Waterman, A. S. (2014). Eudaimonia and its distinction from Hedonia: Developing a classification and terminology for understanding conceptual and operational definitions. *Journal of Happiness Studies*, *15*(6), 1425–1456. https://doi.org/10.1007/s10902-013-9485-0

Kim, C., & Shen, C. (2020). Connecting activities on social network sites and life satisfaction: A comparison of older and younger users. *Computers in Human Behavior*, *105*, 106222. https://doi.org/10.1016/j.chb.2019.106222

Lahey, B. B., Krueger, R. F., Rathouz, P. J., Waldman, I. D., & Zald, D. H. (2017). Validity and utility of the general factor of psychopathology. *World Psychiatry*, *16*(2), 142–144. https://doi.org/10.1002/wps.20410

Lazuka, R. F., Wick, M. R., Keel, P. K., & Harriger, J. A. (2020). Are we there yet? Progress in depicting diverse images of beauty in Instagram's body positivity movement. *Body Image*, *34*, 85–93. https://doi.org/10.1016/j.bodyim.2020.05.001

Licoppe, C. (2004). 'Connected' presence: The emergence of a new repertoire for managing social relationships in a changing communication technoscape. *Environment and Planning D: Society and Space*, *22*(1), 135–156. https://doi.org/10.1068/d323t

Litt, E. (2012). Knock, knock: Who's there? The imagined audience. *Journal of Broadcasting & Electronic Media, 56*(3), 330–345. https://doi.org/10.1080/08838151.2012.705195

López-Guimerà, G., Levine, M. P., Sánchez-carracedo, D., & Fauquet, J. (2010). Influence of mass media on body image and eating disordered attitudes and behaviors in females: A review of effects and processes. *Media Psychology, 13*(4), 387–416. https://doi.org/10.1080/15213269.2010.525737

Magnusson, D. (1981). Problems in environmental analyses – An introduction. In D. Magnusson (Ed.), *Toward a psychology of situations* (pp. 3–7). Mahwah, NJ: Lawrence Erlbaum.

Masur, P. K. (2018). *Situational privacy and self-disclosure: Communication processes in online environments*. Cham: Springer.

McLean, S. A., Paxton, S. J., Wertheim, E. H., & Masters, J. (2015). Photoshopping the selfie: Self photo editing and photo investment are associated with body dissatisfaction in adolescent girls: Photoshopping of the selfie. *International Journal of Eating Disorders, 48*(8), 1132–1140. https://doi.org/10.1002/eat.22449

Meier, A., & Reinecke, L. (2020). Computer-mediated communication, social media, and mental health: A conceptual and empirical meta-review. *Communication Research,* 0093650220958224. https://doi.org/10.1177/0093650220958224

Mingoia, J., Hutchinson, A. D., Wilson, C., & Gleaves, D. H. (2017). The relationship between social networking site use and the internalization of a thin ideal in females: A meta-analytic review. *Frontiers in Psychology, 8,* 1351. https://doi.org/10.3389/fpsyg.2017.01351

Nissenbaum, H. (2010). *Privacy in context: Technology, policy, and the integrity of social life.* Stanford, CA: Stanford University Press.

Orben, A. (2020). Teenagers, screens and social media: A narrative review of reviews and key studies. *Social Psychiatry and Psychiatric Epidemiology, 55*(4), 407–414. https://doi.org/10.1007/s00127-019-01825-4

Orben, A., Dienlin, T., & Przybylski, A. K. (2019). Social media's enduring effect on adolescent life satisfaction. *Proceedings of the National Academy of Sciences, 116*(21), 10226–10228. https://doi.org/10.1073/pnas.1902058116

Orben, A., & Przybylski, A. K. (2019). The association between adolescent well-being and digital technology use. *Nature Human Behaviour, 3*(2), 173–182. https://doi.org/10.1038/s41562-018-0506-1

Perloff, R. M. (2014). Social media effects on young women's body image concerns: Theoretical perspectives and an agenda for research. *Sex Roles, 71*(11–12), 363–377. https://doi.org/10.1007/s11199-014-0384-6

Rauthmann, J. F., Sherman, R. A., & Funder, D. C. (2015). Principles of situation research: Towards a better understanding of psychological situations: Principles of situation research. *European Journal of Personality, 29*(3), 363–381. https://doi.org/10.1002/per.1994

Reinecke, L., & Hofmann, W. (2016). Slacking off or winding down? An experience sampling study on the drivers and consequences of media use for recovery versus procrastination: Slacking off or winding down? *Human Communication Research, 42*(3), 441–461. https://doi.org/10.1111/hcre.12082

Rosenthal-von der Pütten, A. M., Hastall, M. R., Köcher, S., Meske, C., Heinrich, T., Labrenz, F., & Ocklenburg, S. (2019). "Likes" as social rewards: Their role in online social comparison and decisions to like other People's selfies. *Computers in Human Behavior, 92,* 76–86. https://doi.org/10.1016/j.chb.2018.10.017

Ross, L., & Nisbett, R. E. (2011). *The person and the situation: Perspectives of social psychology*. London: Pinter & Martin.

Ryan, R. M., & Deci, E. L. (2001). On happiness and human potentials: A review of research on hedonic and eudaimonic well-being. *Annual Review of Psychology, 52*, 141–166. https://doi.org/10.1146/annurev.psych.52.1.141

Schemer, C., Masur, P. K., Geiss, S., Müller, P., & Schäfer, S. (2021). The impact of internet and social media use on well-being: A longitudinal analysis of adolescents across nine years. *Journal of Computer-Mediated Communication, 26*(1), 1–21. https://doi.org/10.1093/jcmc/zmaa014

Thorisdottir, I. E., Sigurvinsdottir, R., Asgeirsdottir, B. B., Allegrante, J. P., & Sigfusdottir, I. D. (2019). Active and passive social media use and symptoms of anxiety and depressed mood among Icelandic adolescents. *Cyberpsychology, Behavior and Social Networking, 22*(8), 535–542. https://doi.org/10.1089/cyber.2019.0079

Tiidenberg, K., & Gómez Cruz, E. (2015). Selfies, image and the re-making of the body. *Body & Society, 21*(4), 77–102. https://doi.org/10.1177/1357034X15592465

Twenge, J. M., Joiner, T. E., Rogers, M. L., & Martin, G. N. (2018). Increases in depressive symptoms, suicide-related outcomes, and suicide rates among U.S. adolescents after 2010 and links to increased new media screen time. *Clinical Psychological Science, 6*(1), 3–17. https://doi.org/10.1177/2167702617723376

Valkenburg, P. M., Beyens, I., Pouwels, J. L., van Driel, I. I., & Keijsers, L. (2021). Social media use and adolescents' self-esteem: Heading for a person-specific media effects paradigm. *Journal of Communication, 71*(1), 56–78. https://doi.org/10.1093/joc/jqaa039

Valkenburg, P. M., Peter, J., & Schouten, A. P. (2006). Friend networking sites and their relationship to adolescents' well-being and social self-esteem. *CyberPsychology & Behavior, 9*(5), 584–590. https://doi.org/10.1089/cpb.2006.9.584

Vanden Abeele, M. M. P. (2020). Digital wellbeing as a dynamic construct. *Communication Theory*. https://doi.org/10.1093/ct/qtaa024

Veldhuis, J. (2020). Media use, body image, and disordered eating. *International Encyclopedia of Media Psychology*. https://doi.org/10.1002/9781119011071.iemp0103

Veldhuis, J., Alleva, J. M., Bij de Vaate, A. J. D. (Nadia), Keijer, M., & Konijn, E. A. (2020). Me, my selfie, and I: The relations between selfie behaviors, body image, self-objectification, and self-esteem in young women. *Psychology of Popular Media, 9*(1), 3–13. https://doi.org/10.1037/ppm0000206

Veldhuis, J., Konijn, E. A., & Knobloch-Westerwick, S. (2017). Boost your body: Self-improvement magazine messages increase body satisfaction in young adults. *Health Communication, 32*(2), 200–210. https://doi.org/10.1080/10410236.2015.1113482

Veldhuis, J., Konijn, E. A., & Seidell, J. C. (2012). Weight information labels on media models reduce body dissatisfaction in adolescent girls. *Journal of Adolescent Health, 50*(6), 600–606. https://doi.org/10.1016/j.jadohealth.2011.10.249

Whitlock, J., & Masur, P. K. (2019). Disentangling the association of screen time with developmental outcomes and well-being: Problems, challenges, and opportunities. *JAMA Pediatrics, 173*(11), 1021. https://doi.org/10.1001/jamapediatrics.2019.3191

13

"WHAT DOES GOD NEED WITH A STARSHIP?"

A Conversation About Politics, Participation, and Social Media

Nico Carpentier and Henry Jenkins

Henry: Near the end of *Star Trek V: The Final Frontier*, Captain James T. Kirk confronts an entity who claims to be a divine being but who is deceiving his followers into helping him escape from captivity: "What does God need with a starship?" The moment has come to mind recently as I have thought about a similar question: What does the American president need with Twitter?

The two of us have now had several conversations about the nature of participation in contemporary culture and politics and about the ethical norms that might govern meaningful participation (Jenkins & Carpentier, 2013). Summing up a 2019 discussion of participatory ethics,[1] Nico wrote:

> Participation is a concept that loses its meaning if it is pushed outside democratic culture. Of course, there are many grey zones, and there, the discussion is famously complicated, but that should not spoil the fun right now. There is one important addition, and that is that we need to distinguish between progressive politics and democracy. . . . There is now ample evidence that participatory logics can be activated by a wide variety of political ideologies, and that is not the exclusive territory of progressive politics. This, of course, is combined with the realization that civil society is not necessarily progressive, and not even necessarily democratic.
>
> *(Carpentier & Jenkins, 2019)*

As we discussed how to continue this exchange, we both realized that neither of us have had very much to say about participation *in* and *through* social media, and that there was a need to open up this avenue. So, that will be our primary focus here.

DOI: 10.4324/9781003171270-13

I should start by saying that as we are writing this, I am still working through fresh memories of insurrectionists storming the US Capitol on January 6, 2021, inflamed by the deceptions and angry rhetoric of Donald Trump, who has throughout his political career used social media to enhance his ambitions toward autocratic power. Trump is only one of a number of new-style far-right leaders who have seen Twitter, Facebook, and other social media as ideal tools for solidifying their power and mobilizing their supporters. And this situation creates an opportunity to consider how top-down use of social media differs from the ways these same platforms are deployed in the name of reciprocal or bottom-up power.

Trump has often claimed that he uses social media to speak directly to the American people and work around the powerful role of mainstream media gatekeepers. I would argue that Trump used Twitter to invalidate the claims of professional journalists, who he often dismissed as "fake news" or "enemies of the people." He chose a platform that validates individual expression over the collective good and supports uninformed opinion over expert insights. In using Twitter, he was claiming to be a man of the people who was being muzzled by the press, the same press that was broadcasting his every word. He used Twitter to frame himself as an outcast even as he was consolidating power. His use of Twitter allowed him to seem to flatten hierarchies even as he had the capacity to amplify his grievances louder than anyone else. Trump was using what some saw as a democratic platform toward profoundly undemocratic ends.

Now that the tech companies have shut down Trump's various social media accounts, there is a widespread sense that he was misusing and abusing these platforms, yet this would seem to be a debatable proposition (or at least plenty are debating it). How can we distinguish what Trump did from the logics that have shaped social media platforms from the start? How might we think about this top-down use of social media alongside other widespread claims that Twitter has empowered progressive social movements around the world to route around censorship, to organize and mobilize against the powerful and to successfully launch "leaderless" movements for social change?

Nico: It's nice to have another iteration of this dialogue, this time with quite a spectacular (even stellar) title. Before we started writing this text, we had a quick discussion about the title first, and I did (and do) like the title we chose. One reason why I liked the title is that the starship Enterprise has so much to do with social media, at a symbolic level. Space travel is emblematic of the fantasy of exploration, pushing back frontiers and opening up new territories, with its blind admiration for novelty and its strong neglect for its consequences. When social media were new, there was an equally strong fascination for their novelty, combined with a decent dose of optimism and the firm belief that social media would open new frontiers and allow us to participate where we had never participated before.

Social media became our starship. They became our hypnotic disk, spinning in front of our eyes, making us gasp for air because of the sense of endless potentiality they seemingly entailed. Social media became our participatory gods, which absorbed many other forms of participation and their histories. I do understand this fascination for the new, of course, and the need to study social media. But at some point, we should focus our attention on what this "social media turn" means, what we have lost out of sight, and what the cost of this focus is. One issue I would like to raise here is whether we have not brought the twins of technological determinism and media centrism back onto the stage of media analysis. You mentioned your former president ((textual grin)), and I think that we can use that part of the USA's political reality as a starting point (even when we should remain aware that there is still a world outside the USA): Have we really thought through the reception of his tweets, or have we assumed that the vitriolic language would necessarily be poisonous in its effect too? Are we not just returning to a hypodermic needle theory? Of course, yes, people stormed the Capitol, but can we then assume that the behavior of thousands informs us about the interpretations of millions?

Are we not, as an academic field, at the same time strengthening the myth of the mediated center (to recycle my favorite Nick Couldry (2003) concept)? Maybe the media-centric approach has even become narrower than ever, transforming into a "social media-centric" approach. Obviously, we shouldn't give up on media studies, but maybe we can allocate a bit more space to society-centric and process-centric approaches? There are so many assumptions in the (first) analyses of the Capitol riots that still need to be unpacked. If we reduce Trump's ideological project to mere tweeting, aren't we missing out on opportunities for better understanding a highly sophisticated populist ideological project, with an assemblage of political, educational, military, capitalist, and communicative components, among others? When we are focusing on the tweets, aren't we missing the highly complex right-wing chain of equivalence that has been brilliantly created, where very different parts of the (extreme)-right have managed to unite themselves around the empty signifier of Trump, and that thus have moved the center further to the right? Aren't we forgetting how this ideological project still speaks to a middle and working class in economic distress, that is strongly interpellated by this discourse, because it translated their interest into a way of thinking that they can relate to, even when it probably works against their (class) interest at the same time? Have we now forgotten Gramsci's (1971) analysis of Italian fascism?

Shouldn't we think about the articulation of ideology, communication, and technology instead? We have attributed an autonomous force to social media as the ultimate moment of many-to-many communication while we forget how other media technologies were once also articulated as forms of many-to-many communication. Bertolt Brecht's (1983) outcry, in his radio theory of the late 1920s and early 1930s, pleading for rescuing radio from the claws of the capitalist forces that articulated radio as means of distribution, and not as means of communication, is a grim reminder of what was lost when radio became a mainstream medium. Trump's use of Twitter is a form of one-to-many communication, firmly in the tradition of "legacy" mainstream media. It demonstrates how communication technologies can become articulated, materially and/or discursively, in many different ways, ranging from maximalist participatory and dialogical, to authoritarian and monological. Moreover, we should also not remain blind to the assemblage of mainstream media, online and audiovisual, that all direct our gaze to mainstream politics and the horse race logics of the elections. Still, I must confess, I enjoyed watching CNN and Fox during these US elections days, from my comfortable Prague seat. Still, I'm not sure what I actually learned about the USA these days and the everyday lived experiences of (north) Americans at times of the COVID-19 crisis. And I'd like to add that I don't think we should see these evolutions necessarily as a loss and abandon ourselves to nostalgia, but I do think we need to think about the structural processes (e.g., massification, mainstreaming) to better understand what happened, and what is still happening.

Henry: Whenever I talk about the rise of social media, I try to direct people to the larger social, political, and cultural framework you discuss. From a US perspective, I can trace a long history of efforts of everyday people to expand their communicative capacities, to gain greater control over the means of cultural production and circulation, and to assert a right to meaningfully participate in the decisions that impact their lives. When social media emerged (the latest in a series of new configurations of media that have advanced these same goals), it seemed natural that the public would map their hopes onto the affordances of this new media system. Social media platforms enabled networks of people to speak, facilitating some form of collective intelligence, wisdom, ignorance, foolishness (call it what we want). If the medium is the message (always a dubious proposition), the message of Twitter originally was "here it is" (sharing links) and "here I am" (calling for acknowledgment) but increasingly, the implicit and often explicit message of Twitter has become "I'm pissed about this." And the algorithms have been organized to move intensely felt content through the system, drowning out other conversations people want to have.

Recent years have also seen a shift from the idea of Twitter as a grassroots platform and toward Twitter as the space of "influencers" (following its own mass media logic where the value of the content is determined by how many likes it receives). There is no greater influencer than the president who already has access to so many other sources of power – discursive or otherwise – through which to command attention ("Here I am" indeed!) and shape the agenda (Here it is, once and for all). Above all, as the nexus of multiple forms of power, the national leader has an unusual capacity to normalize ideas and practices that might otherwise exist on the fringes of the mediated middle. The insurrectionists operated in the shadows, in semi-public spaces, such as the lesser-known social media platforms (Parler for example) (Miranda, 2020). The president could amplify those discourses, mainstreaming their messages at a time when the news media was covering his tweets as the primary source of news about what the White House was thinking and doing each morning. Whatever the president tweets is de facto news.

I do not mean to be adopting a technological determinist stance here: this is ultimately not an argument about the technology per se but about how these platforms are being used, about who is using them, and about the relationship between social media, the other parts of the media system, and the other sources of power a national leader possesses. If Trump did not respond to actual fault lines in the culture and to a widespread perception among his followers that they have been neglected, dismissed, or simply dissed, then his disinformation would not be effective. But researchers have found a 70 percent decrease in "misinformation" about the election results since Trump's social media accounts were shut down (Garrett, 2020). Trump (and other global leaders) function as nexus points around which these various forces of discontent coalesce. Ultimately, his impact comes from his interventions, forwarding (and thus increasing the visibility of) messages and establishing the discursive norms determining which messages get taken seriously. In that way, the model of the mediated center operated to make white supremacist messages more socially acceptable.

Trump would periodically disavow any direct knowledge of right-wing groups such as Proud Boys, political figures such as David Duke, and conspiracy theories such as Q-Anon. His denials were never fully convincing, but in a way, the truth doesn't matter. He does not need to know who they are; they knew who he was, and they knew how to organize their messaging around his tweets to ensure that they got wider circulation, and he knew enough of their language to ensure that he addressed their concerns and could call on them for support. In describing this dynamic, "Twitter" serves as a shorthand for this larger political-discursive-media configuration securing support for these autocratic leaders (operating in supposedly democratic contexts) and constituting a palpable threat to those who get in their way. So, yes, I am totally on board with your effort to move beyond a media-centric or tech-centric account as long as we recognize that it is through social media that so many of these other forces are coming together right now.

Nico: I think you raise an important point, when you refer to the rise of social media and how they tapped into one of people's most fundamental desires, the desire to communicate. Social media are discursive-material assemblages (Carpentier, 2017) that offer and promise to fulfil that desire, interpolating ordinary people and elites to translate this desire into reality, through social media's discourse of self-expression and through their material interfaces and infrastructures that allow translating this discourse into material practice. And yes, I agree, this is embedded in a history of ordinary people's struggles in order to gain control over their means of communication. If we go back a bit in time, we can find a similar level of enthusiasm with ham radio and free radio activists in the 1970s (and a bit before), even if it was still at a different scale. Your work on *Textual Poaching* (Jenkins, 1992) made the same point in relation to fandom. These were (and are) deeply liberating moments where control was wrestled away from mainstream media elites and "shared with the people", as it was called at that time.

Behind this desire for communication is an even more encompassing desire (and fantasy), and that is the will to power. Not in a Nietzschean meaning, which is very much centered on dominating the other, but in a more positive way, as a desire to control one's own life and destiny. The desire for communication is also about controlling the representations about ourselves and our world. It is about the ability to show who we are, and what matters to us, in a way that we decide for ourselves. It is about no longer being controlled by media elites that communicate their world views, and sometimes show social processes, identities, practices, . . . in awkward ways, at least in the eyes of those who were subjected to this media professional gaze.

Of course, these desires are also fantasies – and you'll have to forgive me for using this Lacanian concept. These fantasies are driving forces that make us act with the objective to realize them. They promise and sometimes deliver pleasure, and we crave to approximate these fantasies. Both the desire for communication and the desire to control our environment are fantasies, I would argue. But this also means that they are permanently frustrated. There is an unbridgeable gap between a fantasy and its full realization, with which we are also confronted. This is the moment when we say (or think) "This is not it!". At the individual level, these are the moments when the social media interface doesn't comply with our wishes, or when we don't manage to produce the perfect photograph or text. These are the moments when there are no likes and no viewers. These are the moments where our perfectly formulated sentences drown in the multitude. At a more societal level, these are the moments where the social media exercise control over us and where we run into the limits of these media.

To return to the second part of your previous answer: I think that the logic of the fantasy also works well to better understand Q-Anon. To be honest, I find most discussions about Q-Anon quite unsatisfying, problematizing, and ridiculing "believers" without generating a deeper understanding of the knowledge structures and fantasmatic logics of Q-Anon. Of course, listening to Q-Anon's alternative knowledge project gives me the same feeling as watching Monty Python. In particular, the dead parrot sketch comes to mind here, where a man who was sold a dead parrot attempts to return it, while the shopkeeper is adamant that the parrot is still alive.[2] Attacking a Washington pizza restaurant with an assault rifle because sex slaves are thought to be in the basement, as part of a child-abuse assemblage controlled by Hilary Clinton, comes pretty close, I would say (Siddiqui & Svrluga, 2016). But this doesn't advance our knowledge about these discourses – or conspiracy theories as they are called – that much.

One entry point into this discussion takes us back to participation. As we have touched upon before, in our earlier discussions, participation is quite a slippery concept. I tend to distinguish between two approaches, a sociological approach focused on participation as taking part and a political studies approach, defining participation as sharing power. I am part of the latter approach. But whatever approach one takes, I have always argued that participation is always participation *in* something, namely in a particular process, that is, in turn located in a particular (societal) field. I would like to suggest that Q-Anon followers are using social media (and other communicative tools) to participate *in* knowledge production. If we bracket the absurdity and the dangerous nature of this knowledge project for a few moments, we can maybe see the pleasure (or even jouissance) of being part of creating a whole new world, or, at least, a whole new understanding of the world. Is this one of the most gratifying things to do? Isn't it extremely empowering to be part of a knowledge production community, to have your voice heard and confirmed, to participate in building this new world of ideas? I think I can see this temptation, which is at the same time the reason why it is so dangerous.

And this brings me to the second entry point, which is populism. I see populism as a vertical structure that (discursively) creates a juxtaposition between people and an (old) elite. I would add that there is also a horizontal structure in populism that unifies the people with a new elite that "truly" represents them. Q-Anon fits this picture quite well, in its rejection of a cluster of elites, including political and media elites. But there is also, and I think that this is important, the rejection of a knowledge elite that is articulated as strange to the people (or "treacherous" or even "dangerous" for the people). In a very different way, this reminds me of John Fiske's (1989) analysis of the excessive (e.g., in *Understanding Popular Culture*), where he argues that the excessive demonstrates the limits of dominant ideology. I think that Q-Anon with its emphasis on the excessive is transgressing dominant ideology, as part of a political–populist project to generate a new hegemony. And this is where Trump, and the horizontal structure of populism, enters on stage, as he (a bit surprisingly for me, I must add) has managed to claim the position of the true representative of the people, the new elite that will lead the people away from the old "corrupt" elite ("draining the swamp"), toward a new hegemony, structured by new ways of thinking and new mechanisms of establishing truth. I should probably repeat that this hegemony would be destroying all that is dear to me as a scholar and as a human, but that doesn't contradict my analysis, I would say.

This then leaves us with the question where social media feature in this analysis. Discourses (and hegemonies) – and here I don't mean statements or utterances, but ideological frameworks or frameworks of intelligibility (see Carpentier, 2017) – have histories of emergence. In other words, they originate through societal processes that take time to become consolidated. Often, a diversity of signifying machines, for example, education, church, and media – Althusser called them ideological state apparatuses – are needed to support this consolidation. These signifying machines coordinate, synchronize, and harmonize this enormous multiplicity of voices and eventually manage to (co-)produce discourses. The interesting thing is that these signifying machines were often aligned with diverse elites, while social media are now acting as grassroots signifying machines that coordinate, synchronize, and harmonize voices and transform them into discourses (e.g., Q-Anon). Of course, these social media processes are not completely autonomous but supported by grassroots movements, mainstream media, and political parties. After all, the presidency is a pretty decent signifying machine in itself. And, second, there is not one discourse that originates from social media but a diversity of discourses that then engage in discursive struggles with each other and that might be defeated or victorious.

Henry: I was sitting down with my wife's family around the holiday season when my brother-in-law asked me which "fact-checker" I used. Taking this as an informational question, I began to discuss the merits of several different fact-checking projects. He interrupted me with a mischievous grin and said that he and his wife used Q-Anon. You can imagine my sputtering spit-take and then my complete silence (deciding not to feed stereotypes of California academics who were unlikely to change things anyway). More recently, you will be pleased to know that his wife told me that they were trying to "minimize" their exposure to social media outrage, having restricted themselves to lists dealing with gardening, freeze-drying food, veteran's health issues, and "of course, the John Birch Society."

The idea that Q-Anon (on social media or otherwise) functions as a "fact-checker" for its participants has haunted me since and goes hand in hand with much you say here. One of the fantasies about social media – one I have personally been drawn to off and on through the years – is the idea of a place where people with different kinds of expertise can pool knowledge, learn from each other, vet information, and arrive at an understanding of the world that goes deeper than the knowledge of any given expert. Couple this ideal of collective intelligence with a populist distrust of experts as part of the "coastal elites" or "deep state," etc., then we can understand why groups who feel that they have been rendered obsolete in the job market, invisible by the mass media, and deplored by political leaders, feel empowered by social media. Many of them felt "seen" (literally and figuratively) by Trump who would retweet messages, seemingly at random, supporting the fantasy that any individual tweet might reach the eyes of the most powerful person in the country. Q-Anon represented a depository of "truths," many of them emerging bottom up (even if the fantasy behind Q-Anon is that Q intel is bravely leaked by some person or people secretly working as a patriot within the "deep state"). This "data" now seems so firmly cemented that it could provide the basis for "fact checking" the claims of other media, whose motives were held suspect. Q-Anon also offers people like my brother-in-law heroic roles to play in its unfolding narrative, ways of connecting with others who think and feel the same way, and ultimately, to put their often-devalued skills to work in the service of a larger "patriotic" cause. This has often been how populism has historically been recruited in the service of authoritarianism as desires for meaningful participation are redirected toward profoundly antidemocratic ends. We might see this wholesale dismantling of democratic norms and institutions as a bottom-up model of how hegemonic power operates.

But how does this differ from the other kinds of social media revolutions, such as the Arab Spring, which many – me among them – celebrated just a few years ago? A second progressive fantasy was that social media would allow the formation of counter-publics where opinion could emerge outside control by the nation-state or news media that were often deeply beholden to the ruling interests. These publics could question what they were being told, forging alternative truths based on their lived experiences, and ultimately, mobilize into the streets and topple governments that were turning their backs on (or were actively repressing) their citizens. Some of these potentials of social media have been realized by social movements around the world – from the Umbrella Movement to Black Lives Matter, from Occupy to the Arab Spring. Such networked movements are often described as "leaderless," reflecting the flattening of hierarchies, but they could also be described as "leaderful," since any given participant could, in theory, emerge as a leader on an ad hoc basis as actions takes place in multiple locations, on multiple scales, and around multiple goals. These modern protests are often coalitions of diverse networks, working together when it makes sense and independently when it doesn't.

The early debate on these so-called Twitter Revolutions centered on risk. On the one side, critics like Malcolm Gladwell (2010) suggested that social media could not sustain meaningful and enduring social movements because people would not take substantial risks on the basis of the relatively superficial social connections forged amongst relative strangers. And on the other, critics such as Evgeny Morozov (2009) asserted that the risks of conducting transformative politics in such a public space were too high, that people were posting information about their associations and movements on Facebook that earlier revolutionaries refused to confess even when tortured. The ground has shifted on both of those critiques: people are willing to risk a lot on the basis of social ties forged on social networking sites, and modern leaders use social media not simply to access covert information but to mobilize supporters behind their interests.

You are right that there will always be some gap between our fantasies of a more participatory culture and the realities of how power actually gets distributed and deployed. I always thought that it was a good thing that our reach should exceed our grasp since this situation motivates continued struggles for progressive change. But it also rekindles the disillusionment that is driving Q-Anon, the Washington insurrection, and other reactionary movements. If there is no guarantee that such struggles will necessarily be progressive, where does that leave us in terms of setting ethical norms about what constitutes meaningful participation?

I confess that another of the fantasies which have driven my own work has been the idea that social norms would emerge within online communities as opportunities for participation expanded to groups that had never had a public voice before. I have been thinking a lot lately about Julian Dibbell's (n.d.) classic essay, "A Rape in Cyberspace." Dibbell depicted how different factions within an early MUD came together to figure out how to address an incident of sexual harassment. It seems like a mythic moment where the transgressor, Mr. Bungle the Clown, was confronted with the democratic impulses of a participatory community that debated what their norms were, what the limits were, and how they were to be enforced. But such debates about the norms of social media are today few and far between in part because these communities no longer play a role in governing the policies that shape their online conversations. Rather, those policies are authored by Silicon Valley companies with more investment in ensuring constant churn and conflict than fostering greater understanding amongst participants.

Nico: Your family story reminded me of an earlier transformation (which was also very much located in families) in Belgium, in the 1990s. When the extreme-right there moved from the fringes to the mainstream, by capitalizing on widespread latent racism, there was a change in (what was considered to be) legitimate speech. Earlier, openly racist statements were often frowned upon (and attributed to the "weird uncle at the Christmas table," even though structural racism was very present at the same time). Slowly but surely, in the 1990s, openly racist speech became more possible and acceptable. One striking part of this process was the pleasure of transgression (the same kind of "mischievous grin" that you mentioned earlier) that accompanied these racist voices. You could feel, and hear, how much they enjoyed saying what had been unsayable before, draping themselves in the aura of resistance. Moreover, these racist voices loudly claimed access to truth, by explicitly referring to the "parlez-vrai" (or truth-speaking) and the need to "say things as they really are" (later combining it with the rejection of "politically correct" speech). In practice, these voices often created an amalgamation of social analysis and normative (racist) evaluations, which turned out highly efficient (even without social media, I should add). The second thing that struck me was the breakthrough effect. There had always been deeply racist voices (and political groups), but they remained at the fringes for a long time. Their continuous attempts for interpellation failed. The breakthrough came when a series of frustrations (caused by, for instance, urban mismanagement and poor anti-poverty measures) were articulated with these racist interpellations and a new common sense could be created. But it is this first phase, where one shifted from drops to a flood, which interests me here. It turned out that the social sanctions, that blocked racist speech for so long, malfunctioned. One argument here is that these racist voices stayed underground for a very long time, and the lack of visibility allowed them to spread. The other argument is that many underestimated the danger of these racist voices and did not bother to respond to them (and thus did not mobilize sufficient social sanctions), at times when these anti-racist responses would have mattered considerably.

This brings me to the discussion about risk. Even if I see the strength of the argument that people need to structurally commit to a particular cause (and a "like" is easy to give), there are a few ideas to add to this analysis, from a more discursive perspective. One thing to be careful with – and I'm not talking about you here, but more in general – is to build an argument on the separation of speech from social/political action. The dichotomy of safe speech and risky action is problematic, I would argue, because, for me, speech is action, and speech can be risky as well. Imagine that Belgian Christmas table in the 1990s, with the racist uncle defending his racist position with fire and conviction. Even at the social microlevel, this is a risky decision, as it might alienate other family members and lead to the uncle being ostracized. Somehow, the 1970s TV series "All in the Family" comes to mind, with the main character of Archie Bunker, who was sometimes described as a "lovable bigot" (Hobson, 1971). Here, we can see the backlash to racist speech, but as was quickly argued (by, for instance, Neil Vidmar and Milton Rokeach (1974)) it also offered points of identification for other (undoubtedly also lovely) bigots.

This then brings me to your other example: the responses to Bungle's virtual rape and the discussion about whether to "toad" Bungle or not. In the "A Rape in Cyberspace" article, Dibbell (n.d.) writes that, for him, the "real magic Lambda-MOO had to offer" was "the conflation of speech and act that's inevitable in any computer-mediated world, be it Lambda or the increasingly wired world at large." What is vital in the account that Dibbell gives us is that the community stood up to condemn the violent speech acts of Bungle's and – as you say – to democratically discuss the consequences of these violent speech acts, both at the individual (to toad or not to toad) and collective level (to regulate or not to regulate). It was, for me, a deeply ethical moment, where violence in a participatory context was rejected. But it also showed the complexities of democratic deliberation, as the community did not reach an agreement about the response to the rape, and Bungle's account was finally eliminated by the action of one individual (at least that is what Dibbell suggests in his narrative). Still, the main point for me remains that violence was considered incompatible with the participatory environment of the MOO.

Taking a bit of a broader perspective and bringing together the threads of the Belgian Christmas table and LambdaMOO, I would like to suggest that these ethical debates have two entry points. One is the *ethical nature of participation*. The position I defend here – and for a more detailed elaboration, I happily point to the introductory essay of the special issue on "Rescuing Participation", coauthored with Ana Duarte Melo and Fábio Ribeiro (2019) – is that participation in itself is ethical. To be more precise: my argument is that the equalization of power (relations) is both wise and ethical, or, in other words, that domination that mutes or incapacitates others against their will is unethical. There is some support for this position in democratic theory. Take, for instance, Dewey's early essay, "The Ethics of Democracy," where he writes:

> [D]emocracy, in a word, is a social, that is to say, an ethical conception, and upon its ethical significance is based its significance as governmental. Democracy is a form of government only because it is a form of moral and spiritual association.
>
> *(Dewey, 1888, p. 18)*

Surely, we need a more expanded version of this, not restricting democracy to government, but I do not think that this expansion alters the key argument about the ethical nature of democracy (and participation) itself.

But I would argue for a second perspective also, and that relates to the *ethics of participation*. For participation to be (and remain) participatory, a particular ethics is required, driving the actions of those involved, combining a series of deliberative norms (e.g., respect, equality, listening). Of course, there are a multitude of complexities to be considered, but I, for instance, would find it hard to say that people who are storming parliament are enacting a participatory logic. Surely, they are intervening in a political process, but storming a parliament is not participatory in itself, simply because the violence of the political act catapults it outside the realm of participation and democracy through the violation(s) of the ethics of participation. In a similar way, I would not call Trump's tweets participatory. This was a leader speaking to the people in a way that left no space for negotiation, listening, respect for diversity, equality, and so on. Sure, this was access and interaction, which are two crucial conditions of possibility for participation, but they are different from participation as such.

And this then brings me to the last step in my argument, because we run into what Karl Popper called the "the paradox of tolerance." As Popper wrote: "if we extend unlimited tolerance even to those who are intolerant, if we are not prepared to defend a tolerant society against the onslaught of the intolerant, then the tolerant will be destroyed, and tolerance with them" (1947, p. 226). In other words, an ethics of participation also has to be protective. This does not imply that all conflict and difference have to be eradicated – definitely not; it means that participatory processes need to be protected from forces that can destroy them from within. This is where the Belgian uncle and LambdaMOO meet. But this is also where time becomes a relevant factor: anti-participatory forces tend to grow stronger over time, and early responses tend to be more efficient and seem to have a higher chance of success.

Henry: I was at MIT when the events in Dibbell's essay unfolded. I've had a chance to speak to some of the key participants through the years. You remind me here of the role of individual action in resolving this particular incident. But we hoped and believed that such ongoing conversations about democratic norms, the ethics of participation, respect and restraint, were essential if the fantasy of online community was going to be an achievable utopia, to use Pierre Levy's (1999) term. But these early experiments in online community were highly localized and in retrospect, involved elite participants (located at research universities or the military-industrial complex). The Internet expanded in scope and scale at a rate few had anticipated, making it harder to inculcate new members into shared norms. Online community gave way to social media, which, as danah boyd (2006) noted, constituted "ego-centric" networks where individuals share their own thoughts on their own platforms without necessarily developing strong connections to a larger community or holding shared goals and expectations about the nature of the communication taking place.

Rather than the grassroots systems represented by the early MUDS and MOOS, these social media sites were overwhelmingly commercial enterprises with vested interests in expanding their membership and little investment in "toading" anyone. Without established norms to draw on, any attempt to regulate transgressive behavior was decried as "censorship" or more recently, "cancel culture." The so-called cancel culture can be a tool for the marginalized and oppressed to share information vital to their survival in the face of failure of institutions to hold the powerful accountable for their actions. "Cancel culture" (especially as exercised through social media) may also be a form of mob violence directed against individuals when divorced from any democratic norms and without regard for its long-term consequences for community life.

All of that has given rise to a world where Mr. Bungle or his descendants run roughshod over any effort to maintain civil conversation across our differences, and no one has the will to toad in defense of democratic norms. Mr. Bungle now operated from the White House. We are now at a crisis point where we need to revisit what we mean by social media. I am not ready to give up on the participatory fantasies that draw so many of us to these platforms, but we need to ask whether the current platforms are serving us.

On my podcast, "How Do You Like It So Far?", Eli Pariser and Talia Stroud (2021) from The Civic Signals Project suggested that rather than remaining obsessed with the problems in current practice (as, I confess, I have been throughout this whole discussion), we need to be asking what it is we want from social media platforms and online communities. For starters, we want real diversity. We want social media platforms that are governed by motives other than commercialism. We need platforms that are run by nonprofit organizations, that emerge from grassroots collectives, that are housed by faith-based organizations, that adopt explicitly democratic or educational goals, and so forth.

We need social media platforms with articulated norms for participation, norms that are collectively developed through democratic processes, norms that participants agree to follow and are prepared to enforce where needed to protect their collective interests (responding to Popper's "paradox of tolerance"). The articulation of such norms needs to be ongoing, responding to new challenges and situations, and guarding against various forms of power and privilege that threaten to dominate these conversations. The already powerful do not need spaceships or social media accounts.

We need social media platforms that operate on all scales – some that allow hyperlocal discussions with immediate repercussions on people's lives and others that invite global participants. We need social media platforms that bring together people around shared interests that transcend ideological divides – gardening, fandom, gaming, etc. – although each of these has, from time to time, been deployed as battlegrounds in the ongoing cultural wars and political fractions.

The Civic Signals project has identified four core building blocks that should shape such new platforms: **welcome,** which is based on the goal of greater inclusion and respect for members; **connection,** which seeks to identify common ground amongst participants; **understand** which is both about empathy toward each other and a commitment to maintain accountability over the quality of information we put into circulation; and **act** which has to do with the ways that ideas that emerge through our conversations are deployed in the world. These principals strike me as good starting points for the conversation we need to be having about how to construct social media platforms and practices that better satisfy the democratic and participatory fantasies that drove us to seek such tools in the first place. I am disillusioned by what social media have become, but I am not ready to give up on the project of trying to foster and protect a more participatory culture.

Nico: I agree that giving up is not an option. But the struggles that are ahead of us are considerable. As you so eloquently explain, this is partially an issue of control over media organizations and structures. I am deeply sympathetic toward the idea of having diverse (social) media ecologies. My position, for a couple of decades, has been that we (at least) need a triad of media organizations, complementing commercial media with public media and community media. When discussing social media, I see no reason why this triad (at least as a vision for the future) would be different. Of course, this requires a reconfiguration of our categorization systems, where we give up on the mainstream media/social media dichotomy, and where we acknowledge that we currently, and almost exclusively, are dealing with mainstream commercial social media. That reconfiguration allows us to move away from the idea that social media are necessarily different from mainstream media, and that social media are necessarily participatory and supportive of democracy. This also allows us to better understand that access does not automatically lead to participation. Participation is a process that requires ethics, care, support, skills, and many other components and not just a door that is opened.

But I want to complement this focus on media structures and organizations with an emphasis on audiences/users and democratic cultures. Restructuring the media landscape is only one part of the debate, and also, we need a more society-centered and (democratic) process-centered approach to rethink social media. There are two reconfigurations I want to highlight here. First, there is a need for further agonization. This is very much in line with Chantal Mouffe's (2013) writings about antagonism and agonism, with antagonism referring to the construction to the other as enemy and agonism to the construction of the other as adversary. Of course, there are other (more synergetic) ways of dealing with the other, but what agonism, as a concept, allows us to see is that we need to acknowledge the existence of diversity and the conflict that diversity brings. A world of loving harmony is unlikely to materialize anytime soon, which implies that we need to find ways of taming conflict, and bringing it into the realm of democracy, by acknowledging the legitimacy of other voices, even if they are fundamentally different. But this also implies that violence needs to be extracted from this equation. To return to your point about cancel culture (with its complex set of counter-hegemonic and hegemony-protecting strategies) and to frame my comments in this language: I think we mostly need to cancel violence, in its many forms, including the structural violence to which marginalized groups have been exposed for so long.

The second configuration is very much related, in the sense that it is equally strongly embedded in the democratic-ethical field. I would argue that we need to find ways of strengthening the participatory dynamics in/of social media. For me, this is very much what you mean when talking about a more participatory culture. We have, for a long time, assumed that the provision of access to platforms that enabled self-publication and communication was a sufficient condition for participation. My argument here is that access is a necessary condition for participation but not a sufficient one. To decentralize decision-making practices, more is needed. Again, participatory–democratic control over infrastructures and technologies is important here, but we need to also acknowledge that the strengthening of democratic cultures requires permanent care and effort. Just opening a door does not suffice. Participation requires skills, and this is where formal and informal education matters so much. One of my arguments to defend and promote community media organizations is that they are informal participatory learning environments that allow people to learn about participation by participating. I see no reason why community social media cannot play that role, but I also see no reason why our many different educational systems cannot place more emphasis on participatory literacy. However important media literacy is, it is part of a cluster of literacies (including media, communicative and participatory literacy) that are all vital for citizens to function in their 21st-century societies. But I fear that there is still a long way to go and that the incessant critiques on social media, combined with their profit-seeking strategies, will only end up strengthening elitist positions and decrease participatory intensities in the decade to come, while I would say that we need more participation and not less.

Notes

1. We encourage readers to read these earlier pieces (see Jenkins & Carpentier, 2013; Carpentier & Jenkins, 2019), since this piece will begin where the most recent exchange left off. There we outline some core principles of what we called participatory ethics.
2. Cinematheia (2013, December 6). Monty Python Dead Parrot [Video]. *YouTube*. Retrieved from https://www.youtube.com/watch?v=vZw35VUBdzo

References

boyd, d. (2006). Friends, friendsters, and top 8: Writing community into being on social network sites. *First Monday, 11*(12). Retrieved from https://firstmonday.org/article/view/1418/1336

Brecht, B. (1983). Radio as a means of communication: A talk of the function of radio. In A. Mattelart & S. Siegelaub (Eds.), *Communication and class struggle: Vol. 2. Liberation, socialism* (pp. 169–171). New York: International General and International Mass Media Research Center.

Carpentier, N. (2017). *The discursive-material knot: Cyprus in conflict and community media participation.* New York: Peter Lang.

Carpentier, N., & Jenkins, H. (2019, June 10). Participatory politics in an age of crisis (Part 4). *Confessions of an Aca-Fan.* Retrieved from http://henryjenkins.org/blog/2019/6/8/participatory-politics-in-an-age-of-crisis-henry-jenkins-amp-nico-carpentier-part-v-ftym7

Carpentier, N., Melo, A. D., & Ribeiro, F. (2019). Rescuing participation: A critique on the dark participation concept. *Comunicação e Sociedade, 36,* 17–35.

Couldry, N. (2003). *Media rituals. A critical approach.* London: Routledge.

Dewey, J. (1888). *The ethics of democracy.* University of Michigan, Philosophical Papers, Second Series, Number 1. Ann Arbor, MI: Andrews & Company Publishers.

Dibbell, J. (n.d.). *A rape in cyberspace.* Retrieved from www.juliandibbell.com/articles/a-rape-in-cyberspace/

Fiske, J. (1989). *Understanding popular culture.* London: Routledge.

Garrett, A. (2020, January 17). Election misinformation drops over 70 percent after social media platforms suspend Trump: Study. *Newsweek.* Retrieved from www.newsweek.com/election-misinformation-drops-over-70-percent-after-social-media-platforms-suspend-trump-study-1562206

Gladwell, M. (2010, October 4). Small change: Why the revolution will not be retweeted. *The New Yorker.* Retrieved from www.newyorker.com/magazine/2010/10/04/small-change-malcolm-gladwell

Gramsci, A. (1971). *Selections from the prison notebooks of Antonio Gramsci.* London: Lawrence and Wishart.

Hobson, L. Z. (1971, September 12). As I listened to Archie say 'Hebe' . . . *The New York Times.* Retrieved from www.nytimes.com/1971/09/12/archives/as-i-listened-to-archie-say-hebe-as-i-listened-to-archie-as-i.html

Jenkins, H. (1992). *Textual poachers: Television fans and participatory culture.* London: Routledge.

Jenkins, H., & Carpentier, N. (2013). Theorizing participatory intensities: A conversation about participation and politics. *Convergences, 19*(3), 265–286.

Levy, P. (1999). *Collective intelligence: Mankind's emerging world in cyberspace.* New York: Basic Books.

Miranda, C. A. (2020, November 25). Parler's vibe is MAGA-Red and unreal: Extremism by design. *Los Angeles Times.* Retrieved from www.latimes.com/entertainment-arts/story/2020-11-25/parler-social-media-design-maga-extremism-badge-hierarchy

Morozov, E. (2009). Iran: Downside to the 'Twitter revolution'. *Dissent, Fall,* 10–14. Retrieved from www.evgenymorozov.com/morozov_twitter_dissent.pdf

Mouffe, C. (2013). *Agonistics: Thinking the world politically.* New York: Verso.

Pariser, E., & Stroud, T. (2021). "Hope for new online public spaces with Talia Stroud and Eli Pariser", Episode 79. In H. Jenkins & C. Maclay (Eds.), *How do you like it so far?* Retrieved from www.howdoyoulikeitsofar.org/episode-79-new-online-public-spaces-talia-stroud-eli-pariser/

Popper, K. R. (1947). *The open society and its enemies: The spell of Plato.* London: George Routledge & Sons.

Siddiqui, F., & Svrluga, S. (2016, December 5). N.C. man told police he went to D.C. pizzeria with gun to investigate conspiracy theory. *Washington Post.* Retrieved from www.washingtonpost.com/news/local/wp/2016/12/04/d-c-police-respond-to-report-of-a-man-with-a-gun-at-comet-ping-pong-restaurant/

Vidmar, N., & Rokeach, M. (1974). Archie Bunker's bigotry: A study in selective perception and exposure. *Journal of Communication, 24*(1), 36–47.

14

CONCLUSION

Together We Ascend

Devan Rosen

The Past: The Net's Unbreakable

Our relationship with social media has become a complicated one. This wasn't always the case. Early research (pre-2000) investigating the social uses of information and communication technologies (ICT) were generally centered on the ways that face-to-face communication (FtF) differed from computer-mediated communication (CMC). Could these new technologies effectively help build personal relationships? Is there as much social penetration in FtF conversations as there is in CMC conversations? Are there systematic differences in how we present ourselves in FtF interactions as opposed to online? Theories and methods were developed and deployed that facilitated these comparative investigations, and along with a host of other research streams, results were published and findings debated.

Yet, most of these early debates leaned heavily toward comparisons of FtF and CMC. People were using ICT mostly for love (not necessarily to find love, although that did happen) but out of a love for an affiliation or hobby, a fandom, or an interest group. CMC was driven by love for our friends and family. It seemed that a communication technology had finally emerged that could support a bottom-up, user-generated, networked public. Fortunately, the Internet is a self-organizing socio-technical system (Fuchs, 2003), so the net's unbreakable.

Then came the real money. Not the "pre-bubble-burst venture capital" money that baited well-intended grad students to surrender their ideas to an IPO-carrot on a stick. Rather, this was global dominance-level money. As website and platform utility improved and widespread uses of social-leaning ICT grew, so did the race to harvest our attention, build our platform loyalty, and monetize our personal data.

DOI: 10.4324/9781003171270-14

The transition of ICT from novel and alternative tools for the tech-savvy to becoming the very fabric from which much of our society is woven has greatly complicated the debates about social media. These complications bloomed when the very act of human communication became profitable, when our personal preferences and uniqueness became lucrative, and when controlling the information that we access became commercial. Our agency and relationships became the foundations for business models and bottom lines, and we fell for it. As such, debates about how social media were altering our society, changing our relationships, and affecting our well-being have become even more critical. Debates about the effects on geopolitical issues, changes in the ways that individuals maintain their social resources, the ways that interface designs can manipulate our social tendencies, the corporatization of the public sphere, the ways that content moderation curates the information we access, effects on media agendas, the rise of misinformation and disinformation, consequences for cultural subgroups, and the potential impacts on our mental health.

Clearly, these debates are necessary. Fortunately, scholars from a wide array of fields stepped up. Research into ICT is no longer limited to communication scholars pulling from their sociological and psychological roots to establish a burgeoning scientific field; we have an all-hands-on-deck situation emerging, involving the need for expert investigations and insights from economics, anthropology, political science, computer science, the health sciences, and many other fields. The publishing of this volume is but one of many steps needed to move down the path toward a better understanding of the relationship between technology use and our well-being, with the hope of a healthier society. A path illuminated by a planet of scholars whose research effort is functionally a safety net; the gravity is strong, but the net's unbreakable.

The Present: Together We Ascend

Over the past several years, the opacity of social media's varied effects has begun to wane. The continued diligence of researchers paired with whistleblowers from within social media corporations have led to a confluence of clarity; we know more about how these corporations make their decisions, and we know more about how those decisions have manifested in our society. For years we were smitten by these new technologies but then started to realize there were some confusing and (somewhat) unanticipated outcomes. Together we are starting to ascend from the confusion. Contributions from scholars have followed two clear trajectories, the insights have continued to gain nuance, and the related recommendations have increased in focus. The chapters in this volume are representative of these two gains, summarized in the following and using the authors' own words where possible.

Sarah Myers West's examination of social media companies as geopolitical actors revealed that these large companies rose to become power brokers, and that "this created a single point of failure that enabled nation-states to target social media platforms for surveillance, censorship, and eventually, the spread of disinformation" (West, in this volume, Chapter 2). Further, social media companies shifted from informal policy making to developing a formalized bureaucratic infrastructure focused largely on the United States and the European Union. Moving us forward, West (in this volume, Chapter 2) calls for "incisive, critical research and analysis of companies' and governments' activities, published in highly visible venues that shape global conversations about platform accountability." Further, that publicity can be brought to light by "investigative journalism, rigorous research, and intrepid whistleblowing that brings to light what would otherwise be largely opaque aspects of what social media companies do in the world and the effects they render on our geopolitical environment" (in this volume, Chapter 2).

Michael A. Stefanone and Jessica Covert take a more user-centered approach, focusing on social resources in networked society and how users are afforded increased network monitoring. They conclude that

> [S]ocial media users have unprecedented access to network-related data, and it may be the case that these individuals are building a more comprehensive understanding of the on- and offline social networks they routinely navigate and thus, capitalizing on the opportunities posed by generally public and persistent information about their associations.
>
> *(this volume, Chapter 3)*

Stefanone and Covert proffer that this information can be used to train individuals to advantageously mobilize the social capital embedded in their networks. They go on to point out that this is "specifically important for those individuals belonging to underrepresented or unfairly treated social groups that could benefit from understanding and accessing the social capital embedded in their network" (this volume, Chapter 3).

Elinor Carmi explained that our behaviors in social media can be deviant and can impact social media's political economy, norms, and values. Carmi points out that

> [B]ehaviors are not the only thing that can be deviant, different kinds of design can also have different norms and values engineered into them. . . . Dark patterns influence what we can and cannot do and consequently also shape how we understand these environments.
>
> *(Carmi, in this volume, Chapter 4)*

After unpacking these critical elements of deviant design principles, she moves us forward by indicating that

[J]ust like society constructs specific rules and norms, so do social media platforms. These are not neutral, objective or permanent, but rather, constantly negotiated, challenged and changed according to multiple motives, mainly economic and political. It is important to understand that our social networks are mediated by biased infrastructures that want us to engage and understand our networks, ourselves and these spaces in specific ways.

(this volume, Chapter 4)

In the chapter on public sphere, Christian Fuchs elucidated how the digital public sphere "is both colonialized and feudalized by capital, state power and ideology, and characterized by economic, political and cultural asymmetries of power" (this volume, Chapter 5). He explicates that the Internet and social media are now defined by class structures and inequalities and are dominated by commercial culture and that public service media operate on the basis of a different logic. Fuchs suggests that "development of a public service Internet is a democratic alternative to the capitalist Internet and digital capitalism" (this volume, Chapter 5) and offers examples of independent, critical, non-commercial public service media as an embodiment of the democratic public sphere.

When discussing content moderation, Ysabel Gerrard points out that it is both necessary and also controversial that

[T]he humans undertaking this work are plagued with mental health difficulties, automated moderation technologies famously scrub the wrong things from the internet, public commentators worry about the lack of transparency from social media giants, and the rules governing online communication can create as many problems as they solve.

(this volume, Chapter 6)

Gerrard makes pragmatic suggestions for greater transparency; that listing the number of moderators is important, as is telling us where they are based, and under what contracts and conditions they work. Gerrard concludes that the time has come for social media companies to drastically rethink their approach to content moderation.

Gabrielle Lim, Alexei Abrahams, and Joan Donovan investigated one of the key debates around the ability for influencers to manipulate news media agendas. Their analysis of Twitter hashtags suggested that right-wing influencers may not be manipulating news media agendas as much as had been thought, but they did find evidence that right-wing influencers do affect media coverage independently. The authors recommend future research adopts "a wider aperture so as not to filter out these alternative means of influence" (this volume, Chapter 7).

In writing about mis/disinformation, Melissa Zimdars explained that imposter local news sources exploit a shortage of local news and use social media platforms to spread and generate engagement with mis/disinformation, and that "social media platforms are designed to prioritize the very kinds of emotionally charged, highly partisan, and provocative content that imposter websites and other forms of mis/disinformation are adept at creating and circulating" (this volume, Chapter 8). Zimdars offers some recommendations; that we need more local news sources to serve their communities, that we hold those with power in their local communities accountable, and that journalists take greater care in preventing inadvertent amplification of imposter local news websites and other forms of mis/disinformation. Zimdars concludes with the recommendation that bad actors on social media need to be transparently held accountable or removed from social media platforms, and that for digital media literacy to work "we need structural solutions that begin earlier in the communication process and that reduce the barriers that currently exist to being a responsible news consumer" (this volume, Chapter 8).

In writing about social media and Black digital studies, Francesca Sobande explained that "experiences of social media are often associated with an ability to transcend geo-cultural borders to connect and communicate with people in different parts of the world. However, social media encounters are shaped by various complex geographies, including Black geographies" (this volume, Chapter 9). Sobande writes that engaging with "Black digital studies and Black geographies work which illuminates the (dis)located nature of Black people's experiences, such as how the histories of places, politics, and violence affect the daily lives of Black people" (this volume, Chapter 9). An important contribution from Sobande is related to the limits of academia,

> [T]he work of Black digital studies, which includes iterations of vitality and joy, is often at odds with the foundations of academia. Thus, even when Black digital studies are somewhat located in, or at least, linked to academic situations, they are never fully *of* the academy, nor should they be.
>
> *(this volume, Chapter 9)*

Summarizing research on social media and mental health, Sarah Coyne, Emily Schvaneveldt, and Jane Shawcroft review one of the most fervent debates around social media, the possible relationship to mental health. They report that findings have been mixed, with some researchers finding a strong relationship between social media and mental health while others have found a nonexistent or weak relationship, often using the same datasets. Some elements of social media use were less debatable, such as the addictive nature of social media. The authors use their review to make some concrete recommendations; that individuals avoid social media in the hour before bedtime, turn off all notifications during the nighttime hours, reduce the fear of missing out by improving self-esteem, managing impulsive behavior, and practice self-talk. They also recommend that users strive for active media use, practice mindfulness, and engage in prosocial behavior.

Methodological recommendations are also offered for future research into social media and mental health.

Continuing the section on social media and mental health, Drew P. Cingel, Michael C. Carter, and Lauren B. Taylor highlighted the importance of studying mental health outcomes among adolescents during a critical developmental period, and that social media have the potential to both positively and negatively impact mental health. The authors offer platform-specific effects on mental health, for example, differences between Facebook and Snapchat. Using a Personal Social Media Use Framework, the authors make suggestions that apply to research on social media and also about the platforms themselves. They conclude that "the effects of social media on mental disorders among adolescents are complex, nuanced, and likely idiosyncratic" (this volume, Chapter 11).

Rounding out the section on social media and well-being, Philipp K. Masur, Jolanda Veldhuis, and Nadia Bij de Vaate suggest that research focus "on the intricate relationships between different types of social media uses, content- and person-related characteristics, as well as contextual and situational factors will provide a nuanced insight into how social media use affects well-being" (this volume, Chapter 11), and that simply asking whether social media use negatively affects well-being is oversimplifying. The authors urge for "future research to investigate the intricate combination of personal and environmental factors in explaining heterogeneity in social media use effects" (this volume, Chapter 11).

In the final chapter, Nico Carpentier and Henry Jenkins engage in a conversation about politics, participation, and social media. Through their dialogue, suggestions are offered for a productive way forward for our relationship with social media. Carpentier suggests that *participation* is ethical, that "the equalization of power (relations) is both wise and ethical, or, in other words, that domination that mutes or incapacitates others against their will is unethical" and that "for participation to be (and remain) participatory, a particular ethics is required, driving the actions of those involved, combining a series of deliberative norms (e.g., respect, equality, listening)" (this volume, Chapter 13). Through the dialogue, Jenkins offers the following insights about what we need:

> We want social media platforms that are governed by motives other than commercialism. We need platforms that are run by nonprofit organizations, that emerge from grassroots collectives . . . We need social media platforms with articulated norms for participation, norms that are collectively developed through democratic processes . . . We need social media platforms that operate on all scales – some that allow hyperlocal discussions with immediate repercussions on people's lives and others that invite global participants . . . We need social media platforms that bring together people around shared interests that transcend ideological divides.
>
> *(this volume, Chapter 13)*

Taken together, the debates discussed in this volume point to the interpretation that the social, psychological, and cultural effects of social media are mixed but tend to be problematic. That the corporatized decision-making, overall profit motive, and unregulated deployment of platforms have had a negative effect on our society and culture, but that the social affordances of these tools can have a positive effect on an individual's ability to mobilize their resources and locate communities of affiliation. These conclusions are not surprising. The economic interests of corporations are often at odds with the best interests of society, especially when cloaked and unchecked. Moreover, individuals who care about our culture, and each other, have often tended to uncover problems and work toward solutions. The chapters in this volume suggest that we need a collaboration between the two, that corporations need to act more ethically and responsibly, and that we as individuals have a responsibility to become increasingly media literate. Widespread civic engagement would also increase the likelihood that corporations are held accountable. It is the role of the scholar to help connect these two disparate stakeholders, investigate the situation, recommend solutions, and help to move the debate forward.

The Future: Escaping the Gravity

Our collective understanding of social media and its myriad of effects is growing ever more well articulated and well researched, and the chapters summarized here represent a cross-section of the excellent work being done around the globe. However, the fantastic contributions of the authors in this volume do signify a baseline of the key debates, and since they are assembled into a single place rather than scattered across journals and proceedings, this volume offers a valuable and unique resource. It is in this form, bringing scholars from different fields and perspectives together, that we stand a chance at not only understanding the multifaceted outcomes of social media but capitalize on opportunities to re-create these tools in new forms which promote healthy interpersonal relationships in society (i.e., the bedrock of social capital), opposed to treating users around the world as commodities.

Historically, when society has faced the most difficult problems with the most gravity (e.g., climate change), it was through collaboration and cooperation that we created shared understanding. However, much like the climate change issue, we are most divided when our communication channels are co-opted and the information we access is distorted. It is in this sense that there is such an urgency to the social media debate, and why the existential threats we face today are inexorably bound to social media. The social media ecosystem *is the market in which* our information is shared and our agency negotiated. We have to work together to achieve a common good. Only then will we ascend and escape the gravitational pull of the most powerful corporations in human history.

Reference

Fuchs, C. (2003). The internet as a self-organizing socio-technological system. *Human Strategies in Complexity Research Paper.* Retrieved from SSRN: https://ssrn.com/abstract=458680 or http://dx.doi.org/10.2139/ssrn.458680

INDEX

Note: Page numbers in **bold** refer to tables, and page numbers in *italics* refer to figures.

Abrahams, Alexei 223
Adler, Paul S. 23
adolescence: body image and body
  ideals 177–178, 187, 195–198, 199;
  chat activities 179; definition of
  172–173; development 173; social
  media use and mental health 152–154,
  159, 161, 173–181; *see also* Personal
  Social Media Ecosystem Framework
  (PSMEF)
agenda seeding 97, 98; channels 105–106,
  106; definition of 104; research
  questions regarding 104–105
algorithmic politics 60, **61,** 72
Alibaba 62, 63
alienation: antagonisms in types of
  alienation **58**; digital alienation 61–62;
  main actors in alienated and humanist
  society **59**; Marx on 58, 72; three
  antagonisms of digital alienation **61**;
  three types of digital alienation **61**
Amanatullah, Emily T. 28
Amazon 8, 14, 62, 63, 84
Amazon Mechanical Turk 85
Amazon Web Services 101
Ames, Daniel R. 28
Ammori, Marvin 11
Anderson, Robert 40
antisocial, social media as 60

antisocial behaviors 39–44; disconnectivity
  42–44; flaming 40; groups of 40;
  hacking 40; harassment 40–42; purpose
  of defining 41–42; spamming 40–41;
  trolling 40–41
antisocial interface designs (dark patterns)
  44–50; metrics 44–46; newsfeed
  algorithms 46–48; terms of use 49–50
apparent sincerity 32
Apple 14, 62
application programming interface (API)
  44, 101, 105, 107
Arab Spring 10, 53, 98, 211
Are, Carolina 81
artificial intelligence 62, 82; *see also*
  automation; machine learning
astroturfing 11, 15, 123
Austria 68–69, 73
authoritarianism: antisocial social media
  and 60; in Azerbaijan 14; capitalism and
  69; communication technologies and
  206; digital authoritarianism 60, **61**, 65,
  72; false/fake news and 60; networked
  forms of 10; populism and 210; public
  sphere and 56; "splinternet" and 138
automation: automated algorithms 47,
  60; automated content moderation 78,
  79, 82–84, 85, 86, 91, 223; automated
  disconnective activity 42; automated

memories 46; bias and 47; definition of 83; public service internet and 65, 69
Azerbaijan 14

Bailey, Moya 142, 145–146
Barrera, Manuel 24
Baumer, Eric 42
Baym, Nancy 45
Beer, David 46
Benkler, Yochai 7, 110
Biden, Joe 113; hashtag campaigns against 108, 109, 110, 111, 116n8; misinformation and disinformation regarding 120, 125, 126
"Big Lie" 113, 123, 128
Bij de Vaate, Nadia 225
Black British Twitter 143
Black cyberfeminism 145–146
Black digital diaspora 141, 143–144, 148
Black digital studies 137–149; Black joy and 143–144, 149; COVID-19 pandemic and 145–147; digital diaspora and 141, 143–144, 148; history of in Britain 140–144; locations and locatedness 138–140
Black feminism 140, 141, 144
Black Lives Matter (BLM) 109, 146, 211
body image and body ideals 177–178, 187, 195–198, 199
Bosworth, Andrew 8–9
boycott campaigns 15
boyd, danah 2–3, 215
Brands, Raina A. 29
Brecht, Bertolt 205
Bruce, Keisha 140–141, 144
bulletin board systems (BBS) 2, 6, 77

Cambridge Analytica 60, 64–65
Campbell, Karen E. 26
capitalism, influencer 60, **61,** 72
Caplan, Robyn 85, **87,** 91, 130
Carmi, Elinor 222–223
Carpentier, Nico 225
Carter, Michael C. 225
Casciaro, Tiziana 28–29
Cassidy, Elija 42
Castells, Manuel 7
censorship 11, 55, 86–87, 215, 222
Chaplin, Charlie 10–11
Chen, Adrian 77, 86
China: research on adolescent social media use and mental health 175; "splinternet"

138; teahouses 56–57; Western social media platforms blocked by 81
Chomsky, Noam 66
Christchurch mosque shooting 83
Cingel, Drew P. 225
Civic Signals 216
Classmates 2
clickwrap license agreements 49
Clinton, Bill 8
Clinton, Hillary 208
Club 2 68–72
cognitive social structures (CSS) 21, 28–29, 33
Coleman, Gabriella 40
Coleman, James 24
commercial content moderators (CCM) 48, 85–86
computer-mediated communication (CMC) 190, 220
Computer People for Peace 15–16
Computer Professionals for Social Responsibility 16
content moderation: artisanal approaches to 82; automated content moderation 82–84; borderline content policies (case study) **89;** case study (moderation of healed self-harm scars) 86–90; commercial content moderators (CCM) 48, 85–86; community reliant approaches to 82; content warnings **87;** defining harmful online content 79–81; definition of content moderation 77–78; de-monetization **87;** flagging 80, 84–86, 130; hashtag bans **88;** human review 83, 84–86, 91; industrial approaches to 82; invisibility as sign of good 78; limitations of automation 84; need for content moderation 78–79; outcomes of (case study) **87–90;** pattern matching used for 82; policies and processes of 81–87; regulation of 90–91; scaled up process of 83; of self-harm references 78, 80–81, 86–90; shadowbanning **88, 89;** skin filters used for 82; transparency and 78, 85, 90–91; user suspension or removal 84, **87,** 91; volunteer moderators 82
cookies 41, 138
Couldry, Nick 39, 205
Covert, Jessica 222
COVID-19 pandemic 206; content moderation during 78, 83, 86;

entitlement and digital experiences
during 145–147; Facebook CCM
workers during 86; misinformation
regarding 48, 126; public service media
during 74; Zoombombing during
98–99, 147
Coyne, Sarah 224–225
Crawford, Kate 83, 84, **89**
Creative Commons 60, 61, 67–68
"culture wars" 97
cyberfeminism 145–146

Daniels, Jessie 123, 124
dark patterns 44–50; *see also* antisocial
interface designs (dark patterns)
deregulation 65
Dewey, John 213–214
Dibbell, Julian 211–212, 213, 214
digital acceleration 60, **61,** 72
digital capitalism 8, 59, 61–63, 65, 72–73,
223
digital class relations 59, **61,** 72
digital commons 60, 61, 67–68
digital culture industry 60, **61,** 72
digital defeatism 73
digital fingerprint 83
digital individualism 59, **61,** 72
digital luddism 73
digital surveillance 59, **61,** 72
disinformation *see* mis/disinformation
Donovan, Joan 223
dot-com boom and bust 7–8
Douglas, Mary 38–39
Douyin *see* TikTok
Dunbar, Robin I. M. 28

eating disorders 84, 177, 178–179
economic power of six largest internet
corporations **62–63**
Egypt 10, 12
Ellison, Nicole B. 2–3
Erdogan, Recep Tayyip 12
Eubanks, Virginia 47
Europe: Black Europe 148;
bureaucratic social media
decision-making in 14; Digital
Services Act (DSA) 90; power and
internet regulation in 138–139;
proposed European alternative to
YouTube 68; research on adolescent
social media use and mental health
175; web-cookies and 41; *see also*
individual nations

Facebook: Aquila program 9; Cambridge
Analytica scandal 64–65; Community
Operations 80; content moderation
10, 14, 80–81, 82, 85–86, 91; content
moderator guidelines 85; economic
power of 61, **62,** 62–63; Free Basics
program 9; influence of 3, 8–9;
iniquitousness of 1; leaving Facebook
42; "Like" button 41, 45; mental health
and use of 176–179, 180; metrics
45–46; mis/disinformation and 48,
122, 124, 125, 127, 129, 130; newsfeed
algorithm 47; purpose of 5, 7, 8–9;
rules set by 39; social capital and 26;
social movements and 53; spamming
41; use by far-right leaders 204; Web
2.0 and 5, 7; well-being and use of 187,
190, 191, 193, 195, 196; whistleblowers
13, 85–86
Facebook Demetricator 45–46
Facebook Live 83
face-to-face communication (FtF) 220
fact-checkers 210
fake news *see* false/fake news
false/fake news 53, 60, **61,** 64, 65, 67, 72,
122, 127–128, 130, 204
Faris, Robert 110
Ferris, Gerald R. 32
filter bubbles 47, 60, **61,** 72, 114
flagging 80, 84–86, 130
Flynn, Francis J. 28
FOMO (fear of missing out) 154–155,
157, 177
Foucault, Michel 38–39
Freedom House 11, 14
Friendster 3, 8
Fuchs, Christian 223

Germany 73–74, 90
Gerrard, Ysabel 223
Geybullayeva, Arzu 14
Gillespie, Tarleton 77, 79, 82, 83, 84, **87,
89,** 91, 127–128, 129
Gladwell, Malcolm 211
Global South 13–14
Google 7, 9, 14, 47, 53, **62,** 63, 122, 126
Gorka, Sebastian 96, 101, 102, 103,
106–107, 109, 111
Gould, Roger V. 24
Gramsci, Antonio 205
Granovetter, Mark S. 22
Great Britain 56, 73, 137, 139–145,
147–149, 175

"Great Dictator, The" (film) 10–11, 15
Grosser, Benjamin 45–46
Guha, Palavi 100

Habermas, Jürgen 54, 55–56, 57, 66, 72
Hampton, Keith N. 25
Hartzog, Woodrow 49
"hashing," definition of 83
hashtag activism: agenda seeding channels
    and *106*; hashtags coined and amplified
    by influencers **108**; history of 98–99;
    media mentions of hashtags and share
    of total stories **109**; mentions of
    right-wing Twitter influencers *114*;
    motivations for 99–100; against Ocasio-
    Cortez 96, 98–104, 113; research data
    and methodology 104–107; research
    discussion 112–114; research findings
    107–112; statistics for #AOCLied
    and #AlexandriaOcasioSmollett
    103; time series plots of #AOCLied
    and #AlexandriaOcasioSmollett
    102; Twitter retweet networks for
    #AlexandriaOcasioSmollett (left) and
    #AOCLied *103*; *see also* hashtags and
    hashtag campaigns
hashtag bans **88**
hashtags and hashtag campaigns:
    #AlexandriaOcasioSmollett 96,
    99–104, 113; #antifa 109, 110;
    #AOCLied 96, 98, 99, 100–104,
    113; #bidenbordercrisis 108,
    110, 116n8; #BMM 109;
    #bodiesunderbridges 108, 110,
    116n8; #crowderbidenstream 109;
    #exposeCNN 108, 109, 110–112,
    113, 114, 115; #justanotherdemhack
    109; #NoTechForICE 16; #Pizzagate
    107; #rhod 116n8; #StopTheSteal
    98, 107; trending hashtags 96–97,
    99, 100–101, *102,* 104–105, *106,*
    107–112; #trinidadcarnival2020 **88**;
    #TwitterIsBlockedInTurkey 13
Heal, Alexandra 47–48
Heider, Fritz 28
Her, Eun Ja 25
Hesselberth, Pepita 42–43
Horkheimer, Max 58

imposter websites and news sources 121,
    123–125, 127–131, 223–224
India 9, 12, 85, 100
Indonesia 9, 12

information and communication
    technologies (ICT) 220–221
Instagram: case study (moderation of
    healed self-harm scars) 86–90; influence
    of 3; iniquitousness of 1; mental health
    and use of 172, 175, 176, 177–178,
    187, 188, 190, 192, 193, 196; Ocasio-
    Cortez's Live broadcast 96, 101
instrumental action 21, 22, 23, 25–26
interpersonal influence 32
Iran 10, 98

Jackson, Jasper 47–48
Jacobsen, Benjamin 46
January 6 Capitol Hill siege 96–97, 98,
    100–101, 106–107, 204, 205, 211
Jenkins, Henry 225
Jobin, Anna 47
John, Nicholas 43–44
Johnson, Boris 73
Jones, Naya 137, 139, 143, 148
Jorge, Ana 43

Karppi, Tero 43
Kelly, Kevin 7–8
Klein, Adam 125
Klonick, Kate 12
Knöbl, Kuno 68
Korea 24, 104
Kreuzer, Franz 68
Kwon, Seok W. 23

Lasade-Anderson, Temi 144
Lasswell, Harold 122
Lee, Chul-joo 25
left-leaning media 104, 113, 120
left-wing influencers 102
Lemley, Mark 49
Lewin, Kurt 28
Libya 12
Lievens, Eva 49
Light, Ben 42
Lim, Gabrielle 223
Lin, Nan 22, 25
LinkedIn 3, 53
livestreams 78, 80–81, 82
Livingstone, Jared 49
local news media 121–131, 223–224
Lu, Jessica H. 144
Lukács, György 58

machine learning 83; *see also* artificial
    intelligence; automation

Mackay, Kui Kihoro 141, 144
Marcuse, Herbert 58
Marsden, Peter V. 26
Marx, Karl 55–56, 58, 72
Masur, Philipp K. 225
Matias, J. Nathan 82
McCay-Peet, Lori 3
McGregor, Shannon 99
Media Cloud 97, **109, 112**
media literacy 130, 156, 161–162, 217, 224
Meier, Adrian 190
memory 46, 86
"mental health," definition of 173
mental health and mental disorders 152–162; active social media use 158; Facebook 177; fear of missing out (FOMO) 154–155; gender and 153; Instagram 177–178; limitations of current research on social media and 160–162; mindfulness and 158–159; pathological use of social media 156–157; platform-specific research on 176–178; prosocial behavior and 159–160; protective contexts 157–160; reaching out and 159–160; research on 152–154, 174–180; risky contexts 154–157; sleep and 154–155; Snapchat 177–178; social comparisons and 156; within-platform research on 178–180; see also Personal Social Media Ecosystem Framework (PSMEF); suicide
Microsoft 14, 62, 63, 86
Milne, Esther 40
Milner, Ryan M. 129–130
Minnesota Sun 120–121, 122, 124–127
mis/disinformation 120–121; accountability for 129; cloaked websites 123–125; definition of disinformation 121; definition of misinformation 121; definition of propaganda 121; digital news literacy and 130; imposter websites and news sources 121, 123–125, 127–131, 223–224; laundering information 125–127; legitimizing information 125–127; network ethics and 129–130; social media amplification of 127–128; solutions to 128–131; Star News websites and 120–129, 131
moderation see content moderation
Molyneux, Logan 99
Mouffe, Chantal 216

Napoli, Philip 130
neoliberalism 8, 43, 65, 73
networked public sphere 7
networking ability 32
network monitoring 21, 27–28, 29, 30–31, 32–33, 34, 222
network perception accuracy 28–29, 30
network social awareness 31
newsfeeds 2, 44, 46–50
newsgroups 2
Ngo, Andy 113–114, *114*
Nissenbaum, Asaf 43–44
Noble, Safiya 47
non-disclosure agreement (NDA) 85–86
nostalgia 46, 206
Nyhan, Brendan 127

Obama, Barack 12
Ocasio-Cortez, Alexandra: hashtag campaigns against 96, 98, 99, 99–104, 100–104, 113; Instagram Live broadcast 96, 101
O'Keefe, James 106, 107, 108, 109–111, 112, 113–114, *114*, 116n8
Osei, Krys 141, 144
Owens, Candace 96

Pakistan 12, 15
Palatino, Mong 10
Pariser, Eli 47, 215
Parler 100–101, 206
Parmelee, John 99
participatory culture 59, 64–65, 211, 216–217
participatory democracy 63–64, 67–68, 72
participatory ethics 203, 206, 211–217, 225
participatory governance 8
participatory media 78–79
participatory public sphere 63–64
Personal Social Media Ecosystem Framework (PSMEF) 170–181
personal social media ecosystems (PSMEs) 171–172, 174, 177, 179
Peter, Jochen 173–174
Philippines 85
Phillips, Whitney 40–41, 129–130
Plunkett, Isabella 85–86
Popper, Karl 214, 215
Posobiec, Jack 106, 113–114, *114*
post-traumatic stress disorder (PTSD) 86
propaganda 53, 121, 122, 123
prosumers 67, 79

protests 6; bonding capital and 24;
"The Innocence of Muslims" and 12;
networked protests 10, 211; Occupy
movements 57; public meeting places
and 57; railway protests in Chengdu
(1911) 57
public service internet: Club 2 68–72;
Creative Commons 67–68; YouTube
and video 67–68
public service media 54, 65–72, 73–74,
223; definition of 66
Public Service Media and Public Service
Internet Manifesto 66
public sphere 72–74; capitalist internet
platforms and 59–65; class structuration
and 57, 58, 60; colonization of 57,
59–65; commodification and 57–58; as
concept of critique 54–59; definition
of 54; domination and 57–58, 60–61,
63–64; forms of stratification 57–58;
Habermas on 54, 55–56, 57, 66,
72; ideology and 57–58, 59–61, 64;
limitations on 56; Marx on 55–56,
58; media system and 54–55, **55**; Paris
Commune as 55–56; places of critical
publicity and critical discussion 54;
public service internet 65–72; public
tea house as 56–57; Western-centric
concepts of 56–57; see also alienation

QAnon 98, 101, 107, 207–211
Quan-Haase, Anabel 3

racism: in academia 145, 149; "anti-white
racism" 99; cyber-racism 123; mis/
disinformation and 123, 125; normative
212–213; responding to 212–213;
structural anti-Black racism 146
rational choice theory 20, 21, 22
Reagans, Ray E. 28
Reddit 82
Reinecke, Leonard 190
Renner, Martin E. 73
right-leaning media 120–131
right-wing politics: attacks on public
service broadcasting 73–74; Cambridge
Analytica scandal 64–65; in Germany
73–74; in Great Britain 73; hashtag
campaigns 96–115; influencers 96–115;
in United States 64–65, 96–115
right-wing social media influencers
96–102, 104–114
Roberts, Hal 110

Roberts, Sarah 48, 77–78, 79, 84, 85, 86,
90, 91
Rohanaphruk, Pravit 10–11
Roose, Kevin 47

Schiller, Dan 8
Schvaneveldt, Emily 224–225
science and technology studies (STS) 7
Scottish Twitter 143
self-harm 78, 80–81, 86–90
self-interest 20, 21–22, 23, 29, 34
self-management 43
self-monitoring 27–28, 29–30, 31
Shapiro, Norman 40
Shawcroft, Jane 224–225
Six Degrees 2, 3
SMS 13
Snapchat 1, 176–178, 225
Snowden, Edward 60
Sobande, Francesca 224
social astuteness 32
social capital 20–21; bridging and
bonding capital 21, 23, 24–25, 26,
28, 31; cognitive social structures and
21, 28–29, 33; data 21, 24, 25, 26;
definition of 24; network monitoring
and 21, 27–28, 29, 30–33, 34; rational
choice theory and 20, 21, 22; resource
availability and 21; self-interest and 20,
21–22, 23, 29, 34; self-report data 24,
25; social network analysis and 20–21,
22, 28, 33
social embeddedness 24
social infrastructure, definition of 5
"social media," definitions of and use of
the term 1–3, 53, 190–191
social media moderation see content
moderation
social network analysis 20–21, 22;
definition of social networks 22;
egocentric networks and 22;
measurement of social support 24;
strong-tie and weak-tie contacts 22, 23,
27; traditional approaches to 22, 28
social network attention 30–31
social network sites, definition of 2–3
social structures: cognitive social structures
21, 28–29, 33; definition of 22;
network monitoring and 27; social
network analysis and 22
social support 24, 175, 179, 187, 198
South Africa 15, 54
Splichal, Slavko 66

Starbird, Kate 98
Star News websites 120–129, 131
Star Trek V: The Final Frontier (film) 203
Steele, Catherine Knight 144
Stefanone, Michael A. 222
Stone, Brad 77
Streisand effect 11
suicide: livestreamed 78, 80–81; social
media use and 152–153, 161, 174–175,
187; witnessed by CCM workers 86
Suzor, Nicolas P. 90, 91
Switzerland 73

Tayler, Lauren B. 225
technological determinism 7–8, 205
Tennessee Star 120–121, 122–127, 129
terms of use 49–50
Thailand 10–11, 15
TikTok: content moderation 39, 81,
83; content removed from 81; dance
trends on 79; iniquitousness of 1; inter-
networked posts 172; rules set by 39, 81
Trump, Donald 97, 107; 2016 election
campaign 64–65; 2020 election defeat
of 98, 100; hashtag campaigns and 98,
100–101, 204–205; populism and 209,
210; social media amplification by 127,
204; Twitter account suspended 101,
105, 113, 207; use of Twitter by 105,
107, 204, 206, 214
Tunisia 10
Turkey 10, 12–13, 15
Turow, Joseph 44–45
Twitter: automated removal of user
accounts 84; banned by Erdogan 12–13;
Black British Twitter 143; content
moderation 79, 80, 81, 83–84, 85;
Country Withheld Content policy 12;
iniquitousness of 1; Scottish Twitter
143; suspension of Trump's account
101, 105, 113, 207; trending topics
and hashtags 96–97, 99, 100–101, *102,
104–105, 106,* 107–112; Trump's use of
105, 107, 204, 206, 214; verified users
99; *see also* hashtag activism; hashtags
and hashtag campaigns

United Kingdom (UK) 56, 73, 90, 137,
139–145, 147–149, 175; Online Harms
legislation 90
Usenet 2, 82
user-generated content (UGC) 59, 63,
67, 77, 78, 79, 172, 179–180;

adolescent media use 172, 179–180;
in digital public sphere 59, 63, 67, 77,
78, 79

Valcke, Peggy 49
Valkenburg, Patti 161, 173–174
van Dijck, José 39, 43
Veldhuis, Jolanda 225
venture capital 8, 220
virtual private network (VPN) 81

Walcott, Rianna 141, 144
Wang, Di 56–57
Wardle, Claire 121, 128
Wauters, Ellen 49
Web 2.0 2, 8
web-cookies 41, 138
Weibo 53, 79
well-being 187–199; body image
and 195–198; definitions of social
media and 190–191; hedonic and
eudaimonic 195; holistic model of
effects of social media use on
188–190; influences on well-being
at a given time **189**; moderating
factors on effects of social media use
on 192–194; susceptibility to effects of
social media use on 191–192; types of
194–195
Wellman, Barry 26
West, Sarah Myers 222
whistleblowers 13, 15, 85–86, 221, 222
Wikipedia 53, 61
Wortley, Scot 26
Wright, Keith 138

York, Jillian 12
YouTube: content moderation 83, 85;
digital attention economy of 65; public
service YouTube 67–68; removal
of Great Dictator clip in Thailand
10–11; response to "The Innocence of
Muslims" 12, 15; top ten most-viewed
videos 63–64, **64**; volume up uploaded
content 79

Zenon: Girl of the 21st Century (film)
144–145
Zhang, Sophie 13
Ziewitz, Malte 47
Zimdars, Melissa 223–224
Zoombombing 98–99, 147
Zuckerberg, Mark 7, 9, **89**

Printed in the United States
by Baker & Taylor Publisher Services